Ever since the notorious tip off which led to the defection of Burgess and Maclean, MI5's molehunters have been convinced that their own organisation harboured a traitor.

Now, following the bizarre Peter Wright court case in Australia and the deaths of two crucial witnesses, it is at last possible to expose the whole incredible truth: the plots, the molehunts and the cover-ups – even evidence that Peter Wright was not aware of.

Was Hollis really a spy? Why did Peter Wright break his oath of lifelong secrecy? What was Lord Rothschild's involvement? Leading spy-writer Nigel West uncovers a wealth of new, important and fascinating material.

'Just when we were beginning to believe that perhaps the late Sir Roger Hollis, former head of MI5, really *was* a Russian agent, along comes spy-writer Nigel West to rescue his reputation and pull another espionage rabbit out of thc hat'
Sunday Telegraph

**Also by the same author,
and available from Coronet:**

A MATTER OF TRUST: MI5 1945–72
GCHQ: THE SECRET WIRELESS WAR
1900–86

About the Author

Nigel West is a military historian specialising in
security matters and is the European Editor of
Intelligence Quarterly. He has also written several
controversial histories of Britain's intelligence
organisations, and the *Sunday Times* commented:
'His information is often so precise that many
people believe he is simply the unofficial historian
of the secret services. West's sources are
undoubtedly excellent. His books are peppered
with deliberate clues to potential front-page
stories.'

Nigel West

MOLE-HUNT

The Full Story of the Soviet Spy in MI5

CORONET BOOKS
Hodder and Stoughton

For Venetia Pollock

Copyright © 1986 Westinel
Research Limited 1987

First published in Great Britain in
1987 by George Weidenfeld and
Nicolson Limited

Coronet edition 1987

British Library C.I.P.

West, Nigel
  Molehunt: the full story of the
Soviet spy in MI5.
  1. Espionage, Russian – Great
Britain – History – 20th
century   2. Secret service – Great
Britain – History – 20th century
I. Title
327.1'2'0941   UB271.R9

ISBN 0-340-41984-9

Printed and bound in Great Britain
for Hodder and Stoughton
Paperbacks, a division of Hodder
and Stoughton Limited, Mill Road,
Dunton Green, Sevenoaks, Kent
(Editorial Office: 47 Bedford
Square, London WC1B 3DP) by
Cox and Wyman Limited, Reading,
Berks. Photoset by Rowland
Phototypesetting Limited,
Bury St Edmunds, Suffolk.

Contents

Illustrations

16 Peter and Lois Wright on their way to court in Sydney
     (*Associated Press*)

(Unless otherwise stated, all the photos are from the author's collection)

Acknowledgements

I am indebted to the following people who have been kind enough to help my research: Dr Sarah Street of the Bodleian Library, Oxford; Dr Adrian Hollis; Dr Anthony Glees; Camilla van Gerbig; Dr H. Montgomery Hyde; The Conservative Research Department; the *Illustrated London News*; and the staff of the British Museum Newspaper Library, Colindale.

Finally, my thanks are due to Her Majesty's Stationery Office for permission to reproduce the 1955 White Paper on Burgess and Maclean, and to Admiral W. A. Higgins of the D Notice Committee for his guidance.

DIRECTORS-GENERAL OF MI5

Sir Roger Hollis	1956–65
Sir Martin Furnival Jones	1965–72
Sir Michael Hanley	1972–79
Sir Howard Smith	1979–81
Sir John Jones	1981–85
Sir Anthony Duff	1985–

DEPUTY DIRECTORS-GENERAL OF MI5

Graham Mitchell	1956–63
Martin Furnival Jones	1963–65
Anthony Simkins	1965–71
Michael Hanley	1971–72
Ronald Symonds	1972–76
John Jones	1976–81

INTRODUCTION

On Monday, 28 May 1951, Mrs Melinda Maclean telephoned the Foreign Office in London from her home in
Tatsfield, Kent. In a brief conversation she reported that
her husband Donald had disappeared and would not be
turning up for work.

Her call had been expected, for the Security Service,
MI5, had known of her husband's sudden decision to travel
to the Continent for more than two full days. For Donald
Duart Maclean, then head of the Foreign Office's American Department, was also suspected of having been a
Soviet spy. His decision to avoid interrogation by escaping
abroad, which had not been anticipated by MI5, was to
rock the British establishment. It was also to raise the
spectre that a large number of Britons, with impeccably
respectable backgrounds, had changed their allegiances.
Instead of remaining loyal to their country of origin, they
had opted, for ideological reasons, to serve the interests
of a country with an alien political system.

At first there had been considerable mystery about
Maclean's motives. The speculation increased when it was
revealed that he had gone missing with another Foreign
Office diplomat, Guy Burgess. It was not until the defection of two Soviet intelligence officers, Vladimir and
Evdokia Petrov, some three years later, in April 1954, that
the truth had been learned with any certainty. According to
the Petrovs, both Burgess and Maclean had been long-term
Russian agents, dedicated to the Soviet cause since their
recruitment at university before the war.

The concept of a mole, a deep-cover agent armed with what appeared to be impeccable credentials, was almost completely unknown in Britain. Since the 1917 Russian Revolution, there had been a handful of misguided political zealots who had deliberately betrayed their country's secrets. There were a greater number of naïve individuals who had been duped or coerced into treachery. But the idea of a deliberate, well-organised conspiracy, involving the most privileged in society, was disturbing. When the circumstances of the Burgess and Maclean defections became known, the government was obliged to make a public statement on the matter to relieve anxiety. Had the pair acted alone? If so, how had they managed to evade capture? Had they been helped by another suspect, the so-called third man? These pressing questions were the responsibility of the Security Service, an organisation steeped in secrecy. By convention its directors, staff and functions were concealed within an all-embracing cloak of secrecy. In theory, this was preserved to enable the organisation to operate with complete effectiveness, but gradually the suspicion grew that, far from creating the conditions for maximum efficiency, MI5's secrecy had itself been used to prevent the discovery of hostile moles. Indeed, a few senior officers actually believed that they had uncovered evidence of the KGB's penetration of the Security Service itself.

What was to become regarded as firm evidence of the KGB's influence over MI5's operations was found early in 1963. Its consequence was a highly classified investigation into the loyalties of certain men previously considered to be above reproach. Because they were senior members of the Security Service, the exercise became known as a molehunt. That one had even been contemplated, let alone conducted, would probably have remained one of the realm's most closely guarded secrets but for the belief, held by a sizable proportion of those charged with establishing the truth, that their conclusions had been buried because they were politically uncomfortable.

While the molehunters remained in employment by MI5

they were actively discouraged from taking precipitate action. But upon their retirement a few attempted to bring what they saw as a truly frightening and threatening situation to the private attention of selected politicians. In so doing, they inadvertently touched off a major constitutional crisis which brought the issues of loyalty, public accountability, secrecy and treason back into public attention. Some former suspects felt threatened by the selective leaks used to bring matters to a head. Others, despite being still bound by the formal undertakings of confidentiality required of all servants of the Crown, took the opportunity to disclose relevant details from their own experience. The means chosen ranged from letters in newspapers demanding formal statements from the Prime Minister, to covert arrangements with trusted journalists. Beleaguered, and placed in an impossible position by some of its own former officers, the Security Service responded by persuading a bemused government to initiate a series of half-baked court cases which only served to prime the public's appetite. The result was an incomprehensible jigsaw of innuendo, half-truths, smears and unbelievable revelations which left the nation bewildered, mystified and intrigued. The mole-hunts have now ended, and are of only historical importance, so at last the full, bizarre story can be told.

1

IMMUNITY ACCEPTED

As might have been anticipated, nothing about Kim Philby was quite what it seemed. In January 1963 he had been offered a formal immunity from prosecution, specially authorised by the Home Secretary and the Director of Public Prosecutions, and he had accepted it. He had even made a detailed, preliminary confession of his lifetime's duplicity: his recruitment to the Soviet cause while still at university, his determination to infiltrate the British Secret Services and his success at penetrating the highest echelons of the Allied intelligence establishment.

Nicholas Elliott was the quiet, stooped, donnish figure who had been despatched to Beirut to confront Philby with the evidence of his treachery. Some of it was purely circumstantial and dated back to the defection of Guy Burgess and Donald Maclean in 1951. Their sudden decision to flee to Moscow had compromised Philby and had caused him to be sacked, not just from his post as Britain's principal intelligence liaison officer in Washington, but from the Secret Intelligence Service (SIS) itself. Certainly, he had been implicated by the suddenness of Donald Maclean's decision to escape an interrogation at the hands of MI5, planned for Monday, 28 May 1951. Maclean had been tipped off with just hours to spare, and had fled the country via a cross-Channel ferry with his fellow conspirator, Guy Burgess, who had apparently opted to join Maclean at the last moment. The defection was a hasty affair, but only a handful of intelligence officers had known of MI5's intention to question Maclean. Philby had been an undergraduate at Trinity, Cambridge, with Burgess and had briefly shared a house with him when they had both served at the British Embassy in Washington. Philby was strongly suspected of having sent Maclean a secret warning via their mutual friend Burgess, but there was no definite proof. Those who had attended Philby's interrogation conducted at MI5's headquarters in London in November 1951, after his recall from Washington, by a leading barrister and former wartime MI5 officer, Helenus 'Buster' Milmo, had no doubt of his guilt. But guilt is a legal term and in the espionage world binding or 'smoking gun' evidence is notoriously difficult to find. There was no direct proof of Philby's complicity with Burgess or Maclean which could be presented in a court of law, and those who witnessed his performance knew that he would produce an equally impressive turn before any Old Bailey jury. Hence, four years later, when Philby's name was first mentioned in a Parliamentary Question as the possible 'third man', Eden's Foreign Secretary, Harold Macmillan, was obliged to clear him.

The Question was tabled on 25 October 1955 and was designed to bring the scandal into the open. A government reply was scheduled for 7 November, which gave the Foreign Secretary enough time to consult the Director-General of the Security Service, Sir Dick White. He, in turn, asked Graham Mitchell for his advice. Mitchell was then in charge of MI5's counter-espionage branch and, as such, had been the anonymous author of the government White Paper (Cmd 9577) on the Burgess and Maclean affair.* He had confirmed that 'there was no reason to conclude that Mr Philby has at any time betrayed the interests of this country or identify him with the so-called "third man" if indeed there was one',[1] and in consequence White was obliged to advise Macmillan that, in the absence of any new, hard evidence, the government had no choice but to clear Philby. Mitchell's opinion was repeated by Macmillan in the House of Commons during the White Paper debate on 7 November and gave Philby the happiest moment of his life.

Apart from Philby's involvement with Burgess, only one additional incriminating item had come to light since the

* See Appendix, pages 250–63.

notorious defections. During the Christmas holidays of 1961 a KGB officer named Anatoli Golitsyn had switched sides and had told the CIA that Philby was a Soviet spy of long-standing. But once again, the evidence was third-hand. The defector had no direct knowledge of Philby and his evidence was not admissible in court. The case against Philby remained exactly where it had rested in 1951: suspicion but no proof.

It was not until 1962 that a chance meeting on the Tel Aviv cocktail-party circuit gave the Security Service the opportunity it had been waiting for. Lord Rothschild, another wartime MI5 officer, met Flora Solomon, a senior executive of Marks & Spencer who had once employed Philby's second wife, Aileen. A keen Zionist, who was incensed by the anti-Israeli tone of some of Philby's recent articles in the *Observer* and *Economist*, Mrs Solomon told Rothschild about a curious incident which had occurred before the war. Apparently, Philby had once approached her and suggested that she join him in his 'important work for peace'. The suggestion had been made during one of Philby's many drinking bouts but the meaning had been clear: he was a Soviet agent and wanted to recruit her. She had refused, but had kept silent about his offer. Philby had later confided that he was 'in great danger'. He had not elaborated, but Mrs Solomon interpreted this to mean that he had become a Soviet spy.

Rothschild knew only that Philby had once been under suspicion and reported his conversation with Flora Solomon to Sir Dick White upon his return to London. By this time, in 1962, White had been heading SIS for six years, after a long and successful career in MI5. The Burgess and Maclean scandal had been particularly awkward for him as he had known Burgess and Philby well, and had bungled MI5's only opportunity to capture Maclean.

On the night of his departure, Maclean had been spotted by an alert immigration official at Southampton. A telephone call had been made to MI5's headquarters in London and White had been ordered to Paris in an attempt to intercept Maclean. On his way to the airport White had

realised that his passport had expired, and he was forced
to return to Curzon Street. An attempt was made to obtain
a new travel document from the Foreign Office, but by the
time the appropriate official had been woken up, the
trail had gone cold and both Burgess and Maclean had
disappeared somewhere in France.

Mrs Solomon's information amounted to the first eye-
witness testimony of Philby's duplicity, and it was recognised as such by Dick White when he was told of her
story by Rothschild at his Mayfair home. Furthermore,
Mrs Solomon was willing to sign a formal statement concerning Philby's attempt to recruit her and, if necessary,
appear as a witness against him in court. This was the
long-awaited key needed to 'turn' Philby. Now, at last,
White told Roger Hollis, Director-General of MI5, there
was some solid evidence with which to confront the Soviet
spy.

Following Rothschild's timely intervention, a debate
ensued involving both MI5 and SIS. Philby might try to
deny Flora Solomon's claim, but he would realise that his
usefulness to the Soviets had come to an end. There was
little purpose in a public trial, which would inevitably
embarrass those who had been forced to declare him
innocent only a few years earlier, but maybe there was a
chance to turn the tables on the KGB. If Philby could be
persuaded to co-operate and name names, perhaps MI5
would be in a position to close the Burgess and Maclean
file, and the spectre of Soviet infiltration of Whitehall,
once and for all.

The details of the request for a formal immunity from
prosecution remain secret, but it is known that an SIS
officer, Nicholas Elliott, was assigned the task of extracting
Philby's confession. He was briefed on all the evidence
against his old friend and sent to Beirut, where he made
contact with Philby. Much to his surprise, Philby welcomed
Elliott and almost seemed to be expecting him. When
Elliott explained the purpose of his mission, Philby
promptly admitted his guilt and launched into what he
claimed was a comprehensive statement. Having achieved

his objective, Elliott continued on a journey through Africa, inspecting various SIS stations, and then returned to London to expand on the brief report he had filed by cipher from Beirut.

In the light of subsequent events, Philby's initial confession was shown to be deficient in numerous respects, not the least of which was the extent of his involvement with other KGB agents recruited at Cambridge. His admission to Elliott turned out to be a plausible but incomplete account of his duplicity. Indeed, further analysis suggested that it could not have been the spontaneous document that Philby claimed it to be. Very gradually it was realised that the Soviet master spy had concocted a very incomplete statement of his activities. It was remarkable for what it omitted, an observation that suggested Philby had been quite prepared for Elliott's arrival with the offer of an immunity. Elliott confirmed that Philby had not expressed any surprise at his sudden appearance in Beirut and even volunteered that one of his first reactions was the ambiguous remark, 'I had not expected you so soon.' What had Philby meant? Had he been given advance notice of Elliott's mission? White was unable to put these questions to Philby because he suddenly dropped from sight on the night of 23 January 1963.

Philby's disappearance from Beirut, and his unexplained comment to Elliott, suggested that the KGB had been in control of the whole episode: that they had known of Elliott's offer of immunity and had enabled Philby to prepare a cover story – a plausible but partial confession which would give the KGB time to prepare an escape route and perhaps take other precautions. Upon reflection, Philby's willingness to co-operate with the authorities seemed uncharacteristic. At his interrogation by Milmo in 1951 Philby had fought back, denying every allegation and countering every move. Yet with Elliott his tactics had been markedly different. He acknowledged his guilt without much hesitation and needed little prompting before pouring out the story of his double life. What had caused the transformation? Within MI5's counter-espionage branch there was complete agreement: Philby was well prepared for the confrontation with Elliott and had been fully briefed on the substance of the evidence against him. The logical conclusion of this viewpoint was the existence of another highly placed source within the small group of counter-intelligence experts privy to Elliott's mission. The only question remaining was the name of the culprit.

The idea that Philby had been in a position to rehearse his confession had serious implications for the whole of the British intelligence community. Certainly, there was plenty of evidence to show that the Soviets had been very successful in penetrating other areas of the establishment. Quite apart from the examples of Burgess and Maclean, both senior members of the Foreign Office, there had been the more recent case of George Blake, a career SIS officer who had been exposed as a KGB spy in April 1961. There had also been the as yet inconclusive cases of John Cairncross and Anthony Blunt. Both had been at Cambridge with Burgess and were regarded as probable Soviet agents. Cairncross had served briefly in SIS and had been implicated by documents left behind in Burgess' flat in London. MI5 had hoped to trap Cairncross during a rendezvous with his KGB contact, but the operation failed. When challenged about having supplied Burgess with Treasury papers, Cairncross denied having been a spy and merely admitted to having been a little indiscreet. He had resigned his post at the Treasury and taken a teaching job at Northwestern University in America.

MI5's other suspect, Anthony Blunt, had spent the war in the Security Service and was therefore very familiar with the officers sent to question him about his relationship with Burgess; he also knew the limits of MI5's powers. In the face of his persistent denials, MI5 could do nothing except wait for some incriminating evidence to surface.

The problem confronting the Security Service in February 1963 was the knowledge that neither Cairncross nor Blunt had been in a position to alert Philby to Elliott's impending arrival in Beirut. Only a handful of people had actually known of the offer of immunity, and each of them seemed beyond reproach. But if the Security Service had been penetrated by the KGB, it would explain a whole series of apparently unrelated failures. One of these was the elaborate trap set for Cairncross. MI5 had placed him under intensive surveillance and had discovered from a secret source that he was scheduled to meet his KGB case officer in a London tube station. Cairncross had apparently requested the rendezvous because he was anxious about his position. He had been stunned by Burgess' unexpected defection and desperately needed advice. Had Burgess' escape implicated him? Had he come under suspicion? Cairncross had sought help from the Russians through an emergency procedure and a special meeting had been arranged.

MI5's team of watchers kept Cairncross under discreet observation as he entered the tube station, but his KGB friend failed to turn up. As the agreed time for the rendezvous passed, Cairncross showed increasing signs of agitation and eventually went home. Why had the Russians left him in the lurch? Had they spotted the trap, or had they been warned off at the last moment? Given the legendary skill of the Watcher Service to conceal its activities, it seemed likely that the entire operation had been betrayed, although no one had voiced that opinion at the time.

There were other reasons to believe that MI5 had been infiltrated. During the post-war era, the Security Service had made imaginative efforts to recruit and run a stable of double agents. Most had been businessmen who had succumbed to 'honey-trap' operations while on visits to Moscow. The classic scenario was that of an executive photographed in bed with a male prostitute. The blackmail victim was offered the choice of supplying useful information on his return to the West, or facing exposure when the compromising pictures were circulated to his family and the newspapers. In such cases the wretched subject would agree to the KGB's terms and, once safely home, approach the Security Service via the police. As often as not MI5 took the opportunity to provide the victim with suitable information, thus recruiting him as a double agent in the hope of identifying a Soviet intelligence operative in London. Although the scheme seemed practical, the KGB invariably lost interest in the double agents who had been 'turned' by MI5. Their skill at spotting these agents seemed uncanny, but there were those who believed there might be a more sinister explanation: a Soviet source within MI5's elite counter-espionage branch.

Another oddity explicable by the presence of a mole was MI5's complete failure to attract Russian defectors. Over the years there had been plenty of defectors from the various Soviet intelligence services, but they had all chosen other Western countries. Why had none sought asylum in Britain? When asked, most had replied that it was well known in Moscow that the British had been thoroughly penetrated. In other words, Britain did not have a reputation as a safe haven – in fact, quite the reverse.

Suspicions began to harden in 1962 when the head of MI5's Soviet counter-espionage section visited Washington and interviewed Anatoli Golitsyn. Since January 1960 the head of the D1 Section of D Branch had been Arthur Martin, a quiet, unassuming officer with a background in signals intelligence. In February and March 1962 he had met Golitsyn with a representative from SIS, and together they had extracted various items of circumstantial evidence which suggested the existence of a Soviet spy inside MI5. This material became known as the 'ten serials' and was to be regarded as the best proof of Soviet penetration.

Particularly damning was Golitsyn's claim that he had once glimpsed a top-secret card index in the KGB's headquarters in Moscow. Each card listed a separate document stored in one of two special safes. One safe, about a metre square, was reputed to contain documents from within the Security Service. As Peter Wright later commented:

Golitsyn had seen an index of what was there. One said 'material from the British Security Service'. Raw material or source material and was classified under 'Agents'. He couldn't remember the names of agents. Three or four agents but he couldn't remember their names. Golitsyn was sure the Security Service stuff couldn't have come from Blake. Actually the translation was 'material from the British Security Service – the actual material from spies'.[2]

Most of the card indices had been of a wartime vintage, but Golitsyn recalled the card of one which had a much more recent date. Those bearing a wartime date probably had come from Anthony Blunt, but there was a single card which Blunt could not have provided. Blunt had left MI5 to return to academic life in 1945, and the document listed in the KGB's index referred to a report written twelve years later in 1957. Blunt could not possibly have seen it, and nor could Philby or Blake. According to Golitsyn, he had been consulted to see if he could translate technical details of material in the KGB's British department. The document in question concerned the technical requirements of both MI5 and SIS and included a review of recent technical developments.

Enquiries in London established that this document had been written in 1957 by a member of the Security Service's Scientific Adviser's staff, a recruit from Marconi named Peter Wright. Wright had prepared a top-secret report on the very latest techniques in the field of 'eavesdropping, secret writing, opening locks, detecting microdots, the interception of telephones without taps'. It also went on to describe the resources devoted to counter-intelligence work by the government, including an analysis of costs, amounting to £50 million borne by other agencies to cover MI5's expenditure. One such item was the maintenance of the Security Service car fleet, which was concealed within the Department of Transport's budget. Wright's study gave a detailed account of all such clandestine expenditure, and its disclosure to the KGB suggested 'immense damage' to both MI5 and SIS. A limited number of copies had been made of this unique paper.

Golitsyn had seen one page of it. Golitsyn described this document without prompting. He said the source came from MI5. Everybody maintained it must have been Blake or some other document. I think Martin accepted it was the right document.[3]

Martin questioned Wright about his report and discovered that it had been written to support a claim for more resources to be spent on technical research and development, an issue close to Wright's heart. At first only Roger Hollis and Graham Mitchell had been sent the report, but it soon emerged that a few numbered copies had been circulated elsewhere. Martin was able to trace each recipient and limited the source down to five named individuals and the Defence Research Policy Office. Gradually, Martin began to accept the conclusion that MI5 had indeed been penetrated by the KGB. How else could Golitsyn have known about the report? To eliminate Blake's involvement, an MI5 officer was sent to Wormwood Scrubs prison to see if he had any recollection of it. Blake confirmed having betrayed all the signals intelligence assessments that had passed over his desk, but denied ever having seen Wright's research and development paper.

The more Martin looked, the greater the evidence of penetration. Even MI5's most impressive coups seemed doubtful when dissected. The arrest of Gordon Lonsdale, the Soviet 'illegal' caught servicing the Portland spy ring in 1961, had some unexplained inconsistencies. When taken into custody, he had asked what had taken the police so long and implied that he had been expecting an arrest. Sheer bravado? Perhaps, but why had all his secret ciphers been changed within days of the break-in at his flat when all his one-time pads had been photographed? Had the Soviets learned that his communication codes had been compromised? Certainly, thousands of man hours had been wasted on their analysis. A dispassionate judgement of the Lonsdale episode could not rule out KGB intervention.

Similarly, there was a minority view that the John Vassall case was not quite all it seemed. Vassall had been convicted in 1962 of having supplied the Soviets with secrets from the British Admiralty, but Golitsyn recalled having seen a card index referring to documents describing the Royal Navy's fleet of atomic submarines. A special visit to Vassall in prison confirmed that the homosexual spy had never been privy to atomic secrets. Suspicion grew that another Soviet spy had been working in parallel with Vassall in the Admiralty, and the field was eventually narrowed down to a secretary to the First Sea Lord. He was placed under surveillance and was spotted making covert visits to a basement flat on his way home after work. The same flat was sometimes visited by an identified Soviet intelligence officer. Charles Elton, the MI5 investigator, had sought permission to interrogate the naval officer involved but Hollis refused, saying that there was insufficient evidence to justify such a move. Instead, the officer was given the command of a ship and steps were taken to prevent him from having access to sensitive information for the rest of his career.

Further corroboration of Soviet preknowledge of MI5's operations was offered by GCHQ. Much of this is still too secret to be revealed, but it added to the volume of circumstantial evidence accumulating in Martin's dossier of embarrassing, unexplained incidents in the Cold War. One of the more well-known episodes was that of the Petrov defections in April 1954 in Australia. Vladimir Petrov had been persuaded to switch sides by an Australian intelligence agent, and his wife, Evdokia, had subsequently decided to join him. Both were senior KGB officers and were regarded as valuable catches by the West, but their defections had nearly ended in catastrophe. Just hours before Petrov had made his move, two KGB thugs had arrived in Sydney determined to escort him and his wife home. What had prompted their sudden appearance? Once again it looked as though news of Petrov's intended defection had leaked to Moscow. Upon enquiry, Martin discovered that both Mitchell and Hollis had been entrusted with details of Petrov's declared intention to seek asylum in Australia.

When Arthur Martin totted up MI5's failures, it began
to look as though the argument for current or recent Soviet
penetration of the Security Service was an established fact.
He had moved from the realms of speculation into the
dangerous, paranoid 'wilderness of mirrors', in which even
the most experienced of counter-intelligence officers start
putting a sinister interpretation on the most innocent of
incidents. When viewed objectively, the Philby, Lonsdale
and Petrov affairs were only completely explicable in terms
of a Soviet source high in MI5. If the double-agent failures
and GCHQ's secret contribution were added to these, the
case seemed unanswerable.

There was also some indication that an operation in
Canada, codenamed KEYSTONE, had been compromised. This was a complicated plan involving GIDEON,
a Royal Canadian Mounted Police (RCMP) double agent
who had returned to Moscow after a lengthy mission to
Montreal lasting three years. With GIDEON's help, the
RCMP had thoroughly infiltrated the KGB's networks in
North America, yet he disappeared soon after his return
to Moscow in 1955. The RCMP concluded that he had
been betrayed by a well-placed traitor and it was known
that both Mitchell and Hollis had taken an extraordinary
interest in KEYSTONE's progress.

The more Martin looked, the more weight was added
to the proposition that MI5 was penetrated at a high level.
Indeed, when he investigated the more sensitive, technical
operations conducted by the Security Service, the more
suspicious he became. He found that quite separate failures
could be linked by the common strand of betrayal. Operation CHOIR, the insertion of a probe microphone into
the wall of the Soviet Consulate in London, proved an
abject failure; the Russians had stopped using the relevant
room soon after the operation had got under way. In a
similar incident in Canada, masterminded by Wright, the
new Soviet Embassy in Ottawa had been wired for sound.
The original building had been burnt to the ground in an
accident and the RCMP had taken the opportunity of
putting its own eavesdropping experts on to the new site.

Guided by Wright, the RCMP engineers had placed six of the very latest, supposedly undetectable, bugs in the rooms set aside for the KGB. When the Embassy was finally opened for business, the KGB moved its offices elsewhere. It was almost as though the Soviets had known about the exact location of the technical coverage long in advance. The most logical explanation was betrayal: a single, well-placed source inside MI5 who might have been responsible for every failure. With this thought in mind, Martin initiated an extraordinary exercise which was to become known as a molehunt.

A comprehensive analysis of Martin's catalogue of Security Service failures to find a potential traitor would have been an almost impossible task because of the great number of personnel involved. But if his suspicions about Philby's confession were true, then the field was much smaller. In fact, he soon realised that, apart from himself, there were only four other MI5 officers involved, and perhaps two or three secretaries. They were the Director of MI5's D Branch, Malcolm Cumming; the Deputy Director-General, Graham Mitchell; the Director-General himself; and Martin's own assistant, Evelyn McBarnet. If Philby had been tipped off from within MI5, one of these individuals was likely to be a Soviet spy.

The flaw in Martin's thesis was, of course, the small group of outsiders who had been consulted on the question of an immunity from prosecution for Philby. The Attorney-General, Sir John Hobson, and the Home Secretary, Henry Brooke, could reasonably be excluded as suspects, as could the Deputy Director of Public Prosecutions, Maurice Crump. Sir Charles Cunningham, the Permanent Under-Secretary at the Home Office, had also been let in on the secret, but he too was regarded as above suspicion. That only left Sir Dick White and Nicholas Elliott. Martin reasoned that they too could be ruled out as they had only been brought in at the very last moment and were anyway above suspicion. In that situation, the spotlight was fixed firmly on the original MI5 list.

It could have been argued that the warning to Philby was, perhaps, an isolated incident and one that could be explained by some unintentional indiscretion, but once the idea had germinated in his mind Martin became convinced that the tip-off fitted into a definite pattern. Others also were later to reach the same, irresistible conclusion. Although there had been other suspicious events in the past, this mishap was the first to really stand out and, more significantly, the first that could be traced back to a very limited group of participants. In this instance a deliberate leak depended upon the notion that Philby had actually received advance notice of MI5's intentions. At this stage proof of this was lacking, but it was to follow later, as we shall see.

Martin decided to narrow the field further by eliminating his own trusted assistant, whom he had known for many years, and concentrating on Malcolm Cumming. An Old Etonian and graduate of Sandhurst, Cumming had joined MI5 in 1934, aged twenty-seven, after just seven years' service with his regiment, the 60th Rifles; he had later been appointed Director of MI5's administration division. In 1935 he had recommended Dick White for recruitment into the Security Service. While, superficially, Cumming seemed a reasonable candidate, in spite of his background, it was soon realised that he had not had sufficient access to exert an influence over so many operations thought to have been sabotaged. His career was one of steady, if lacklustre, achievement, and he was quickly eliminated as a suspect. Martin then settled on the last two remaining officers, Mitchell and Hollis.

Graham Mitchell had been born at Kenilworth on 4 November 1905 and had been educated at Winchester, where he was an Exhibitioner, and Magdalen College, Oxford, where he read Politics, Philosophy and Economics. While still at school he had developed polio, which left him with a limp, but this had not prevented him from becoming a keen yachtsman, sailing for Oxford, and an enthusiastic golfer. In 1930 he won the Queen's Club men's doubles lawn tennis championship. He was also an accomplished chess player, at one time being ranked fifth in the world in correspondence chess, a game at which he represented his country. Before the war he had worked for the *Illustrated London News* and the Conservative Research Department, before joining MI5's F Division, the counter-subversion branch, in November 1939. There he concentrated on the surveillance of Fascist extremists and gained something of a reputation as a Leftist. His post-war job, until his promotion to Deputy Director-General in 1956, was Director of D Branch, MI5's counter-espionage department. In terms of access to sensitive information about current anti-Soviet operations, Mitchell unquestionably had by far the best knowledge of Martin's three original suspects.

Roger Hollis had been born in Wells on 2 December 1902, the third son of a cleric who was later to become Bishop of Taunton. He was educated at Clifton College, Bristol, and Worcester College, Oxford, although he went abroad to China before completing his degree course. There he worked for a subsidiary of the British American Tobacco Company, but contracted tuberculosis and underwent treatment in Switzerland before finally joining MI5 in 1938. He went straight into F Division to concentrate on monitoring the activities of the extreme Left, including the Communist Party of Great Britain (CPGB).

Since both Mitchell and Hollis were thrown together in F Division, this is a good moment to explain the work of the entire department, which was sub-divided into four main sections. The organisational chart will help to give an overview of the Division's responsibilities. F1, headed by Colonel W. A. Alexander, dealt with military security within the forces and kept a watch for troublemakers and potential mutineers. His brief also extended to government establishments, such as arsenals, which employed civilians as well as military personnel. Alexander's experience in the field had dated back to before the 1931 Invergordon Mutiny, in which he had played an important role, preventing the discontent from spreading beyond Scotland. F2, which was to be Hollis' section, kept a watch on Communism through three smaller units: F2(a), run by an officer named Clarke, which monitored the CPGB's policy activities; F2(b), where Millicent Bagot kept an eye on the Comintern and Communist refugees; and F2(c), headed by Mr Pilkington, which maintained files on Soviet intelligence organisations. F3, where Mitchell worked as an assistant to its head, a distinguished barrister named Aiken Sneath, was responsible for pro-Nazi suspects, the nationalist political parties and the movements of the Right. Finally, F4, in the hands of (Sir) Roger Fulford, dealt with pacifists, peace movements and the revolutionary Left. Other wartime personnel such as (Sir) Blanshard Stamp, Kemball Johnson and the Hon. Hugh Astor spent brief periods in F Division, but the officers mentioned above were regulars who formed the Division's backbone.

Wartime Structure and Responsibilities
of F Division of the Security Service

Deputy Director
Roger Hollis

Assistant Directors
Blanshard Stamp
Graham Mitchell
Roger Fulford

F1	F2	F3	F4
Internal Security in HM Forces	Communism and Left-Wing Movements	Right-Wing Nationalist Movements; British Union; Scottish Nationalists; German and Austrian Right Organisations; Pro-Nazi Individuals	Pacifists; Peace Groups; Revolutionary Movements
	Roger Hollis Hugh Astor		
Colonel W. A. Alexander			Roger Fulford
		Aiken Sneath Graham Mitchell Kemball Johnson	

F2(a) — CPGB Policy

Mr Clarke

F2(b) — Comintern Communist Refugees

Millicent Bagot

F2(c) — Soviet Intelligence

Mr Pilkington

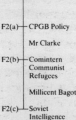

Although Mitchell and Hollis were engaged in monitoring the two opposite ends of the political spectrum, they worked closely together throughout the war years when their office was moved away from London to Blenheim Palace, the Oxfordshire seat of the Dukes of Marlborough. By the end of hostilities Hollis had risen to Deputy Director rank, in charge of F Division, and Mitchell was his principal assistant. Thereafter their careers parted briefly, with Hollis moving to C Division, the physical security advisory service, and Mitchell entering the elite D Division.

The turning-point in Hollis' career took place in November 1952 when Guy Liddell retired as Deputy Director-General of the Security Service. He was then only sixty, but he knew that he had no hope of succeeding Sir Percy Sillitoe as Director-General. Instead, he transferred to the Atomic Energy Authority to head its security department. Dick White, who had been directing MI5's counter-espionage division since 1946, was promoted to take Liddell's place; when he succeeded Sillitoe upon the latter's retirement in 1953, he appointed Roger Hollis as his deputy.

White's choice was unusual in the sense that Hollis had virtually no experience of MI5's most important function, counter-espionage. He had specialised on the political Left during the war, and latterly had run the rather mundane C Division. Only two episodes in his career to date stood out: his involvement in the Gouzenko case late in 1945, and his advisory role in the formation of the Australian Security and Intelligence Organisation (ASIO) in 1948.

The Gouzenko case concerned a twenty-six-year-old Russian cipher clerk who, in September 1945, had defected from the Soviet Embassy in Ottawa, taking with him a batch of secret military documents. Igor Gouzenko himself had little first-hand knowledge of espionage, but his stolen files offered a wealth of valuable information about a Soviet spy network in Canada masterminded by the local GRU *rezident*, Colonel Nicolai Zabotin. One of Gouzenko's first tasks was to explain to the Royal Canadian Mounted Police how the Soviet Embassy housed two sep-

arate but parallel espionage organisations. He knew little
about the activities of the NKVD, the KGB's forerunner,
but he was intimately involved with the GRU, the Red
Army's military intelligence directorate. No fewer than
eighteen people had been named in the 109 pink, blue
and white sheets of paper removed from the Embassy's
coderoom, including a Canadian Member of Parliament.
Many of the suspects were well-known members of the
Canadian Communist Party and Hollis, as MI5's expert on
Communist affairs, was selected to assist Peter Dwyer, the
SIS officer already on the scene, to debrief Gouzenko.
Hollis seems only to have had one brief interview with
Gouzenko, which took place in the presence of Gouzenko's Russian-speaking RCMP bodyguard, Mervyn
Black. Hollis was unimpressed by the youthful codist, and
his subsequent report of that meeting included a reference
to an absurd claim attributed to Gouzenko that the GRU
'knew all about the British spies in the Kremlin'. In fact,
there were none to be known about.

If fantastic statements like this one tended to discredit
Gouzenko as a source, his papers did not, for they were
full of clues to well-placed spies.Of immediate interest to
Hollis were two Britons referred to by the cryptonyms of
ALEK and ELLI. ALEK turned out to be Dr Allan Nunn
May, a distinguished Cambridge-trained physicist then liv-
ing in Montreal with access to important atomic secrets;
ELLI was revealed as Kay Willsher, then secretary to
Malcolm MacDonald, Britain's High Commissioner to
Canada. Both were arrested in March the following year
and convicted of betraying classified information.

One inconclusive item of interest to the Security Service
concerned an allegation made by Gouzenko to Peter
Dwyer. As a young Red Army cipher clerk, Gouzenko
would not normally have enjoyed access to the GRU's
sensitive secrets, or been in a position to betray individual
agents; however, he did recall an illicit conversation held
with an indiscreet friend at GRU headquarters in Moscow,
before his departure to Canada in June 1943. Gouzenko's
friend had boasted of the existence of a valuable Soviet

spy inside British counter-intelligence, apparently also codenamed ELLI. The allegation was a serious one for at that time neither Anthony Blunt, nor Kim Philby had been identified as Soviet spies and either might have fitted that description. When, after Blunt's eventual confession, it was realised that both he and Philby had worked for the KGB, rather than the GRU, Gouzenko's statement about ELLI was to be re-examined in extraordinary detail, as we shall see.

Apart from his brief involvement with the Gouzenko case, Hollis' other work overseas concerned ASIO. In 1948 he had travelled to Australia with Robert Hemner-Scales to take the first steps in the transformation of the country's military Commonwealth Investigation Service into the civilian Australian Security and Intelligence Organisation, which came into formal existence on 2 March 1949 under the leadership of a respected judge, Sir Geoffrey Reed. The decision to create ASIO had been made by J. B. Chifley, the Labour Prime Minister, and was the result of intensive lobbying and the recognition that the Soviets had already embarked on an espionage offensive in Australia, as disclosed by a series of extremely secret intercepted wireless signals. Codenamed VENONA, this material had originated in Australia from an undercover radio receiving station outside Darwin maintained jointly by the British and the Australian armies. The source known as VENONA provided convincing evidence of the KGB's commitment to subversion and the existence of an intelligence-gathering structure within the Soviet diplomatic mission in Canberra. The combination of VENONA and Hollis' advisory team proved irresistible: in spite of some initial reluctance, Chifley's administration authorised ASIO's creation, born in MI5's image. It was also to prove a major boost for Hollis' career, because on his return to London he was established as the Security Service's leading expert on Soviet-inspired Communist subversion and promoted to be one of MI5's six directors. His appointment as Deputy Director-General was to follow four years later.

2

OPERATION PETERS

Arthur Martin's dilemma centred on the relative seniority of his two main suspects. Hollis and Mitchell were Director-General and Deputy Director-General, respectively. That one or both of them might be a traitor seemed incredible, yet, if the penetration theory was correct, they were by far the most likely candidates. There was also some evidence from Martin's own personal experience. According to office gossip, Mitchell 'had had the reputation of being a Marxist during the war', and of Hollis, Martin later commented, 'I could only say that I found his complacency towards the threat of Russian espionage, as reflected in the policy of the Service since he became Director-General, inexplicable to me and to many of my colleagues.'

Aware that he could not seek help from his immediate superiors, in case Mitchell or Hollis were tipped off, in April 1963 Martin approached Sir Dick White, then Chief of the Secret Intelligence Service. He explained that there was growing evidence to show that MI5 had been penetrated at a high level, and that Mitchell or Hollis seemed the best suspects. White thought the matter over for twenty-four hours and then instructed Martin to tell Hollis that Mitchell might be a Soviet spy. Both agreed to conceal the fact that Hollis was also under suspicion and that Martin had been to see White. Hollis heard Martin's analysis in silence, and then invited Martin to join him for dinner at the Travellers Club in Pall Mall later the same evening.

Dinner passed in embarrassing small-talk, with Hollis eventually instructing Martin to tell no one of his suspicions. He would call for him to discuss the matter of Mitchell later the following week.

Five days later Hollis called a secret conference at his home in Campden Hill Square which was attended by Martin, who was invited to repeat his thesis, and Martin Furnival Jones. The latter had served as Malcolm Cumming's predecessor as Director of the Security Service's counter-espionage branch and had been switched to MI5's C Branch. By the end of the meeting it had been decided that Martin should embark on a discreet investigation of Mitchell, who would henceforth be known as PETERS, and report regularly to Furnival Jones.

This arrangement worked well, for Furnival Jones was a respected MI5 officer with plenty of counter-espionage experience. Before the war he had worked as a solicitor with a large firm in the City, and was acknowledged as a skilled intelligence officer who could examine evidence and sift facts.

By the beginning of May Martin had uncovered some odd aspects of Mitchell's behaviour, including his habit of taking counter-surveillance measures on his way home after work. Mitchell lived on the edge of Chobham Common and usually caught the same train each evening from Waterloo, but he often took elaborate precautions to prevent anyone from tailing him to the railway station. This seemed rather strange considering that Mitchell was a desk man and had never run agents in the field. Where had he picked up such tricks? Furthermore, Mitchell was drinking heavily at home and showed unmistakable signs of stress. In anticipation of the investigation proceeding a stage further, Martin asked Furnival Jones for additional help, and a D Branch case officer, Ronald Symonds, was brought in. Symonds was part of the new breed of professionals recruited after the war. He had been educated at Rugby and New College, Oxford, and had joined MI5 in 1951, following the defections of Burgess and Maclean. In his first assignment as a case officer, Symonds began building up a dossier in order to confront Mitchell. In addition, a small group of 'watchers' had been recruited by White from SIS to monitor Mitchell's movements. In order that Mitchell could be kept under constant surveillance, two officers with technical expertise were brought in to complete the team: Hugh Winterborn, who was transferred to D Branch from MI5's technical operations section; and Peter Wright, who was seconded from a joint MI5–SIS technical operations unit, headed by Dr Hector Willis.

Of Martin's team of molehunters, Wright was the most recent recruit into the Security Service. He had joined from the Marconi electronics giant, where he had worked at its headquarters in Chelmsford on several classified government projects. His father, G. M. Wright, was a senior executive with the Marconi company and had been responsible for several important breakthroughs in the wireless communications field. Following one particular success, codenamed Operation SATYR, a sophisticated, remote-controlled microphone made in the Soviet Union had been dismantled and studied. The listening device had been found in 1952, concealed inside a cavity hollowed out of the American great seal which had hung over the ambassador's desk in the US Embassy in Moscow. The transmitter had apparently been activated and powered from a distance, using microwave beams, and it had been Peter Wright's task to discover its secrets. He did so, and his subsequent report so impressed MI5 that he was offered a job as 'Scientific Adviser'. When, in April 1963, Arthur Martin needed to use eavesdropping equipment in the PETERS case, Wright was selected to supervise the technical side. He was regarded as the leading expert in his field and had undertaken numerous clandestine operations for the Security Service. Although Arthur Martin was not aware of it at the time, Wright had also sensed unease about the high failure rate of MI5's anti-Soviet activities. As yet he had not articulated his growing anxiety about hostile penetration of the organisation, but Wright was destined to become an obsessive molehunter.

As far as the PETERS case went, Wright was restricted

by limitations imposed on him by the Director-General. For example, Hollis had been extremely reluctant to confide in any outsiders, and had refused to approach either the Home Secretary, Henry Brooke, or the Prime Minister, Harold Macmillan, for permission to place a wiretap on Mitchell's home telephone. However serious or immediate the circumstances, the Post Office engineers always insisted on seeing an interception warrant signed by the Secretary of State before granting MI5 access to its telephone exchanges or cables. Evidently Hollis, who had been thoroughly preoccupied by the public unfolding of the Profumo scandal since January, was not prepared to undermine MI5's precarious position by disclosing details of PETERS to a minister at such an awkward time. Mitchell, of course, had played an important role in the Profumo affair and had even visited Downing Street early in February to discuss certain developments with the Prime Minister's staff. Understandably, Hollis was loathe to suggest that Mitchell was untrustworthy until he had some firm evidence. Martin insisted that such evidence would be impossible to secure without a telephone tap. Hollis was adamant, so the molehunters were forced to settle for coverage of Mitchell's office telephone. As an additional measure, a special closed-circuit camera was rigged behind a two-way mirror over Mitchell's office door in order to keep him under observation while at his desk. The video monitor was placed on the sixth floor, directly above Mitchell's office. On one occasion Mitchell was seen to break down, with his head in his hands. Moments later he looked up, evidently in mental agony, towards the communicating door in the Director-General's office and was heard to gasp in a tormented voice, 'Why are you doing this to me?', as though Hollis was torturing him in some way. Certainly, pressure of work was not an adequate explanation for Mitchell's unexpected loss of composure.

Technical coverage was considered extremely important because, soon after Operation PETERS had started, Mitchell had suddenly asked for early retirement. This was regarded as a very unwelcome development by the molehunters and some of Martin's investigators suspected that he had learned of the PETERS enquiry. After all, why should Mitchell seek early retirement? He was not due to go until his sixtieth birthday, in November 1965, and he had no satisfactory explanation to offer. Why, at the very peak of his career, should he want to pack it all in? Had he spotted the surveillance? When asked, Mitchell simply said that he was tired of his work and wanted to spend more time playing correspondence chess. Faced with no alternative, Hollis had agreed that his deputy should retire on 6 September 1963, twenty-four years after he had joined MI5, but this decision severely handicapped the operation. Indeed, some of the molehunters believed that Mitchell's timely request had been privately welcomed by Hollis as a convenient solution to a potentially explosive situation. Much later, he was to be accused of actually tipping Mitchell off about Operation PETERS.

The PETERS team knew that they had only a limited period in which to build a case against Mitchell, and they recognised that a hostile interrogation could only be conducted effectively while he was still a member of the Service. After his retirement, he would be free to refuse to attend an interview, or could simply walk out of one if it got too sticky. MI5 had virtually no sanctions to apply once Mitchell had left the office for the last time and not even his pension could be used to threaten him. Like all other Civil Service pensioners, he was automatically entitled to 1/80th of his final year's salary for every year of service. Thus, after twenty-four years, he would get rather more than a quarter of his final salary, which could not be touched. Any attempt to remove it would involve justifying a case to a Civil Service tribunal, which would, of course, demand firm evidence of serious misconduct if Mitchell decided to appeal.

In retrospect, it may seem extraordinary that Hollis should have been so unwilling to tell either Brooke or Macmillan of the PETERS investigation, but a short re-view of the political events of the previous twelve months puts his hesitation into context. In March 1962 George

Blake had received a record term of imprisonment for
betraying SIS secrets to the KGB; early in 1962 Sir Charles
Romer's Committee of Enquiry released its findings on
the Portland spy ring; in September 1962 John Vassall had
been arrested, and in December 1962 Barbara Fell had
been imprisoned for passing information on to her
Yugoslav lover; Dr Giuseppe Martelli, an atomic scientist,
was arrested on espionage charges in April 1963 (and was
later acquitted); in the same month Lord Radcliffe had
published his tribunal's conclusions on the Vassall affair,
and at the end of June Lord Denning was appointed to
look into the security implications of the Profumo affair.
To many observers it seemed as though the country had
gone spy mad.

Quite apart from the above, Hollis had his own internal
troubles. Philby had disappeared at the end of January,
soon after taking his immunity from prosecution and volun-
teering a confession. At about the same time Westminster
was seething with rumours about Profumo's alleged involvement with a call-girl. The Director-General had even
been hauled in to see the Home Secretary on 27 March
just to confirm that MI5 had not been responsible for
writing a series of anonymous letters to Mrs Profumo.

Hollis was fighting a rearguard action on the Profumo
matter so as to conceal, or at any rate play down, the
involvement of a D Branch case officer, 'Woods', who had
recruited Stephen Ward as an MI5 informant more than
three years earlier. Ward had played a key role in the
scandal and was to commit suicide on 3 August 1963,
convinced that 'Woods' had deliberately abandoned him
because of the police's interest in Ward's call-girls. By that
time Denning had already started hearing evidence and
had made two visits to MI5's Mayfair headquarters,
Leconfield House, to see Hollis, Mitchell and 'Woods'. If
all this unwelcome attention was not enough, another
D Branch officer, Charles Elton, was convinced of the
existence of another Soviet spy, apart from Vassall, inside
the Admiralty. During a short visit to London, Anatoli
Golitsyn had confirmed having once seen Royal Navy

papers referring to atomic submarines. When shown
copies, Golitsyn had picked out a batch which had had
only limited circulation. They had not been seen by any of
the Portland spy ring, which had been rounded up in
January 1961, and when Elton visited Vassall in prison he
had denied ever having had access to such material. After
a lengthy search a good suspect had been found, but Hollis
had ordered the investigation to be dropped. Instead, the
naval officer at the centre of the enquiry was given a
command at sea, thus placing him out of harm's way. He
was to stay in the Royal Navy until he retired with the
rank of admiral. He is still unaware of the suspicions held
against him.

    In the midst of all these anxieties, Hollis was facing a
revolt by the molehunters, who had become increasingly
frustrated by the lack of 'technical facilities'. Martin
eventually reported to Furnival Jones that unless the
Director-General obtained authorisation for a tap on
Mitchell's home telephone, he would resign from the case.
Wright tried to talk Martin out of this precipitate action
and instead arranged for the PETERS team to appeal to
Sir Dick White. When, one Sunday afternoon in his London flat, White was told of the crisis involving PETERS,
he agreed to intervene with Hollis. Shortly afterwards,
Hollis explained the situation to the Prime Minister and
obtained permission to tap Mitchell's home telephone line
and plant bugs in his house. Hollis must have felt increasingly isolated, especially when, in June 1963, his colleague
Malcolm Cumming was told of the PETERS case for the
first time. Cumming was astonished and angered that such
an enquiry could have been undertaken by his own Branch
without his knowledge, but at first he appears not to have
realised that briefly he too had been under suspicion. He
was to take early retirement in 1965, after thirty-one years
in the Service. One reason for his bitterness had been
the molehunters' use of the 'barium meal' technique, in
which a select group of officers were given specific
items of traceable information to see if any of it reached
the Soviets. When Cumming learned that he had been

subjected to this treatment, alongside Mitchell, he had been furious.

By early August the PETERS operation had progressed so far that one participant commented, 'None of us engaged in the investigation had any serious doubts of Mitchell's guilt. Our fear was that we would not be able to produce evidence sufficient for prosecution except by successful interrogation.' It was, nevertheless, a case based on circumstantial evidence. In summary, it consisted of background material which could also have fitted Hollis: Gouzenko's claim about ELLI; the failure of so many operations during Mitchell's tenure as Director of MI5's counter-espionage branch; the marked reluctance of defectors to seek refuge in Britain; the vague allegations of numerous defectors; the specific charges made by Golitsyn; the loss of the KEYSTONE double agents; the exposure of the CHOIR surveillance systems; and the bogus nature of Philby's prepared confession. All these items amounted to a general indication of current or recent hostile penetration. The evidence pointing to Mitchell was more detailed: Mitchell's recorded support for Philby in 1951 and again in 1955; his scepticism of Golitsyn's *bona fides*; his habit of playing postal chess with Russians; his personal recommendation of a security clearance for Bruno Pontecorvo, the atomic physicist who subsequently went to live in the East in October 1950; his deliberate falsification of Pontecorvo's personal file in which he had confirmed the completion of a certain field enquiry although it had never been conducted; the unexplained resignation of two of his colleagues after office rows; his extraordinary lapse in the drafting of the White Paper on the defection of Burgess and Maclean, in which he stated erroneously that Maclean had attended Trinity College, Cambridge.

Some of these items could have had perfectly innocent explanations. The embarrassing slip in the government's White Paper was probably nothing more sinister than a stupid mistake, but such official documents are not supposed to contain blunders. Certainly, it exposed MI5 to the charge that it did not know the difference between

Trinity Hall and Trinity College. At the very least this indicated poor research or inept double-checking. The other matters would require detailed answers, and the revelation, by Mitchell's former secretary, that he had deliberately faked an entry in Pontecorvo's dossier, seemed damning. Clearly an interrogation was called for so that Mitchell could be given the opportunity to defend himself by giving a full account of his actions . . . or to make a detailed confession.

This being the case, it was proposed that the Americans be informed so as to retain their confidence. Obviously, the prospect of breaking the news of Mitchell's duplicity was unpalatable, but when the suggestion was made the molehunters were totally unprepared for Hollis' reaction. According to Furnival Jones, who conveyed the news, the Director-General 'was not yet convinced either that the case was strong enough to justify interrogation or that it was necessary to inform the Americans at all'. The PETERS team was stunned, especially since Martin had personal experience of lying to the CIA and the FBI after the defections of Burgess and Maclean in 1951 in a clumsy attempt to conceal MI5's inefficiency. He and the then Director-General, Sir Percy Sillitoe, had made a half-hearted attempt to palm off the FBI with some suitably 'sanitised' files, but it had failed. The Americans had spotted the flaws straightaway, and the incident had damaged the long-established mutual trust between the two Allies.

Determined not to be placed in the same position again, the molehunters demanded a meeting at the Director-General's home one Saturday morning and individually announced their intention to resign from the Service unless action was taken to let the Americans in on PETERS. Hollis made no immediate reply to the threat, but the following week consulted with Dick White and sought an interview with the Prime Minister. At that meeting Macmillan apparently agreed that Hollis should tell the Americans about MI5's suspicions against Mitchell, but not until the end of September.

The net result of this episode was a further postpone-
ment of the decision to interrogate Mitchell. When the
molehunters pressed Hollis for permission, he explained
his new position: no interrogation would take place before
Mitchell's departure from MI5 on 6 September, and a
detailed report was to be prepared of the entire investigation. Once he had studied the report, he would consider
recalling Mitchell for an interview. This was very unwelcome news for the PETERS team, which realised that the
odds against Mitchell confessing would lengthen once he
had reached the safety of retirement. As an experienced
MI5 officer he was fully aware of the organisation's shortcomings, and in particular its inability to detain and question suspects. He would always have the option of declining
to co-operate, leaving the molehunters in the worst possible position of abandoning yet another case without reaching anything even resembling a definite conclusion. In spite
of the team's reservations on the issue, Symonds was
promoted to head the D1's investigation sub-section, and
selected to prepare the PETERS case history. This was
completed quite quickly.

This document became known as the Symonds Report
and was initialled by both Dick White and Roger Hollis
late in September 1963, shortly before the latter flew to
Washington to explain the PETERS episode to the Director of Central Intelligence, John McCone, and the Director
of the FBI, J. Edgar Hoover. The fact that Hollis endorsed
this remarkable document, and then reported its contents
to the Americans, is itself a bizarre event. He must
either have been extraordinarily confident of his own
position, or thoroughly convinced of Mitchell's guilt. The
absence of any dissenting attachment by him indicates
that he was perfectly prepared to undergo a molehunt
himself.

Although appalled by the damage Mitchell might have
done, in terms of compromising sources and jeopardising
shared agents, the Americans appreciated the trust shown
by the Director-General and his D1, who flew out the
following day to reassure his bemused opposite numbers

that Mitchell would be called in for intensive interrogation shortly.

In fact, no such interrogation was to take place for several years. Towards December 1963 Symonds began to have second thoughts about the strength of the evidence against Mitchell and, in January 1964, following a conference at an SIS safe-house in Sloane Square, the Director-General commissioned a new report from him and prohibited him from consulting either Martin or Wright. Symonds completed it in March 1964.

In May 1964, following further developments, it is believed that a third and final report was written. Although Hollis said nothing about it at the time, he later revealed that he had consulted the Prime Minister who, allegedly, had advised against a confrontation with Mitchell in case he defected. Nothing of this was known when PETERS was examined for the third time. On this occasion a couple of minor errors were pointed out in the original PETERS case history, and greater emphasis was placed on the success of several cases in which Mitchell had either played a part or had seen sensitive papers. The best example seemed to be the Petrov defections in Australia in 1954. Mitchell had been fully indoctrinated and knew that Vladimir Petrov did not intend to return to Moscow at the end of his tour of duty. The fact that both Vladimir and Evdokia Petrov had made good their escape was surely proof of Mitchell's loyalty? If the PETERS case officers had been given the chance, they would have pointed out that the unexpected arrival of two KGB thugs named Karpinsky and Zharkov tended to show that the Soviets had some foreknowledge of the Petrovs' intentions. In the event, the KGB had tried to hustle Evdokia Petrov out of the country without her husband, but the attempt had been frustrated by ASIO's last-minute intervention. Whatever the truth of the Petrov affair, a report was submitted to Hollis in August, by which time Mitchell had long gone and Furnival Jones had become Deputy Director-General in his place. Symonds, who had been appointed Director of C Branch, cleared PETERS. Thus, with the consent of Hollis,

Symonds had apparently executed a complete *volte-face*. What had initially seemed a good case against Mitchell, or anyway enough to convince all those engaged on the operation, had been transformed into something rather less substantial, although there was no escaping the final truth: there had been post-war penetration and, as well as pursuing PETERS, the molehunt must be extended.

What makes this conclusion so extraordinary is the Director-General's apparent willingness to endorse it. He had been told by Furnival Jones in the very earliest days of the PETERS enquiry that he had been one of Martin's two best candidates, so he must also have known that the inescapable logic of his acceptance of the third and last report was to focus the molehunters' attention on to him.

The final Symonds Report resulted in a winding-up meeting held in September 1964 at which all those involved in the PETERS molehunt were present. It proved to be a controversial affair, in part because Martin and Wright only became aware of Symonds' decision shortly before the meeting opened. They were both highly critical of one piece of evidence prepared by Dr Hector Willis. He had been given a memorandum prepared by Wright on the case of Gordon Lonsdale which argued that the Soviets had deliberately discarded him so as to throw MI5 off the scent of more important spies. This theory was based on an analysis of Soviet wireless signals soon after Lonsdale's flat had been broken into surreptitiously by D Branch investigators and Lonsdale's one-time pads had been found and photographed. According to Wright, the quality of the information contained in Lonsdale's signals went into sharp decline soon after the burglary. He interpreted this as further proof of MI5's penetration, but Willis disagreed. He argued that Lonsdale had simply outlived his usefulness and his communications reflected his low standing with the KGB.

One reason for Wright's certainty that there was something peculiar about the Lonsdale affair was the reaction of the KGB's *rezident* in London. He had been at home, watching television, when the news broke that the Portland spy ring had been arrested. Those monitoring the bugs placed in the KGB man's flat were astonished when he made no attempt to telephone his Embassy where he was accredited as a first secretary. Why the obvious self-restraint? Wright was convinced that the only plausible explanation was the fact that the KGB was expecting Lonsdale to be caught. Indeed, Lonsdale himself let slip a remark to his MI5 interrogator, Charles Elton, that he could not understand why the Security Service had waited so long to arrest him. With this disturbing knowledge, neither Martin nor Wright could bring themselves to accept the Willis viewpoint and refused to endorse the Symonds Report while the Willis appendix was attached.

The Symonds Report also took issue with Wright's interpretation of the case of Brian Linney in 1958. Linney had been an electrical engineer with a Rolls-Royce sub-contractor who had been recruited in 1955 by Colonel Oldrich Prybl, a Czech intelligence officer under military attaché cover in London. Prybl's role had been revealed by a defector to the FBI and Linney had been placed under intensive surveillance in the hope of catching him passing secrets to Prybl. In what amounted to a re-run of the aborted Cairncross rendezvous in 1951, Prybl failed to turn up at the appointed hour. A leak was suspected in MI5's Watcher Service, but an internal enquiry declared the elite unit clean. Wright believed this was further evidence of a mole at work at a higher level.

There were other flashpoints during this crucial meeting. The latest Symonds Report contained both conclusions and recommendations. Its main conclusion, of course, was the verdict that the molehunters' case for penetration was unproven. Hollis asked those present to sign a minute agreeing that there was no longer any direct evidence of recent Soviet penetration. Martin was astonished by this suggestion and pointed out that on Golitsyn's testimony alone, the first 'ten serials', there was more than enough evidence to make a *prima facie* case for penetration. Symonds, on the other hand, felt that most of Golitsyn's information was attributable to known spies such as Philby.

In particular, he pointed to Golitsyn's claims about a KGB agent codenamed DIAMONT. After a time-consuming analysis, Symonds had demonstrated that DIAMONT had actually been George Blake. Martin protested that there were other 'serials' of equal significance. Undeterred, Hollis asked another D Branch officer, named Stewart, to prepare a detailed review of all Golitsyn's allegations and to 'find the weight of evidence'. Finally, Hollis stated that he did not believe there was anything to support the molehunters' penetration theory.

Those present believed the truth was somewhat different: Hollis did not want to admit to the new Labour Prime Minister, Harold Wilson, that MI5 was in a state of morale-sapping crisis. It was an attitude that Symonds certainly understood, and perhaps explained why he had received promotion from Hollis and had been placed in charge of the molehunters, in spite of the greater experience of Martin and Wright. Although these two 'terrible twins' rejected Symonds' conclusions, they were prepared to accept his principal recommendations: that the PETERS enquiry should be terminated and that Mitchell be spared interrogation.

Since the Director-General appeared to be so determined to bury the matter, Wright approached Furnival Jones after the winding-up meeting to suggest the creation of a joint MI5–SIS working party to look at all the evidence again, instead of simply leaving Stewart to examine the Golitsyn file in isolation. The Deputy Director-General agreed to put the idea to Dick White, who gave his approval and suggested that Peter Wright be its chairman. (In October the previous year Wright had been appointed to run D3, the Soviet counter-espionage branch's research unit.) The new group's codename was the FLUENCY Committee, and it was destined to meet, in secret session, at Leconfield House after working hours once a fortnight for the next five years. Its membership included Evelyn McBarnet and Stewart from MI5, and Terence Lecky and Stephen de Mowbray from SIS.

Even before the FLUENCY Committee had held its

first meeting, Arthur Martin had scored an important
success during his visit to America to explain the outcome
of the PETERS enquiry to the FBI. He had taken the
opportunity to visit John Cairncross, who had taken a
teaching position with Northwestern University, Cleve-
land. Cairncross was an experienced, Cambridge-educated
Whitehall insider who had worked in the Treasury, GCHQ
and, for a short time at the end of the war, in SIS. In 1951
he had been implicated by Guy Burgess, who had fled
leaving a collection of incriminating documents in a case
under his bed. Among these papers were a set of handwritten notes detailing recent Treasury decisions. None referred to classified information, but it was clear that the
source was well placed and obviously willing to share
everything with Burgess. A short investigation had led to
Cairncross who, it will be recalled, had sought a meeting
with his Soviet controller. At the appointed time Cairncross had shown up, but his KGB contact had not kept the
rendezvous. This incident was among the items listed by
Martin as evidence of a betrayal from within MI5, and he
was determined to get at the truth. When Cairncross had
been confronted in 1951, he had simply issued a firm denial
of ever having passed secrets to Burgess and then resigned
from his job. Since Martin was already in the United
States, he decided to have a second bite at the cherry. His
hunch paid off and Cairncross proved far more forthcoming, apparently feeling more secure in America and
the passing of so much time. He acknowledged having
been recruited by Burgess in 1935 while still at Cambridge,
and recalled the incident in the tube station in 1951. He
felt he had been 'left in the lurch' by the Soviets, whom
he had turned to for help after hearing of Burgess' defection, but he could not explain why his KGB case officer
had not turned up at the agreed meeting-place. To Martin
this was additional proof that the Russian had been warned
to stay clear of Cairncross because he had come under
surveillance by MI5.

   On his return to Washington Martin briefed William
Sullivan of the FBI on this latest development, and was

introduced to another former Trinity, Cambridge, undergraduate, Michael Straight. It was to prove an historic
meeting.

Without prompting, Straight volunteered a wealth of
information about a Communist cell at Trinity College
before the war. Some of his closest friends at Cambridge
had subsequently worked in British intelligence, including
Anthony Blunt, Guy Burgess and James Klugmann. Incredibly, Straight confirmed Martin's suspicions about
Blunt: not only had he been a spy, but he had attempted
to recruit Straight into a KGB network. As he later recalled
in his autobiography, *After Long Silence*:

Had Guy selected me as the first of the undergraduates to be
brought into the network? Had he instructed Anthony to become
a close friend of mine in order to draw him in? Was that why I
was invited to spend an evening with them? I think so. It was
from then on that Anthony took a close interest in me. And
James, whom I loved, did he know what was going on that
evening? Was he part of the snare?[1]

Straight told Martin that before the war Blunt had asked
him to undertake a secret mission for 'our friends in the
International, the Communist International', which involved cutting his ties with the CPGB in Cambridge,
staging a breakdown and moving to a useful post in
America.

This was the bargain that was offered to me. My part of the
bargain would, I knew, be painful. Yet in a way it accorded with
my own state of mind. I had never supposed that my ties to the
Communist movement would outlast my student days. And, in
a sense, they were already broken. In the course of a week, I
had moved out of the noisy crowded world of Cambridge into a
world of shadows and echoes.[2]

Straight followed Blunt's instructions and, having met a
mysterious Soviet intelligence officer with Blunt at a road-
house on the Great West Road, eventually took an unpaid
job in the US State Department in Washington. The Soviet
contact had given him a short course on basic security

procedures, such as the advisability of using public telephone boxes and recognition signals. In April 1938 a
mysterious Eastern European calling himself Michael
Green telephoned him at home in Washington and
suggested that, 'when interesting documents passed my
desk, I should take them home to "study"'.[3] Straight is
deliberately vague about his continuing relationship with
Green, but says that he

appeared and disappeared in the months after I left the State
Department. He had understood that I left the government for
good but he kept in touch with me. He wanted to take me
to dinner with Earl Browder, the secretary of the American
Communist Party. When I turned down his invitation, he insisted
on taking me to dinner in New York with his wife.[4]

Publicly Straight has admitted having been recruited by
Blunt and having volunteered for a job within the State
Department. In the latter post he 'had kept clear of sensitive departments of the government', but had been in a
position to write and circulate 'strictly confidential'
minutes. These apparent contradictions were not a matter
for Martin, not least because Straight offered to confront
Blunt in person and accuse him of having been a Soviet
spy.

Armed with this valuable information, Martin returned
to London and informed Hollis of this remarkable development. For the first time there was hard evidence with which
to confront the one suspect who had consistently denied
ever having spied for the Russians. Over the years Blunt
had been challenged, without success, by Dick White,
Courtney Young, Jim Skardon and numerous other
counter-intelligence experts. Certainly, the two senior investigators into the Burgess and Maclean fiasco in 1951,
James Robertson and Felix Johnston, had concluded that
Blunt had been a spy. Ronald Symonds had reviewed the
evidence against Blunt while researching his first PETERS
report and had found the case proved. Yet there was
still no evidence which could be presented in a criminal
prosecution.

Apart from the lack of first-hand testimony or a trap in which a suspect could be caught red-handed, MI5's dilemma really centred on the very secret source codenamed VENONA. This windfall was a large volume of Soviet diplomatic wireless traffic intercepted and decrypted by GCHQ in a joint operation, codenamed BRIDE, with the American National Security Agency. The 'V-traffic' had been sorted into 'illegal' signals, codenamed VAROOCH, and the KGB's regular communications which shared diplomatic channels. A study of the V-traffic showed the existence of nearly 200 individual KGB agents around the world, but unfortunately each was referred to by a cryptonym so as to protect them. Occasionally there were lapses, of the kind that linked the spy codenamed HOMER with Donald Maclean and eventually led to his investigation. GCHQ continued to monitor the V-traffic from June 1944, when Churchill had first authorised the interception of Soviet wireless signals, to a point in 1956 when the Soviets suddenly changed all their procedures, thus terminating the source. Wright maintained that in 1956 Mitchell had recommended that MI5 stop investigating leads from VENONA. Apparently, 'GCHQ said they didn't think they were getting anything from it and Mitchell said OK.' A further study, organised in 1966, showed that messages from a total of eight important KGB agents could be separated from the rest. Three cryptonyms, STANLEY, HICKS and JOHNSON, were found to be Philby, Burgess and Blunt, and two others were later found to be Cairncross and an elusive scientist. When the VENONA files were re-examined by the FLUENCY Committee in 1966, it was realised that there had been enough material on STANLEY in 1947 to pinpoint Philby who, at that time, was serving as SIS Head of Station in Ankara. In retrospect, it seemed odd that Mitchell should have been so keen to terminate such a productive source.

The molehunters were painfully aware that, until they could persuade a key member of Burgess' ring to switch sides, they would be fumbling in the dark. Martin's unexpected help from Straight had served to confirm the case

against Blunt. Now all that remained to be done was to
obtain his co-operation. Following the example of Philby,
Hollis sought and obtained another formal immunity from
prosecution and, on Wednesday, 22 April 1964, Martin
was ushered into Blunt's study at the Courtauld Institute.

Between the defections of Burgess and Maclean in May
1951 and Arthur Martin's confrontation in April 1964,
Anthony Blunt had undergone no fewer than eleven separate interviews. Some had been conducted by Jim Skardon,
MI5's office interrogator who had successfully extracted a
confession from Klaus Fuchs, the atom spy, in 1949. Others
had made less formal approaches, but Blunt had taken
great care to avoid making any compromising slips.
   Blunt, of course, knew exactly how the Security Service
operated, having spent five years in the organisation during
the war. He was on good terms with many of its personnel,
not least of whom was Guy Liddell, then Sillitoe's Deputy
Director-General. Accordingly, he was also aware of the
restrictions which handicapped MI5. He knew that a persistent, blank refusal to admit anything more damaging
than an apparently harmless friendship with Burgess and
Philby would prevent any legal action from being mounted
against him. In the absence of any direct evidence, MI5
required a signed confession before there was any hope of
preparing a criminal prosecution, let alone obtaining a
conviction. With this in mind, Blunt was supremely confident of his position. Indeed, he had every reason to be. His
initial interviews, immediately following Burgess' escape to
Moscow, had been on the basis that he was in a good
position to assist MI5's investigation. He had co-operated
fully, even to the extent of opening Burgess' flat up for an
illicit search. At first he was regarded as a key witness,
helping to reconstruct the complicated jigsaw of espionage
and homosexuality that dominated Burgess' life. It was
only after the intervention of Goronwy Rees that MI5's
attitude to Blunt changed, and he too was regarded as a
probable Soviet mole.
   Goronwy Rees was a brilliant, eccentric Welsh academic

and former covert supporter of the CPGB. Soon after the notorious defections in May 1951, Rees volunteered a statement to Dick White, then Director of the Security Service's counter-espionage division, in which he denounced the members of a KGB spy-ring recruited at Cambridge. He later said that 'a sense of desperation and urgency' had compelled him to seek White's help and gave this explanation of his motives for denouncing Burgess *et al.*:

The guilt I felt in regard to Guy and my dealings with him was exacerbated by a more general sense of guilt which was inspired by the support and approval which, in the 1930s and even later, I had given to the Communist Party of the Soviet Union.[5]

Rees said that MI5 had reacted with 'a hardly concealed disbelief in my motives for offering information at precisely the moment when it was too late'. Certainly, individual MI5 officers had shown little but contempt for Rees' motives, but his information was regarded as vital. Burgess had been at the centre of a Soviet espionage system, claimed Rees, and the other members included Professor Robert Zaehner and Anthony Blunt. Rees had known Burgess for years and had been with him during his last weekend in England. Others on Rees' list included another distinguished Oxford don, Stuart Hampshire, who had served in the Radio Security Service during the war and was subsequently completely exonerated. Although Rees never admitted to it, MI5 accepted that his information must have been based on first-hand experience, and that he too had been a Soviet spy, perhaps when he had undertaken wartime intelligence work. Rees, of course, was careful not to let his belated allegations incriminate himself. It was only discovered much later that Rees had continued to maintain contact with the KGB up until at least 1964, by which time he had resigned his post of Principal at the University College of Wales, Aberystwyth. As word spread of the help he had given to MI5, Rees' friends ostracised him.

When in 1972 Rees published his autobiography, *A Chapter of Accidents*, he made a bitter attempt to justify his behaviour and revealed his suspicions about MI5:

It seemed highly probable that if Guy and Maclean had been recruited as spies, so had others, and that, if they had vanished, others remained. But who? I had the uneasy feeling that the likeliest place to look was in the ranks of the security services themselves.[6]

Rees' list of suspects was far from complete, but Blunt, Hampshire and Zaehner came under MI5's immediate scrutiny. Of the three, only Zaehner still had access to secrets. In fact, he was working for SIS, under diplomatic cover as acting Counsellor, at the British Embassy in Tehran. When MI5 delved further, it turned out that Zaehner had already been named as a possible Soviet spy. In September 1945 a KGB officer named Konstantin Volkov had attempted to defect in Istanbul and had given clues to various agents operating in London. One had been described as working in British counter-intelligence; another had actually been named as Robert Zaehner, then SIS's man in Tehran, masquerading as the press attaché. The list of traitors had been Volkov's meal-ticket to a new life in the West, but his case had been handed to Kim Philby to deal with. Philby embarked for Turkey but, by the time he had arrived, Volkov had disappeared. Philby reported Volkov to SIS headquarters as an inconsequential 'no-show' who had changed his mind, but years later he was to boast of his narrow escape. He had reported Volkov's offer to defect to Moscow and arrangements had been made to bundle him on to a plane bound for the Soviet Union. Thanks to Philby's intervention, Zaehner's career had been uninterrupted, but Rees confirmed his guilt and added a few important details: Zaehner had been recruited at King's, Cambridge, and had then organised his own cell at Oxford, where he had been Senior Scholar at Christ Church. A brilliant linguist, Zaehner had been snapped up by SIS in 1942.

Zaehner was confronted with Rees' accusation, but his denials ruled out a prosecution. Instead, he was quietly returned to academic life at Oxford, where he was appointed the Spalding Professor of Eastern Religions and Ethics.

In 1951 Stuart Hampshire was a Fellow at New College, Oxford, having left the Radio Security Service at the end of the war, and he was not interviewed until March 1969, by which time he had taken up the post of Professor of Philosophy at Princeton University. Hampshire was an old friend of Blunt's and used to travel to France with him. He had also been close to Burgess, Blunt's friend Ben Nicolson, and a high-ranking member of the CPGB, James Klugmann. Hampshire denied ever having been approached by Burgess, although he later recalled having attended a slight* odd dinner party with Burgess in 1938 where some fairly ambiguous suggestions had been made.

All in all the Rees list proved a disappointment for MI5, although Blunt was to be marked down as a probable Soviet spy. The real evidence against Blunt was only to emerge from Michael Straight early in 1964, and it was his testimony that Arthur Martin confronted Blunt with in April.

At mid-morning on 22 April Arthur Martin called on Sir Anthony Blunt at the latter's bachelor apartment in the Courtauld Institute, overlooking Portman Square. Armed only with the verbal immunity from prosecution and a bulky, reel-to-reel tape recorder, Martin told the Surveyor of the Queen's Pictures that he was now satisfied that Blunt had acted as an agent for the Soviets both before and during the war. Blunt raised a hand in protest, as if to remonstrate that he had heard all this nonsense before from Courtney Young, Jim Skardon *et al.*, but before he could answer Martin continued: 'I have been to see Michael Straight in Washington recently and I am now in possession of sufficient evidence to prove the case. However, before you reply, you should know that I have been authorised to offer you a formal immunity from prosecution. No proceedings will arise from any admission you care to make.'

Blunt slowly got up from his desk, walked over to a tray of bottles and poured himself a stiff gin, apparently deep in thought. As he did so he turned and said, simply, 'It's true.'

Martin's bluff had worked. Just as the threat of Flora Solomon's testimony had been enough to crack Philby, the prospect of being challenged by Michael Straight had proved sufficient to convince Blunt that further denials would be of no use. The trump card had been the offer of immunity from criminal prosecution. If self-preservation was to be a factor in Blunt's motivation, the carrot dangled so skilfully by Martin contained everything he might be seeking: no embarrassing police involvement; no public humiliation; no obvious betrayal of friends.

Within half an hour Martin was on his way back to Leconfield House to report to the Director, D Branch, Malcolm Cumming, completely confident that Blunt would co-operate with the Security Service. The first part of the exercise was to get the magnetic tape transcribed by one of D Branch's confidential typists. Thereafter, with Blunt's admission on record, there would be no opportunity for him to change his mind. Before parting Martin had taken the precaution of playing back the crucial tape and obtaining Blunt's confirmation that it was a true and accurate account of his decision to accept a formal immunity from prosecution. In fact, Blunt later considered asking for some kind of document, perhaps an official letter, setting out the details of the immunity, but he was too embarrassed to ask. Nor did he seek any undertakings concerning his knighthood, which had been awarded in 1956, or even his position within the Royal Household. His understanding of what had taken place was straightforward: the agreement was a private matter between himself, a former member of the Security Service, and his former employer. Like most of MI5's dealings, there was no question about it ever being made public.

MI5 took much the same view although it was believed, within the closed circle of those privy to the secret, that Blunt would be under continuing pressure to help Martin. A criminal trial was, of course, ruled out by the terms of the immunity, but the Security Service was now in a strong position to demand his co-operation. The only issue at stake was D Branch's determination to take full advantage of the situation before the Russians learned that Blunt had switched sides.

At Blunt's first full debriefing, conducted by Arthur Martin two days later, a statement was completed outlining his recruitment by Guy Burgess in 1936, his espionage while working for MI5 during the war, and his direct involvement in the defections of Burgess and Maclean in 1951. He also made two dramatic revelations. Firstly, he acknowledged his own role in relation to Kim Philby. Apparently, he had always been aware of Philby's activities and, on one occasion after the war, had conveyed a message to him from his Soviet contact. But the admission that Martin found utterly devastating, and seemed to confirm his worst fears, was Blunt's description of a conversation he had held with Burgess in 1945. Blunt had asked Burgess to persuade the KGB to let him leave MI5. He wanted to return to academic life, but he realised that the Soviets would probably want him to stay on with the Security Service and continue his espionage long into the post-war era. It had already been made clear to him that there was a job available if he chose to make MI5 his career. It was not unknown for the long-serving office personnel to sometimes refer to Blunt as the most intelligent man ever to have worked for MI5. Blunt had anticipated a row and had sought Burgess' assistance in the belief that he might be able to persuade the KGB to release him. Burgess agreed to intercede on his behalf and, to the apparent astonishment of both, Burgess quickly had obtained the KGB's consent to Blunt's plan. Blunt later admitted that there was only one possible explanation for this extraordinary development: evidently, the Soviets must have had other, perhaps even better, sources already well established inside MI5.

This added to the weight of evidence for current penetration of the Security Service, as did Blunt's close involvement with Philby. He told of an incident in 1954 when a KGB case officer had approached Blunt, after a public lecture on Italian baroque art, in an attempt to get a message to Philby. He had identified himself to Blunt with a postcard on the same subject. On the reverse, handwritten by Guy Burgess, were the words, 'Angel, meet me at 8 o'clock tonight.' The Russian had been unwilling to contact Philby direct because he suspected MI5 surveillance, but had given the details of a rendezvous at the Angel, Islington, to Blunt to pass on. Blunt had then telephoned Philby and had met him for lunch in an Indian restaurant in the King's Road in Chelsea. The restaurant had been too full, so they had strolled to a nearby pub for a quiet drink. During their conversation Philby had suggested that a Soviet intelligence officer was about to defect in Australia. This, of course, was some weeks before the Petrovs had finally decided to make their move. When Blunt was shown the passport photographs of various senior KGB case officers, he selected the picture of Yuri Modin as Philby's contact. Modin had previously served at the Soviet Embassy in London during the war and had been known to Blunt simply as PETER. In 1951 Modin had ordered Blunt to follow Burgess and Maclean, but he had decided against defection, preferring to outwit MI5.

The significance of this episode did not lie in the behaviour of the Soviets, but rather the omission of Blunt's role as a link-man from Philby's 'confession' the previous year. If Philby's preliminary, two-page statement had been authentic, why had he left out Blunt? His failure to name him to Elliott, when it was now certain that Philby had known of Blunt's guilt, was further proof that the so-called confession was little more than an elaborate sham. And if Philby had been able to prepare an authentic-sounding statement, it followed that he must have been tipped off in advance. In other words, there was still an active mole inside MI5. Further supporting evidence could be seen in Blunt's claim that Philby had demonstrated advance knowledge of the Petrov defections. Only a tiny number of people had been let in on that particular secret, and it seemed to explain the sudden appearance of the two KGB thugs who had so nearly wrecked the entire operation.

Blunt and Martin continued to meet every two or three days so that the self-confessed traitor could give a comprehensive account of his work for the Soviets. This was Martin's particular responsibility. He told Blunt that a specialist from F Branch, MI5's political subversion division, would pursue questions relating to his CPGB membership at Cambridge. His help would be needed to reconstruct the CPGB's underground cells at the university, and he would also be required to go through lists of individuals suspected of having concealed their support for the CPGB. Meanwhile, Martin instructed his research section to clear the decks for a lengthy analysis of the names already offered by Blunt.

No sooner had this new, enlarged molehunt begun than MI5's Director of Personnel, John Marriott, summoned Cumming and Martin to break the news that the D1 section was to be slightly reduced in size. He announced that a key member of Martin's team of investigators was to be appointed as MI5's Security Liaison Officer in Washington. Since this was generally considered a plum appointment, the best of a diminishing number of Security Service posts abroad, the candidate had already accepted the offer without hesitation. Martin was furious because he regarded him as a man he could trust completely, partly because they had both served in Kuala Lumpur and were therefore members of an elite group within MI5 known as the 'Malaya Mafia'. A few D Branch insiders also knew that this particular officer had been involved in the investigation into the second Soviet spy in the Admiralty, the search which had been abandoned so abruptly after Vassall's conviction on orders from Hollis. Was the sudden transfer to America (where he was to remain for the next five years) a clumsy attempt to remove Martin's key officer from a crucial position in London at a critical moment?

Martin was bitter about the loss and made his feelings plain to Cumming, who decided to report Martin's comments to the Director-General. He also prepared a short memorandum in which he stated that Martin's obsessively secret molehunting activities were disrupting the office. A heated exchange followed, in which Martin accused Cumming of misrepresenting his motives to Hollis. A tense meeting in the Director-General's office was held the following Monday afternoon. Hollis stated that he was no longer prepared to tolerate Martin as a 'focal point for dissention in the Service', and Martin was suspended from duty for a fortnight. In spite of his objections, he was also told to stop meeting Blunt for the duration of the suspension. Martin explained that he would like to maintain contact with Blunt, working from home, but Hollis ruled out the idea. This was particularly inconvenient as Martin had embarked on an exercise to test Blunt's good faith. Hollis ordered Martin to telephone Blunt and make an excuse of being sent on a mission that would take him away from London for a couple of weeks. As regards the debriefing, he was told, another D Branch member would take up the threads. The officer selected was Peter Wright, then head of D3.

The roots of this bizarre episode can be traced to the original PETERS enquiry, and the resentment felt by Martin and others in his team of the way Ronald Symonds had reviewed the evidence against Mitchell. Some believed that his second report, which had effectively cleared Mitchell in May 1964, had also belittled their own efforts to identify the elusive mole inside MI5. Wright had even referred to it derisively as 'the case for the defence'. With Blunt on the point of giving a detailed confession and naming names, the tension had become almost unbearable. Martin sensed a breakthrough which he considered more important than office politics and then, at the worst possible moment, his unit was to endure a cut in manpower. An experienced officer was to be removed and no replacement was to be provided. Something was bound to give and it was Martin who boiled over. His reaction was a human response to a difficult set of circumstances, but it was to have wide implications.

Martin returned to Leconfield House immediately after the Whitsun holiday, following his two-week suspension, and found Wright already hard at work with Blunt. In fact, Martin had been kept in constant touch with the office throughout his absence, partly thanks to his wife, Joan, who had once been Guy Liddell's secretary, but mainly through calls from his own loyal subordinates who knew the true background to his suspension. One useful development was Peter Wright's introduction to Blunt. The two men seemed to get on well together, and the D3 section was fully occupied pursuing his leads. Wright was eventually to put in around 200 hours of taped interviews with Blunt.

Blunt wasted little time in naming several people as having been important Soviet spies: Goronwy Rees and Stuart Hampshire headed the list, followed by John Cairncross who had been 'talent-spotted' by Blunt for Guy Burgess while still an undergraduate. He also identified two other King's College graduates that had so far escaped suspicion: a former military intelligence officer named Leo Long, and a senior Admiralty scientist, Alister Watson.

In the case of Leonard Henry Long, the investigation was quite straightforward. He had become a civilian again in the late 1940s after a wartime career in MI14, the military intelligence sub-section devoted to the study of the enemy's order-of-battle. After the war he had been posted to the Intelligence Division (ID) of the Control Commission for Germany, a small counter-intelligence unit which bridged the gap between the British military government and the peacetime Secret Intelligence Service. Run by Brigadier John Lethbridge, the Control Commission's ID had run agents into Soviet-occupied territory with a remarkable lack of success. Long had continued to work for the ID in Germany even after his return to civilian life, and in 1952 he had applied for a transfer to MI5 but had been turned down. Instead, Long got a job in the City and then joined an international film company as an administrator at its headquarters in London.

Because Long had no access to classified information, and denied having had any contact with the Soviets for more than a decade, he was of only limited interest to MI5. On Blunt's advice Long had sought an immunity from prosecution, but Martin could only reassure him that no criminal prosecution was contemplated. Apparently satisfied, he made a series of detailed statements and was allowed to go home, keeping his treachery a secret even from his wife.

The Watson case, however, was rather different and infinitely more serious. Dr A. G. D. Watson was a brilliant mathematician and a respected science don at King's College, who had twice been elected secretary of the *Conversazione* Society, the secret Cambridge club known as the Apostles, which had included Burgess, Blunt, Straight and Long among its members. Indeed, Watson had originally been identified as a possible spy by Michael Straight earlier in the year, but to date there was no evidence with which to confront him. Straight had listed him as having been an underground member of the CPGB's clandestine cell at King's, but so far no action had been taken against him, in spite of his important position in the Admiralty's sensitive research laboratory at Teddington. Watson had been engaged on secret, submarine research for much of his career, and MI5 discovered that he had failed to disclose his CPGB involvement on the Positive Vetting questionnaire which he was obliged to complete periodically, as a matter of routine. After a lengthy surveillance operation supervised by Wright, in which the scientist was found still to be in sympathy and even occasional touch with current members of the CPGB, the scientist was interrogated over three days at Brown's Hotel in Mayfair. Blunt also attended, standing at the back of the room passing questions written on pieces of paper to Wright. Watson denied ever having betrayed any secrets, but he did admit to having met two of Blunt's Soviet contacts, both known to be KGB case officers, outside the gates at Teddington. This partial confession was enough to justify Watson's immediate transfer to the National Institute of Oceanography, where he was excluded from access to classified papers. When informed of MI5's decision, Watson was given the opportunity to appeal to a special Civil Service tribunal, which adjudicates when an employee feels that he has lost his security clearance unfairly. Nobody was surprised that Watson decided against an appeal, and Blunt observed that, having heard Watson's lame performance under interrogation, he was convinced that Watson had been a spy as well as an underground supporter of the CPGB. As Wright later commented, 'If Watson wasn't a spy, why else was he meeting Russian intelligence officers?'[7] The conclusion that Watson had been a spy neatly took care of one matter that had been the cause of some anxiety to Wright's D3 team. Burgess, Maclean, Philby and Cairncross had all been members of the group known as the Ring-of-Five. Five separate spies, all known to each other, had been spotted in the Soviet VENONA signals traffic, and the fifth was known to have been a scientist. Anatoli Golitsyn had also confirmed the existence of a university-based Ring-of-Five, although he had only had a chance to learn the true identities of Burgess and Maclean. This had not been of much help at the time of his defection back in 1962, although his description of the third man as having been 'high in operations in the Middle East' had helped to implicate Philby. Lord Rothschild had been a candidate for the fifth member of the ring even following his vital contribution to obtaining the lever for Philby's confession the previous year, for he had originally recommended Blunt for entry into MI5 in 1940, which was bound to count against him, and furthermore, as a scientist, he fitted the profile of the fifth member of Golitsyn's Ring-of-Five. However, one important consequence of Blunt's confession was to confirm that Rothschild had never been a spy.

Rothschild's elimination as a suspect must have come as a great relief to Roger Hollis, who was then nearing his retirement and anxious to start the Director-General's traditional world tour to say farewell to Allied organisations and MI5's far-flung representatives. He made no secret of his distaste of his last year in office, and often remarked to his family that he was literally counting the hours until his final retirement. He could hardly wait to leave Leconfield House for the last time and devote himself to country pursuits in Somerset, and his beloved game of golf.

One possible reason for Hollis' discomfort during his final

year as Director-General was the prospect of a further spy scandal, perhaps one that would be even more far-reaching than the disastrous Profumo affair. With Blunt's help D3 was sifting through dozens of suspected spies, any one of whom was a possible Soviet mole. Many had once held deep left-wing convictions or had associated with known CPGB activists. Among those who were investigated and scheduled for interview were such distinguished figures as Sir Anthony Rumbold, Sir Edward Playfair, Sir Dennis Proctor, Mrs Jenifer Hart, Bernard Floud MP, Stuart Hampshire, Cedric Belfrage, James Klugmann and James MacGibbon. All had held (and in some cases still held) important positions of trust, and all had come under suspicion. To Hollis, D3's determination to pursue these leads must have appeared dangerous and potentially explosive. They had to be handled with tremendous tact, a quality which Arthur Martin could not be said to have exhibited in his dealings with either Malcolm Cumming or Ronald Symonds. The latter's argument for the PETERS case to be terminated in September 1964 had sparked off yet another crisis of confidence within D Branch. Eventually, in mid-November 1964, the atmosphere in D Branch became stifling, with the operations and investigations halves of the D1 section barely communicating. This led to Martin's transfer, initially on a two-year secondment, to the Secret Intelligence Service. After his departure, it fell to Wright's team of D3 researchers to bypass Hollis and his scarcely concealed reluctance to investigate allegations of Soviet penetration of the British establishment. And while the friction continued, Symonds was left in sole charge of what remained of the PETERS case upon which so much seemed to hang.

By this time, in September 1964, Mitchell had been gone for a year, but the PETERS enquiry was still operational, much to the Director-General's obvious disapproval. Hollis had even been known to use the word 'Gestapo' to describe the group of counter-intelligence experts who gathered in secret, under the codename FLUENCY, to debate the various avenues that might be examined.

3

OPERATION FLUENCY

The FLUENCY Committee's task was twofold: to evaluate the evidence accumulated against particular top-level Soviet spy suspects and to assess the possibilities of current penetration of MI5. Under the chairmanship of Peter Wright, the six counter-intelligence experts operated as a working party, conducting individual investigations for their respective organisations but secretly comparing notes at their regular fortnightly meetings.

FLUENCY's first, basic task in the molehunt was to gather together all the evidence of Soviet penetration and to see if the allegations could be explained away by spies that had already been discovered. This had in part been undertaken by Stewart, who had been ordered to study Golitsyn's 'ten serials' at the meeting held in September 1964 to wind-up the PETERS operation. Stewart's eventual report, based on Martin's debriefing of Golitsyn, was to contain 256 specific allegations, of which a significant number were considered to be relevant to FLUENCY's special area of interest. It was an awe-inspiring document but, in deference to its unique sensitivity, it was not circulated beyond the small group of those indoctrinated into the secret of FLUENCY's existence.

From the start the FLUENCY Committee was desperately unpopular with those who knew something of its activities. All its SIS representatives had been deeply involved in the organisation's 'house-cleaning' operations, which had resulted in various senior officers being called in to give an account of their friendships with identified suspects. One early victim was Tim Milne, a boyhood friend of Philby's who had also spent his career in SIS. Although he had been cleared of any suspicion, he had been asked, unfairly, to resign from the Service. So had a dozen others and, as a consequence, morale had suffered at the expense of being able to assure the CIA that an extensive purge had eliminated any possible contamination. A similar exercise happened inside MI5 following the retirement of Roger Hollis late in 1965, 'and four senior officers, all of whom had been recruited into the Security Service during the war, were sacked. The final departure of Hollis led to the appointment of Martin Furnival Jones as his successor, and the promotion of Anthony Simkins, the Director C Branch, as his new Deputy Director-General. Neither showed enthusiasm for what Peter Wright subsequently called 'cleaning the nest', but, because of Dick White's powerful influence from SIS's headquarters across the river, the molehunting continued.

The two chief contributors to FLUENCY's list of suspicious episodes were Peter Wright, whose expertise was in the technical field, and Arthur Martin, who retained his membership of the committee even after his transfer to SIS in November 1964. Although now officially the Head of SIS's Registry, Dick White had nominated Martin as his representative on the FLUENCY Committee.

Wright reckoned that over the years he had come across no fewer than thirty unexplained cases indicating Soviet penetration. Some of the claims were really too vague to pursue but nevertheless were included, such as the breathtaking speed with which the Soviets had discarded MI5's double agents. There was also the negative evidence that no Soviet spy had ever been found in GCHQ, although the organisation was obviously a key target for penetration. After all, before Philby had joined SIS in 1941, he had applied for a post in the government's wartime decryption department then based at Bletchley Park. Fortunately, he had been rejected on that occasion, but why had the Soviets allowed John Cairncross to switch from GCHQ to

SIS in 1944? One possible explanation might have been the existence of an as-yet undiscovered mole.

Wright also produced good, but circumstantial, evidence to demonstrate that the Portland spy affair had come as no surprise to the Soviets. Quite apart from the apparent calm of the KGB *rezident* in London when the arrests were first announced on television, and the reaction of Lonsdale when confronted by Elton, there was also practically no perceptible change in the pattern of signals transmitted from the Soviet Embassy in London during the critical period when a sudden increase in messages might reasonably have been expected. Wright was sure it showed that the KGB knew an MI5 investigation was well under way.

There were three other incidents that were close to Wright's heart. One, years earlier, involved the unsuccessful bugging of the Soviet Consulate when the Russians had simply plastered over a microphone within a few days of its insertion. At the time, Wright had written off the matter as just bad luck, but in retrospect it seemed odd.

Then there was the extraordinary matter of Wright's private safe which, he believed, had been tampered with. After he had first offered his controversial thesis about the Lonsdale case, he had set a trap in his office. He had placed thirty-eight files in his safe in a predetermined order, with all the corners on an exact square, and then photographed the pile with a Polaroid camera. A short time later, after his presentation, he had unlocked the safe and found that the files had been moved. Wright took a second Polaroid to show that someone had been interfering without his authority. The only two other people in the building who knew the safe's combination were Hollis and Mitchell. He had said nothing at the time, but he was sure that his two pictures were clear proof of a spy at work.

Finally, there was the suspicion that a tape-recorder had been concealed in MI5's boardroom at Leconfield House. During the PETERS investigation Wright had obtained Hollis' permission to search the room used by the Deputy Director-General to chair the weekly session at which MI5's various operational sections submitted requests for coverage by the Watcher Service. If there were insufficient watcher resources available, Mitchell would adjudicate, decide on the priorities and allocate the personnel. In the day-to-day operations of the Security Service this 'bids' meeting was of considerable importance. It would also have been of great interest to the KGB because it was the one moment when MI5's branches combined to agree future plans. If a spy had access to the bids meeting, he could anticipate operations conducted by those sections to which he was unable to elicit current information.

These meetings took place every Friday morning, and Wright found an opportunity to go through the room the night before one was scheduled. Against one wall was an ancient desk, once used by Guy Liddell, a previous Deputy Director-General. Wright picked the lock and found what he thought were four distinct marks in the dust. He believed that they might have been the legs of a small tape-recorder which had been removed soon after he had obtained the Director-General's consent to a search. Had Hollis been secretly taping the meetings chaired by Mitchell? Once again, Wright reckoned he had found important evidence.

Golitsyn's complete list of incidents suggesting Soviet penetration totalled 256 separate items, but when the cases were studied in detail just twenty-eight were left for thorough examination. A great deal, of course, hung on Golitsyn's reliability as a source, and Mitchell had not been the only person to express scepticism about some of his allegations. The problem with Golitsyn was the wide variation in the quality of his information. When the defector confined himself to matters of fact about his own, first-hand experiences while serving in the KGB, he was generally found to be accurate, but whenever he strayed into political issues he became a trifle eccentric. Many of his opinions stemmed from a top-level conference he had attended in 1959 at KGB headquarters in Moscow at which a secret, long-range master-plan to subvert the West had been unveiled to those assembled. A major disinformation offensive had been prepared, and the KGB management announced its intention to distract and confuse the Allied intelligence services by all sorts of ingenious means, including the aggressive, mass deployment of false defectors. Golitsyn insisted that Oleg Penkovsky, the GRU colonel who had kept SIS and the CIA supplied with top-level secrets throughout the crisis year of 1961, was really a KGB plant. This novel explanation convinced only a handful of Western counter-intelligence experts, but among them were Wright and Martin. After all, they argued, when Penkovsky's information was analysed, it had never actually contained anything to betray individual Soviet agents. At least in that respect Golitsyn had a proven track record and had been responsible for the identification of more than a hundred KGB spies around the world. When Dick White first learned of Golitsyn's view of Penkovsky he rejected it, remarking that 'too many knighthoods depend on this one'.

Certainly, if a profit-and-loss account was made of Penkovsky's net worth, it seemed that events could be revised so as to demonstrate a sophisticated, KGB-inspired deception operation. Perhaps Penkovsky had been deliberately manipulated during the Cuban missile crisis so as to convey information straight to the White House? When all was said and done, the West had been left with a blown SIS agent, Greville Wynne, imprisoned in the Soviet Union. The case was particularly relevant because, in April 1964, Wynne had been swopped in a spy exchange for Gordon Lonsdale. Penkovsky was rumoured to have been executed in Russia in 1963 but, according to Golitsyn, he was probably still alive, possibly even enjoying his new status as a much-decorated hero for having completed so delicate a mission.

One of Golitsyn's weirder ideas concerned the much-publicised Sino–Soviet split. He would tell anyone willing to listen that the public division between the Russians and the Chinese was actually a complicated strategy to dupe the West. Political analysts gave such opinions short shrift and, when Golitsyn's views were made public, they were used to ridicule him. His full proposition was never released, but in 1984 two of his most loyal supporters in Britain, Arthur Martin and Stephen de Mowbray, edited a shortened version, *New Lies For Old* (Bodley Head), and persuaded an old schoolfriend of de Mowbray's to publish it.

Notwithstanding the obvious objections to Golitsyn, the FLUENCY Committee set about reviewing a total of 270 claims of penetration. After much research, it was conceded that seventy items could be attributed to either Blunt, Blake, Burgess, Maclean or Philby. That left 200; gradually this figure was reduced to twenty key incidents. After further study, just three specific allegations were left, which appeared to be unanswerable.

First on the list was the Konstantin Volkov incident in September 1945. Volkov had offered to denounce various spies in return for a new life in the West, and Philby had been given the assignment of negotiating his defection. As Philby later boasted in his KGB-authorised autobiography, *My Silent War* (MacGibbon & Kee, 1968), he ensured that 'the case was dead'.[1] Volkov's original message had taken ten days to reach SIS headquarters, thanks to his insistence that the British diplomatic ciphers had been compromised and that a diplomatic pouch be used to communicate with London instead of the usual telegraphic channels. Then Philby had taken a week or so to reach Istanbul where Volkov had been stationed. The delay had given Philby more than enough time to tip off his Soviet contact and arrange for Volkov to be spirited back to Moscow.

On the face of it the Volkov affair was a straightforward offer of a meal-ticket followed by a betrayal by one of the very agents he had intended to expose, but upon further examination there was rather more to the incident than that. Volkov's own *bona fides* had been established by his reference to Robert Zaehner, who had indeed turned out to have been a spy. But what exactly had Volkov offered? In Philby's account he recalled that 'two Soviet agents in the Foreign Office, one head of a counter-espionage organisation in London!' had been mentioned, so a check was made on the text of the first message as received from

Istanbul. It was compared with the original which had been typed by Volkov and handed in to the British Consulate before his disappearance. A slight discrepancy was noticed in Volkov's Russian original. He had mentioned a total of five agents in British intelligence and two in the Foreign Office. However, the translation of a crucial sentence read, 'I know for instance that one of these agents is fulfilling the duties of Head of a Department of British Counter-intelligence.'[2]

Philby's treatment of this vital passage was interesting because his record omitted mention of the five moles in British intelligence and implied that the 'Head of a Department of British Counter-intelligence' was a reference to himself. Certainly, Philby was then head of Section IX, a counter-intelligence department of SIS. The point was pursued by Terence Lecky and Wright, with further help from GCHQ's Russian-speaking expert who made a new attempt to translate Volkov's original message. The second translation altered its accepted meaning by reinterpreting the critical sentence to read, 'I know for instance that one of these agents is fulfilling the duties of acting Head of a Department of the British Counter-intelligence Directorate.' Wright believed that far from implicating Philby, who had served in SIS, Volkov had actually been referring to someone in MI5. The 'Head of a Department in British Counter-intelligence' might well be said to refer to SIS, but there could be no mistaking the author's intention when he mentioned the 'British Counter-intelligence Directorate'. He must have had MI5, not SIS, in mind. And that someone in MI5 could hardly have been Blunt, because he had never been head or acting head of any section of the Security Service. In short, Volkov may have been trying to warn of a spy in MI5, not in SIS. Just to be on the safe side, Golitsyn was invited to make his own translation of the key sentence, and he came up with an identical phrase. While this was far from conclusive, it did tend to confirm the existence of an unknown mole. Unfortunately, both Hollis and Mitchell fitted the bill, so the matter could be taken no further. In August 1945

Hollis had been head of MI5's F Division with the rank of Deputy Director, and Mitchell, as his subordinate, had been head of F3, with the rank of Assistant Director. Volkov's description could be said to have fitted either man.

The second of the three final 'serials' was the ELLI allegation made by Igor Gouzenko, also in September 1945, but from Canada. He had revealed the indiscretion of a GRU colleague who had once boasted of having handled the radio traffic of the mole inside MI5. Blunt, of course, had not been run by the GRU but by its 'neighbours', the KGB (or rather its predecessor, the NKVD). It therefore followed that, if Gouzenko had told the truth, the GRU had been in touch with a mole in MI5 other than Blunt. Once again, this was circumstantial evidence of penetration, but did not point directly at either of the two candidates.

Finally, there was the third, apparently damning, evidence of penetration supplied by Michal Goleniewski, the Polish defector who had originally tipped off MI5 about the Portland spy ring. According to Goleniewski, who made his escape to West Berlin in December 1960, the KGB had a middle-ranking agent inside MI5 codenamed HARRIET. He could only offer a limited number of clues as to the spy's identity, and the investigators eventually, by a process of elimination, narrowed the field to just two suspects: one had an English mother and a Latvian father; the other had an Indian wife. The best candidate was discovered to have undergone psychiatric treatment following a major nervous breakdown, and was now actually heading a section of D Branch. Further, exhaustive enquiries were made and it was determined that, although Goleniewski had been utterly sincere in his disclosure, he had probably been fed the information by the KGB as a disinformation ploy.

When the final three conclusions were delivered in a unanimous FLUENCY Committee report to the Director-General, Martin Furnival Jones, he rejected the first two propositions as 'grotesque'. He refused to sanction an investigation into Hollis but he did agree to a detailed look into HARRIET, which was conducted throughout 1966.

However, once the HARRIET matter had been cleared up, the FLUENCY Committee demanded permission to follow up the historical evidence from Volkov and Gouzenko and, with great reluctance, the Director-General gave his consent. As a first move, Graham Mitchell was invited to visit Furnival Jones at Leconfield House. After a brief chat Mitchell was escorted to a safe-house at 33 South Audley Street, Mayfair, just around the corner from the office, for interrogation.

The venue was an elegant, if sparsely decorated, house which had been 'wired for sound'. Every room had been bugged, and there was a special listening room packed with sophisticated recording equipment. There Peter Wright sat hunched over his machines, headphones clamped to his ears, while John Day took Mitchell through all the evidence accumulated during the PETERS operation.

Many of the points put to Mitchell were relatively easy to answer. He gave convincing replies when asked about his decision to terminate MI5's study of the VENONA signals traffic, and justified his opposition to Golitsyn. He gave stock answers, as any professional intelligence officer in his position might have done, but where he was most convincing was when the questions turned to his own personal behaviour. Three items had been listed for special attention: his obvious anxiety in private, his habit of taking counter-surveillance precautions, and a curious incident involving a hand-drawn map.

During the early summer of 1963 Mitchell had been seen to prepare a map on a blank piece of paper while at his desk. He had completed it late in the afternoon, just before his regular train was due to leave from Waterloo, but he had suddenly torn it up and thrown it away before leaving the office. The PETERS team had retrieved the scraps from Mitchell's waste-paper basket before they were incinerated and had reconstructed what was undoubtedly a map bearing the two distinct letters 'RV'. Had this stood for 'rendezvous', perhaps a prearranged meeting with a Soviet

case officer? Mitchell had been under observation by the
PETERS watchers at the time, but he had never been
spotted contacting anyone suspicious. When challenged
about the discarded map Mitchell hesitated for a moment,
apparently making an effort to recall the episode, and then
gave a detailed explanation. He had been preparing a
paper-trail for his children across Chobham Common and
he had been planning a route for them. He had been so
absorbed by it that he had almost missed his train.

Mitchell gave equally good accounts of the other points
raised by Day. It had always been his custom to check to
see if anyone was following him. He regarded this as a
sensible precaution and something that every Security
Service officer ought to do. And as regards his misery
while Director-General? That was also easy to explain: he
had hated Hollis.

This last disclosure came as something of a surprise to
those present. Mitchell owed his promotions to Hollis and
for much of his career had been inextricably linked to him.
They had worked together early in the war when both had
been based at Wormwood Scrubs, and had shared offices
when F Division had been moved to Blenheim Palace in
1940. They had also worked closely for the seven years
when Hollis had appointed him Deputy Director-General.
Mitchell explained that Hollis had never delegated any
responsibility to him and so, therefore, he felt he never
had enough work to keep fully occupied.

The other issues raised in the interview were relatively
trivial in nature, and Mitchell disposed of them all. It
certainly looked as though the PETERS case had indeed
been brought to a close at last, although when Wright
listened to the tapes again he thought he detected some
uncertainty in Mitchell's voice whenever the conversation
turned to Hollis. 'I believed he suspected something was
wrong but did not know what to do,' was his verdict.

With Mitchell formally cleared, the FLUENCY Committee turned to concentrate on the spy referred to by
Volkov and Gouzenko, and a molehunt codenamed Operation DRAT was initiated.

4

SMOKING GUN
EVIDENCE: DRAT

Graham Mitchell's official clearance by the FLUENCY Committee left Martin Furnival Jones with a dilemma. There were still three indisputable pieces of evidence pointing to post-war Soviet penetration of MI5, and a larger number which, though more circumstantial in nature, tended to support the theory. Once Mitchell had been passed by the interrogators, there was little alternative but to embark on yet another painful molehunt.

Furnival Jones' reluctance to participate in D Branch's internal politics was largely born from his concern about morale within MI5. Molehunting had proved itself to be a thoroughly destructive occupation, sapping confidence at every level and undermining that most essential of assets in the intelligence community: trust. As things stood in D Branch, mutual suspicion seemed the commodity in greater supply, and at least two senior officers – Ian Carrel, the Head of Registry, and the Deputy Director-General, Anthony Simkins – were known to have voiced anxiety about FLUENCY's debilitating effect. In an attempt to minimise the damage of the new molehunt, Operation DRAT, Furnival Jones obtained the consent of the new Director of D Branch, Michael Hanley, to a restructuring plan. Henceforth, MI5's Soviet counter-espionage department would be known as K Branch, and it would contain an entirely new section, designated K7 and headed by John Day, to look into claims of hostile penetration.

Of FLUENCY's three remaining 'proofs', only the Gouzenko matter looked even remotely promising unless additional material surfaced unexpectedly. In the absence of some unforeseen development, the clue of a GRU mole codenamed ELLI seemed the best prospect. Goleniewski's HARRIET had been exhausted and Konstantin Volkov was presumed to have been executed. After all, Gouzenko was still alive, living under the RCMP's protection just outside Toronto, and the fact that Hollis, now DRAT's chief suspect, had conducted the original interview on behalf of MI5, made further investigation essential.

Igor Gouzenko defected from the Soviety Embassy in Ottawa on 6 September 1945 and took with him his meal-ticket, the batch of sensitive documents he had already earmarked for removal. When the RCMP eventually re-alised the extraordinary windfall Gouzenko represented, he was taken into protective custody and driven to a motel, accompanied by his pregnant wife, his two-year-old son, and a pair of RCMP bodyguards. Later they were all transferred to more secure accommodation – a secret training-camp just outside Oshawa, on the north shore of Lake Ontario – and debriefed.

So much has been written about Gouzenko, especially in connection with Hollis, that it would be wise to put the case into its proper perspective. This has not always been possible in the past because Gouzenko enjoyed a well-earned reputation for being highly litigious and, until his death, by natural causes at his home in suburban Missis-sauga, on 25 June 1982, he often sued authors and others critical of his behaviour. He invariably won substantial damages, so commentators were naturally hesitant to be entirely candid. The need for such discretion on that score is now past.

When Gouzenko sought political asylum in Canada, he was just twenty-six years old. He had been in the country since June 1943 and had worked as a confidential cipher clerk, chiefly for Colonel Nicolai Zabotin, the GRU *rezident* at the Embassy who operated under military attaché cover. Originally, Gouzenko had joined the Red Army from the Young Communists and, after a period of training, had been sent to the front as a clerk. A year later, holding the rank of lieutenant, he was recalled to Moscow and assigned to the GRU headquarters before being selected for an overseas posting.

Gouzenko's decision to defect certainly took the Canadian government and the RCMP by surprise. At first, when Gouzenko spoke of the papers he had stolen from the Embassy, there was serious thought given to the idea of handing him back to the Russians. One reason for this was the RCMP's relative inexperience in intelligence matters. Indeed, the RCMP's entire Intelligence Division only consisted of two people: Superintendent Charles Rivett-Carnac, the younger son of an English baronet, and Inspector John Leopold, a Czech-born agent who had once penetrated the Canadian Communist Party during the 1920s. Certainly, the RCMP's wartime efforts at counter-intelligence had been appallingly amateurish and had led to the first permanent posting of an MI5 liaison officer in Ottawa to supervise their activities. However, early in September 1945, the officer concerned was in mid-Atlantic, already on his way back to London to be de-mobbed. In his absence, the RCMP contacted the joint MI5–SIS office in New York headed by Sir William Stephenson.

The first two British officers involved in the Gouzenko case were Peter Dwyer and Jean-Paul Evans, then both members of British Security Co-ordination, Stephenson's cover organisation in New York. They flew up to Ottawa, but neither of them ever actually met Gouzenko face to face. Instead, John Leopold translated their questions and then reported Gouzenko's answers. Later a Russian-speaking RCMP officer, Mervyn Black, took over Leopold's role as Gouzenko's translator.

Dwyer's prime concern centred on Gouzenko's allegations about two Britons. One was Dr Allan Nunn May, who was then working on an atomic research project and had apparently sent Zabotin a sample of Uranium 235 taken from the atomic plant at Chalk River, Ontario. The physicist was due to take up a teaching job at King's College, London, and on 17 September flew back to England, where he remained under discreet surveillance until his first interview with MI5 on 15 February the following year. The other Briton named as a Soviet spy was Kay Willsher, a forty-two-year-old unmarried graduate of the London School of Economics, who held the rank of Deputy Registrar in the British High Commission. According to the defector, May and Willsher were Communists and part of an enormous Soviet espionage network.

On 4 February 1946, some five months after Gouzenko's defection, Prime Minister Mackenzie King informed his Cabinet, for the first time, of the existence of a Soviet spy ring in Canada. He told those assembled that there was a mass of evidence to support the charge and, omitting any mention of Gouzenko, went on to announce that a Royal Commission would be appointed the following day, headed by two respected judges, Mr Justice Robert Taschereau and Mr Justice Kellock. The two Commissioners began taking evidence *in camera* two days later, and Gouzenko appeared in person on 13 February to give his oral testimony. By the end of his second day of evidence, the Commissioners ordered the immediate arrest of thirteen men and women identified by Gouzenko and his documents as Soviet sources. More arrests followed as the Commission heard more details, and the Prime Minister finally made the first public statement on 15 February.

The Royal Commission issued an interim report on 2 March 1946, which led to the formal arrest of Allan Nunn May a couple of days later in London; and on 14 March it was disclosed that so far a total of forty-eight witnesses had been called to give secret evidence. The final report was released to the public on 15 July, but it was an edited account of the Commission's proceedings. The full 6,000-page transcript of the evidence taken was to remain a classified document until 1981.

As a result of Gouzenko's revelations, twenty Canadian

Communists were charged with offences, and eleven Soviet agents were convicted of espionage and imprisoned. The convictions of two were quashed on appeal, and seven were acquitted. Allan Nunn May, arrested and convicted in England, received the longest sentence, ten years.

More than forty years later it is easy to take defectors and their all-important meal-tickets for granted. Their *prima donna* antics and outlandish claims have all become commonplace, but in September 1945 there had never been such an opportunity to gain an insight into the Soviet intelligence system. Indeed, at that time it was hardly appreciated that Moscow operated two parallel espionage networks, run by the GRU and the NKVD, world-wide. In fact, if Gouzenko had not been equipped with his valuable documents, he might easily have been disbelieved.

The decision to send Hollis to Ottawa to interview Gouzenko followed a semi-official letter sent by Philby, who was then about to fly to Istanbul to deal with Volkov. Philby passed the case on to Hollis because the latter was then the Assistant Director of F Division, in charge of investigating political subversion. As Philby observed in *My Silent War*: 'We both served on the Joint Intelligence Subcommittee which dealt with Communist affairs and never failed to work out an agreed approach to present to the less well-informed representatives of the service departments and the foreign office.'[1] There was, therefore, nothing odd about the selection of Hollis to go to Canada.

Exactly what took place when Hollis arrived is not known for certain, beyond the fact that he met Gouzenko for a short interview in the presence of Mervyn Black, and obtained a written statement from him which was signed by all three men. In addition, Hollis wrote a somewhat disparaging report on Gouzenko himself.

The allegation that Hollis was there to investigate centred on the mysterious spy codenamed ELLI. Gouzenko was later to testify about this individual to the Royal Commission on 15 February 1946, when he confirmed the existence of two Soviet agents with similar codenames. The following exchanges were recorded when Gouzenko was giving evidence on Exhibit 23–J, an embassy telegram, numbered 12200 and dated 24 August 1945, addressed to Colonel Zabotin. An extract of the text was read out by the Commission's Counsel, E. K. Williams KC:

WILLIAMS: 'In answer to No. 248.1. In telegram No. 8267 of 20th June you were instructed as to the inadmissibility of disclosing to the ambassador our agency network. The handing over to the ambassador of Wilgress' report of 3/11/44 about the financial credits for assuring trade between the USSR and Great Britain after the war, in the same form as it was received, has uncovered the identity of our source on the objective ELLI'. What should those words be?

GOUZENKO: 'On the object of ELLI . . .'

WILLIAMS: Does that mean the purpose?

GOUZENKO: That means that the ambassador will be able to surmise that where ELLI works, the Soviet government has an agent.

KELLOCK: That is, that the Soviet government has a secret agent in England going under the name of ELLI?

GOUZENKO: Not in England; in Canada.

WILLIAMS: And you have identified ELLI as Kay Willsher, who works in the office of the High Commissioner in Ottawa?

GOUZENKO: That is right. In other words, it means that the ambassador can realise that in the office of the High Commissioner there is a secret agent.

TASCHEREAU: He was not supposed to know that?

GOUZENKO: No.

KELLOCK: I suppose it might read 'has uncovered the existence of our secret agent ELLI'?

GOUZENKO: No. That is not correct. He does not know about ELLI. By this document he will understand that in the office of the High Commissioner there is somebody who can give this document of Wilgress' to Zabotin.

TASCHEREAU: And the ambassador will know that?

GOUZENKO: After Zabotin gives him that document.

KELLOCK: I suppose it means, 'has disclosed the fact that Zabotin has an agent or a person acting as an agent in the office of the High Commissioner in Ottawa'?

GOUZENKO: That is right.

KELLOCK: And while the ambassador does not know the name or the cover name of that agent, in fact it is ELLI?

GOUZENKO: That is right.

WILLIAMS: Do you know whether ELLI was used as a nickname or cover name for any person other than Miss Willsher?

GOUZENKO: Yes. There is some agent under the same name in Great Britain.

WILLIAMS: Do you know who it is?

GOUZENKO: No.

At this point Mr Williams returned to the text of the telegram, but later the same day Commissioner Taschereau again took up the subject of Kay Willsher who, at that stage, was under surveillance, still at work in the British High Commission.

TASCHEREAU: This is a Kay Willsher, who is known under the cover name of ELLI. She is secretary to the High Commissioner here in Ottawa.

GOUZENKO: That is right.

TASCHEREAU: And there is also a cover name ELLI, and I understand that he or she, I do not know which, has been identified as an agent in England?

GOUZENKO: That is right.

TASCHEREAU: Would that be the same person?

GOUZENKO: No.

TASCHEREAU: Are you sure of that?

GOUZENKO: As far as I know.[2]

This laborious cross-examination conclusively demonstrates that, at least as early as 1946, Gouzenko was convinced that there were two undercover Soviet agents codenamed ELLI. Obviously this was bound to lead to some confusion so, for the sake of convenience, the codename referring to Kay Willsher was altered to ELLIE, although the copy of the incriminating telegram quoted above, which was shown to her when she appeared before the Commission, was left intact with the original spelling. She was not, of course, told of the second ELLI and anyway pleaded guilty when, on 3 May 1946, she was charged with having breached the Official Secrets Act. She was sentenced to three years' imprisonment and, upon her release after maximum remission in August 1948, she returned to England where she married.

Gouzenko's information about the second ELLI was apparently gleaned from a colleague working in the GRU coderoom in Moscow. The spy worked for 'British Counter-intelligence', had access to files on Soviet personnel in Britain and evidently worked for the GRU rather than the NKVD. Exactly how much of this information was given to Hollis is unclear, but in May 1952, in an attempt to link either Philby or Blunt to ELLI, the Security Service asked the head of the RCMP's Special Branch, Superintendent George McClellan, to obtain a second, detailed statement from Gouzenko about ELLI. Gouzenko responded with enthusiasm, placing the blame for MI5's lack of action on his previous allegations on to the mistaken decision to leave the original investigation in MI5's hands.

In Gouzenko's statement to McClellan, he attributed his information about ELLI to an indiscreet cipher clerk named Lubimov and gave several useful clues to the spy, as well as confirming that the mole had been in MI5 specifically (and not 'British Counter-intelligence') around 1942 or 1943. Certain deductions could reasonably be made from Gouzenko's latest recollections. He suggested that the mole had something Russian in his background and had avoided personal meetings by communicating through dead-letter drops. A favoured location was a particular tomb in a graveyard.

The first question to be answered by the DRAT investigators was whether or not any of Gouzenko's statements could be applied to Hollis, rather than to Blunt or Philby. At first glance it seemed possible. Since his confession in April 1964, it was known that Blunt had been run by the KGB and the NKVD, as opposed to the GRU. Philby too had worked for the KGB. This tended to rule out both as candidates for ELLI. Furthermore, Blunt had nothing remotely Russian in his background, apart from a visit to the Soviet Union in 1935, and he had been based in

London, not Blenheim, where the Soviet intelligence files had been kept during the relevant period. In theory Philby, whose job in SIS during 1942–3 involved counter-intelligence against the Nazis, would not normally have had unrestricted access to Soviet material, but he later admitted to having studied SIS's Soviet source books which were 'far outside the normal scope of my duties'.

In contrast, Hollis would have had a free hand among the Registry's Comintern dossiers while he was at Blenheim and he had also visited Russia once, on his return from China.

Much hung on Gouzenko himself, so in 1972 Stewart flew to Toronto to interview the defector. They met, in the presence of three armed RCMP Security Service officers, in the Royal York Hotel, and Stewart read Gouzenko a copy of Hollis' original report dated September 1945. Gouzenko denounced the report as a fabrication, and insisted that the remarks attributed to him by the author were bogus and had been manufactured with the intention of discrediting him. When asked about the authenticating signatures, Gouzenko insisted that they were forgeries. Was this more evidence of DRAT's duplicity, or simply additional proof of Gouzenko's paranoia?

When considering Gouzenko's original allegations it should be remembered that he was then a celebrity, the object of considerable attention. When he had given his evidence to the Royal Commission back in 1946, he had impressed everyone who heard him. He was blessed with almost total recall and had given a superb performance as a witness. Indeed, some RCMP officers conceded that without his direct evidence more of those prosecuted would probably have been acquitted. Yet Gouzenko had never met any of those charged. The one person he did meet, at a purely social gathering, was the only individual to have all the charges against him dropped. In other words, Gouzenko's value was not so much his own first-hand knowledge of agents, but his interpretation of documents and his memory of events inside the Embassy coderoom. Indeed, years later Gouzenko brought a successful legal action for defamation against a Canadian newspaper that had described him as having been a spy. He had never been anything other than a confidential cipher clerk, albeit one with a good memory for detail.

Gouzenko's secret testimony to the Royal Commission in 1946 hardly shed any light on the second ELLI in England. He was not prompted to volunteer a comment when Commissioner Taschereau had remarked on his own ignorance of the spy's gender. If Taschereau had been fishing for more information on ELLI, he must have been disappointed. Gouzenko had denied knowing who the spy was. Why hadn't he at least mentioned that ELLI worked in British counter-intelligence or, even better, MI5? Why the reticence when, just six years later, his memory had so improved? What had happened in the intervening years?

In fact, quite a lot had happened to influence Gouzenko. After his brief moment in the limelight as a witness before the Royal Commission and giving evidence in various spy trials, Gouzenko and his wife Svetlana tried to build a new, anonymous life. If this was truly his intention, he was unsuccessful.

The RCMP did its best and gave him a permanent bodyguard and a new identity, complete with false documentation that showed him to have been born of Ukrainian parents near Saskatoon, in Saskatchewan, where there were many of a similar background. He was also bought a house, with the deeds held in trust in the name of a Mountie, and a large car. In spite of these comforts, Gouzenko proved extremely difficult to handle. He frequently ignored the RCMP's advice on security matters and, once he began to realise his value, it was difficult to prevent him selling interviews. At first he found the concept of 'exclusive' a little hard to grasp, but after a few rows he caught on. At the same time, he learned the principles of defamation. When his first libel action was brought against the *Toronto Star* for reporting his differences with the RCMP, it was settled out of court for $4,000 and a front-page apology. After this early success, he started to take an interest in litigation. Thereafter, he brought dozens of libel suits for the most trivial of reasons. He said the word 'defector' was pejorative and insisted that he had escaped, not defected. Once he even issued a writ when *Maclean's* magazine suggested, with some justification, that his whereabouts were an open secret. Gouzenko was outraged, claiming that the article had jeopardised his family's future because it would encourage his neighbours to be indiscreet.

Gouzenko's unique status as Moscow's first post-war defector made him the object of great attention from the press. The precautions taken by the RCMP to ensure his safety only added to his media value. He would only appear on television wearing a pillow-case with eye-slits over his head to disguise his features, and in later years he demanded a special throat microphone to distort further his already heavy accent. What with his strong RCMP protection, each appearance was a sensation.

In November 1946 he sold a long interview to *Cosmopolitan* for $50,000. The film rights to his first book, *The Iron Curtain*, were purchased by Twentieth Century Fox for $75,000. A movie was made, starring Dana Andrews playing Gouzenko, but it was a flop at the box office. Gradually, as the public's appetite for adventure stories about Gouzenko waned, so his frustration and nuisance value increased. When, during the McCarthy era, the US Senate formed a Subcommittee on Internal Security, Gouzenko told the Chicago *Tribune* that he had valuable new information to give. This was a considerable embarrassment for the RCMP, because Gouzenko had assured them that he had already told them everything he knew. It also posed a constitutional problem, because Gouzenko would not travel to Washington and the Canadian government was reluctant to let the American Senate conduct a judicial hearing on Canadian territory. The FBI was also baffled because it had interviewed Gouzenko as recently as August 1951, and it was widely believed that every last grain of value had been extracted from him. When challenged, Gouzenko denied having supplied the *Tribune* story, but when a retraction was printed and he was asked to comment, he could not resist repeating the original version. Sympathetic American commentators interpreted these contradictions as proof that the Canadian administration had something to hide and was determined to gag Gouzenko. A political rumpus followed and, in the end, after lengthy negotiations, Gouzenko was questioned under oath by a Canadian judge before two US senators. But instead of making new disclosures, Gouzenko simply delivered a well-rehearsed diatribe about what he considered to be the right and wrong ways to attract Soviet defectors.

Gouzenko's entire attitude was of someone who had never been given the recognition he deserved. He suffered from a colossal, over-inflated ego and had convinced himself that he had been treated shabbily. His historic public service of exposing the Soviet spy networks ought to have been rewarded properly and, in his view, his literary efforts, the novel *The Fall of a Titan* and his self-serving autobiography, *This Was My Choice*, merited attention of a much greater magnitude than they ever received. In fact, both were best-sellers and brought him substantial royalties, which he had squandered immediately. He claimed that it was impossible, for security reasons, to get a regular job, and that his index-linked, tax-free government allowance of $1,050 a month was not enough to live on. Such gripes cut little ice with his bodyguards, who knew of Gouzenko's bizarre, spendthrift lifestyle and whose own salaries were considerably less than his income. Gouzenko habitually borrowed money and then failed to repay his debts. Few of those who knew him at all well liked him except, of course, his loyal children and his long-suffering wife whom he had been known to assault. No one who had any dealings with him believed that he had defected for ideological reasons, as he invariably claimed. Instead, most agreed that Gouzenko was nothing more complicated than a typical Slav from a peasant background who was ruthlessly determined to avoid starvation and make a better life for his family in a land of comparative plenty.

As an author, Gouzenko often compared himself with Tolstoy and, undeniably, *The Fall of a Titan* was an impressive book, a saga not unlike *War and Peace*. However, those close to him knew that it had largely been written by his ghost-writer, John Dalrymple, and his RCMP translator, Mervyn Black, himself a talented writer who had spent many years in Russia. Black died of a heart attack soon after *The Fall of a Titan* was published. In addition to Dalrymple and Black, *The Fall of a Titan* benefited from the editorial skill of a distinguished journalist, Laurie McKechnie. After publication Gouzenko only acknowledged Black's contribution and threatened to sue anyone who suggested that the book was not all his own work. He was hypersensitive on this subject, especially after the *New York Times* had compared the defector to Dostoevsky. Indeed, the review went completely to his head and prompted an unsuccessful, one man campaign to have the book nominated for the Nobel prize for literature.

The Fall of a Titan's literary acclaim was not reflected in its financial return. A film option was bought for $10,000, but the movie was never made. Gouzenko was soon broke again, borrowing money from those who could least afford to lend. The ever-patient RCMP intervened and, for a while, a job was found for him working at Malton airport as a member of the security staff: He was eventually sacked for poor attendance. At one stage it was realised that he had no fewer than 114 loans outstanding, totalling $153,000, to banks, mortgage companies, lawyers, businessmen and private individuals in Canada's Ukrainian émigré community.

To add to his imaginary troubles, as well as his real ones, Gouzenko developed diabetes and was warned to undergo a course of medication and to cut down on his drinking. But, characteristically, he refused to take any advice and eventually went blind. When he finally died, he had just received a cheque for $10,000 from Harper & Row, the American publishers of *Wilderness of Mirrors* in which the author, David Martin, had referred to Gouzenko, disparagingly in his view, as a defector.

This, then, is the true background of Gouzenko. The power of his lawyers was feared (he was not averse to suing even them for malpractice), and anyone unwise enough to comment on him knew the consequences. He craved publicity, but brought lawsuits against anyone he thought had trespassed into his private life. Privately, the RCMP believed that he was a classic egotist who had succumbed to 'defector syndrome', a combination of paranoia, self-righteousness, persecution mania and an overwhelming desire constantly to be the centre of attention. Certainly, his political analysis was nowhere near as sophisticated as Golitsyn's, who followed his example and defected fifteen years later. Where Golitsyn perceived conspiracies and complex stratagems on a global scale, Gouzenko only saw the threat of personal violence. He was sure that the RCMP had been thoroughly penetrated by Philby-like moles and always thought that even Superintendent McClellan of the Special Branch was a probable spy, controlled by the KGB. During the Liberal Party's convention in 1968, he printed and distributed pamphlets accusing Pierre Trudeau of being a covert Communist bent on turning Canada 'into a second Cuba'.

Given Gouzenko's cranky behaviour, how did the DRAT molehunters come to take him so seriously? Certainly, he was extraordinarily persuasive. His performances before the Royal Commission and in court were completely convincing, and there is no denying that he knew every word of every one of his 109 stolen documents by heart. His memory had a prodigious capacity and, whenever he appeared for the prosecution, he was the consummate expert witness. In later years, anyone tempted to doubt the relevance of his opinions was reminded of the string of convictions obtained on his testimony and his fondness for litigation. Thus, there was virtually no detrimental material about him on the public record. Anyone seeking to research Igor Gouzenko only found compliments, or a libel lawyer. In time, even the

RCMP's most hardened officers grew wary of their charge. Gouzenko was conscious of every slight and innuendo, real or imagined, and would not hesitate before approaching opposition MPs to lobby the administration for better treatment. He was treated with extreme caution by virtually everyone he came into contact with, leaving the British Security Service with something of a dilemma when his help was needed. MI5's investigators were duty-bound to take each fresh allegation seriously and, although Gouzenko did not become aware of his position for some time, he was a key element in Operation DRAT.

Gouzenko was always available for a press comment and followed the developments of the Cold War with interest. The machinations of the KGB were to be seen everywhere, and he was hardly alone in his theories about Soviet penetration of the British Security Service. Few people, even in England, believed that Burgess and Maclean had acted alone in 1951, and speculation about the possible involvement of a third man had been rife, at least until Philby's official clearance in 1955. It is, therefore, hardly surprising that Gouzenko felt compelled, when approached by the RCMP on MI5's behalf in 1952, to elaborate on his original remarks about ELLI. He had, however, forgotten the codename: 'I forget the cover name. You mentioned it in your letter and that looks like it, but since I forget, I won't repeat it. However, the cover name is not so important in this case.'

In the years since his statement to Hollis, the mysterious mole in England had definitely become a member of MI5 rather than 'British Counter-intelligence'. He even reckoned that his information had narrowed the field to just two or three suspects, and he was able to name his former colleague Lubimov as his source. Now Lubimov had already played a part in Gouzenko's autobiography, *This Was My Choice*, published in 1948, and had been described as 'Liubimov, a veteran now taking the cipher clerk course' at GRU headquarters. Several colourful anecdotes were ascribed to 'Liubimov', including his participation in the murder of a German prisoner of war on the Caucasian front, but the author had not made any reference to the curious ELLI. Was the 'Liubimov' of 1948 the 'Lubimov' of 1952? Perhaps, but what is a little odd, considering that Gouzenko had recalled stories about several other Soviet agents such as ALBERT in Harbin, MAR in Berlin and FELIX in Rome, is the omission of anything about ELLI in England. Yet when called upon by MI5's molehunters to elaborate four years later, Gouzenko was to explain exactly how 'Lubimov' had told him all about the spy in MI5. Apparently, both had shared a table in the GRU's coderoom during the war when Lubimov had been employed on the decryption of telegrams from secret agents in London. Yet, according to Gouzenko, 'my work was on telegrams from and to Germany and Switzerland'. Perhaps it was the GRU's practice to mix together clerks dealing with messages from different countries, but it smacks of unusually poor security, especially in an organisation which prided itself on high standards. Certainly, the penalties for lapses were severe. Gouzenko himself described an incident in which a fellow lieutenant had been executed by a firing squad for nothing more serious than misplacing a signal.

Could the young, inexperienced Lubimov really have been entrusted with access to such sensitive messages? In *This Was My Choice* Gouzenko gave an account of the precautions taken by the GRU specifically to prevent such breaches:

To protect workers from determining the identity of an agent or the exact location of his activity, each operative branch had a 'security reader' who was responsible for obliterating any identification words or symbols. He kept a secret record which was turned over to the proper authorities who would later, if necessary, identify the source of any document. It sounds complicated, but actually the organisation seemed to be operating smoothly and on an ever-increasing scale throughout my year on the 'inside'.[3]

With such elaborate arrangements it is remarkable that Lubimov acquired so much information about a single agent, ELLI, and risked passing it on to his friend. And if he did, what made Gouzenko decide not to mention him in his book? Or could it be that Gouzenko had not thought about ELLI since his cross-examination by the Royal Commission back in February 1946, and had chosen to give an embroidered account when given the opportunity?

Even supposing that Gouzenko's claim about ELLI was true, and that he did learn of a Soviet spy in MI5 in 1942 or 1943, the only reason to believe that this valued source was not Philby (who was then working in 'British Counter-intelligence') or Blunt (then similarly employed in MI5) is the certainty that neither had been run by the GRU. But had their messages never been routed through GRU channels? Gouzenko had something to say on this point too although, of course, he did not know of either Blunt or Philby by name at the time, in 1948. He explained that when Stalin had abolished the Comintern in the war, there had been a major reorganisation of responsibilities within the Soviet intelligence structure:

Some idea of the magnitude of this new Intelligence set up supplanting the 'dissolved' Comintern may be gleaned from the fact that there were approximately five thousand people employed in Moscow headquarters! Military intelligence took over the old chores of the Comintern. It became an active part of the Soviet Fifth Column in democratic countries.[4]

In the shake-up of Moscow's intelligence-gathering system, the GRU had taken over at least some of the Kremlin's overseas assets. Could anyone be absolutely certain that a handful of KGB messages had not been transmitted by the GRU? Although unusual, it was not entirely unknown for the agents of one organisation to be taken over by its rival.

One interesting aspect to the case, and perhaps further evidence of Gouzenko's tendency to embroider a good story, is Chapman Pincher's version of how Gouzenko first heard of ELLI. In *Too Secret Too Long* he tells of how Gouzenko and Lubimov shared a table while 'on the night shift in the Moscow headquarters of the GRU on Krapoykinskaya Boulevard'.[5] Apparently, the 'Special Communications Division' in which they served was accommodated in the ballroom of a palace once owned by a Czarist millionaire. This information was volunteered to Pincher in September 1981 by Gouzenko, but in 1948 Gouzenko had already described the two buildings where he had worked during the war, just before his transfer to Canada: one was at Kropotkin Gate, the other at Znamenskii 19. Neither was the palace with elaborate ceilings or ballroom later described to Pincher.

When arriving at a conclusion about Gouzenko's reliability, and the relevance of his statements about ELLI in relation to Operation DRAT, there is one additional factor requiring consideration. Gouzenko developed diabetes in about 1952 and later suffered severe eye damage because of his failure to take his prescribed medication. He eventually went blind and had to learn Braille. Nevertheless, he continued to write letters to lawyers and others using a Braille typewriter. While he was alive this was a closely guarded secret, because Gouzenko believed that if word of his handicap leaked out it might assist the KGB to trace his new identity. 'How many blind Russians living in or around Toronto are there?' he used to ask. His condition was therefore concealed, apparently even from MI5, because in 1973 Stewart, a member of the DRAT investigation team, flew to Toronto to suggest that Gouzenko sift through a collection of photographs in order to see if he could identify Hollis as the MI5 officer who originally had questioned him for three minutes in September 1945. Needless to say, Gouzenko was unable to pick out Hollis' picture.

Before Stewart's first visit to meet Gouzenko in Toronto in 1972, MI5 had virtually no knowledge of the defector's case, apart from the original assessment written by Hollis and the RCMP's second-hand offerings. Up until April 1964, when Blunt gave the first detailed insight into the activities of the KGB's Ring-of-Five mentioned in the

VENONA traffic, it had been assumed that Gouzenko's claims about a spy in 'British Counter-intelligence' had referred exclusively to Philby. He, of course, had worked in SIS's counter-intelligence section during the relevant period, in 1942 and 1943, and had been sacked from SIS in the wake of the Burgess and Maclean defections in 1951. Several other possible suspects had also had their contracts terminated as a result of SIS's house-cleaning exercise. At least one other could have fitted the bill. When Gouzenko revised his original comments in May 1952 and spoke of ELLI having been in MI5, it was widely assumed that, in all probability, the source had been Blunt. But Blunt's own account made him an unlikely candidate for ELLI. Little thought was given to the possibility that Gouzenko might have altered the story, substituting MI5 for the vaguer term 'British Counter-intelligence'. That possibility certainly existed because the newspapers had been full of references to MI5 since the previous June, when the disappearances had been made public. Gouzenko could hardly have missed the stories and may have been tempted to add some extra colour to his original claim. At that stage he could not really have been expected to know that the wartime Secret Intelligence Service had also contained a counter-intelligence section.

When Furnival Jones finally authorised Operation DRAT, he could not have anticipated that the litigious Russian would play such an important role in implicating the recently retired Director-General. When the issue first came up, he had called the scenario 'grotesque', yet there was undeniable evidence that the KGB and the GRU had gone to considerable lengths during the 1930s to recruit moles, as well as to operate the scattershot principle: that if enough talented people were developed, at least one or two would end up in useful positions. On that basis the Soviets must have approached dozens of suitable recruits, because more than thirty were eventually persuaded to make full or partial confessions. This was the exercise that had been assisted by Blunt and involved MI5 interrogators extracting admissions from those named by him. Blunt recalled that anyone admired by Burgess was approached. Anyone praised by him had probably been signed up for the Comintern. Dozens of likely leads were pursued, but some investigations were handicapped by what Wright interpreted as the hierarchy's reluctance to sanction awkward enquiries that might prove politically embarrassing.

At least one such case ended in tragedy. Furnival Jones obtained permission from the Prime Minister, Harold Wilson, to seek an interview with Bernard Floud, the Labour MP for Acton since 1964. Soon after taking office Wilson had instructed Hollis to obtain his consent if MI5 wished to investigate a Member of Parliament. This convention applied to his successor and was made public by the Prime Minister in November 1966. The following year, after Floud had been implicated in an Oxford-based underground CPGB cell, he underwent a series of interviews but, unknown to MI5, he was also suffering from severe depression. On 27 October 1967, soon after the death of his wife, Floud returned home from an interrogation and gassed himself.

Several other public figures were interviewed by MI5 and a number of suspect civil servants were switched from sensitive Whitehall posts so as to prevent them from having access to classified documents. Some of the K Branch researchers regarded such solutions as profoundly unsatisfactory, because shifting someone away from secrets was only a short-term expedient. It removed the individual to a place where the nation's security was not at risk, but it did little to improve MI5's knowledge about widespread penetration of Whitehall by covert Soviet sympathisers. Indeed, not all the suspects were civil servants. A few were newly elected Labour Members of Parliament and the Prime Minister's ban had effectively restricted Furnival Jones' freedom of action. In practical terms it meant that MI5 would only step in if, as happened with Floud, a suspect became a candidate for promotion to ministerial office.

MI5's only trump card – its depth of knowledge about the CPGB's clandestine membership – came from copies of the organisation's confidential files which had been copied illicitly in 1955. Codenamed Operation PARTY PIECE, the Security Service had been given the opportunity to photograph the CPGB's entire membership roll which had been left unattended overnight in the Mayfair flat of a wealthy CPGB supporter. A secret annexe to the main list was found to contain the dossiers of underground supporters who had concealed their true political allegiance by joining the Labour Party. Because the original effort to copy the files had been illegal, and had involved a break-in, their existence was a closely guarded secret even within MI5, and the resulting intelligence was severely restricted. On the rare occasions it had to be circulated, it was attributed to one of several agents who had been infiltrated into the CPGB's headquarters. Although technically 'deniable', in that MI5 invariably took steps to ensure it could dissociate itself if anything went wrong, operations like PARTY PIECE were extremely rare events and required permission from the top. In more than one case an illegal, surreptitious break-in was approved by the Permanent Under-Secretary at the Home Office.

It was K Branch's contention that Soviet penetration of the Civil Service could not be detected or thoroughly investigated without resort to such methods, but the Security Service management was understandably wary of high-risk ventures. The Director-General's reluctance to give his approval to certain K Branch proposals led to frustration among some members of K3, the operations section, and K7, the molehunting unit.

Much of this frustration resulted from senior management's blank refusal to sanction full-scale investigations into high-ranking suspects. Sir Anthony Rumbold, Britain's ambassador to Austria until 1970, was just such an example. He had been named as a Soviet source as long ago as 1940 by a Soviet agent who had defected in 1936. The allegation had been dismissed out of hand and the information buried in the files, but the molehunters backtracked and, once the link was found, were anxious to question the diplomat about his long friendship with Donald Maclean, who had been best man at Rumbold's first

marriage. Rumbold had been given a perfunctory interview soon after Maclean's defection when MI5 had not
fully appreciated the extraordinary scale of the KGB's
recruitment campaign during the 1930s. Permission to
question him again was denied. In the case of Sir Dennis
Proctor, an interview was only sanctioned after he had
retired as Permanent Under-Secretary at the Ministry of
Power in 1965. A former Apostle and undergraduate of
King's College, Proctor had been a close friend of Guy
Burgess', and a letter from Proctor had been found in
Burgess' flat. When Proctor retired from the Ministry of
Power, Peter Wright travelled down to his new home in
the South of France and interviewed him. Wright concluded that he had not been a spy, as such, but had never
had any secrets from Burgess. K7 marked this down as a
partial confession and obtained a list of other members of
a Fabian-style discussion group which had flourished in
Whitehall before the war.

Proctor was not told that a confession had already been
extracted from Blunt, but Victor Rothschild was. Writing
in his autobiography, *Random Variables*, published in
1984, Rothschild recalled the shock which seemed 'devastating, crushing and beyond belief':

I found it almost impossible to believe and, childishly, felt like
telephoning Blunt to ask him if this appalling news was true. But
there was no doubt; why should 'they' wish to play a cruel and
meaningless practical joke on me? What might I be stimulated
to confess in return? The short answer was: nothing. As 'they'
knew, I was not a Soviet agent.[6]

Nevertheless, MI5 was keen to tap his prodigious mind:

The 'authorities' knew, of course, that many years before I had
been a close friend of Blunt, though we drifted apart in about
1950; and they were therefore interested in anything, anything,
I could tell them about him, his friends and acquaintances. So
appalled was I by their news as I am sure they expected, that I
found it essential to help them in every possible way; and this I
did within the limits of an imperfect memory.[7]

Not surprisingly, the Security Service was very anxious to keep the news of their molehunting activities from the public. Rothschild, as a former MI5 officer himself, was treated differently, but was expected to keep the matter to himself. Charges of McCarthyism had never been levelled against MI5 and there was no wish to attract such criticism now. The system of security clearances, known as Positive Vetting, which had been masterminded by Graham Mitchell and introduced after the defections of Burgess and Maclean, had gradually extended without public comment. Instead of the 2,000 names originally contemplated, more than 58,000 individuals had undergone the screening process. Only a tiny handful of those discreetly rejected had sought to appeal, and none had been reinstated. In other words, the vetting system worked. If one or two senior suspects had slipped through the net, there was still an opportunity to manipulate their transfer into non-sensitive posts, as had happened to the two Treasury officials who found themselves moved sideways into the Department of Trade. Delicate matters demanded tact, and it was argued that a witch-hunt would prove counter-productive, both politically and professionally. Indeed, the need to maintain secrecy about Blunt's confession was essential if the Russians were not to be alerted.

Another difficulty hampering the molehunters was the lack of information concerning penetration of MI5 itself. A few of those who had given full or partial confessions had named other covert Communists, but none had implicated anyone in two of the KGB's most obvious targets, GCHQ and MI5. With so few clues to work on, a K7 case officer paid a visit to Jane Sissmore, MI5's expert on the Comintern. Long since retired, she was living in an old people's home in the West Country. Like John le Carré's character, Connie, she had lost none of her faculties and, after listening to a series of decoy questions, asked, 'Why on earth do you think Roger was a spy?'

Almost in desperation, K7 took the matter up with Blunt in order to obtain his opinion. John Day, who conducted the interview on that occasion, went to some lengths to conceal the fact that Hollis had become the focus of Operation DRAT, but none the less Blunt quickly realised what the officer was driving at. He could not understand how Hollis had become a suspect, but he found the situation startling, not to say slightly ludicrous. His own private view was that Hollis was too stupid to have been a spy, although he was not prepared to rule out the idea completely.

Curiously, in 1971 K Branch initiated a new assessment of Blunt which came to some depressing conclusions. Written by another K Branch officer, Ann Orr-Ewing, the report claimed that Blunt's confession in 1964, and his assistance to Peter Wright, had been entirely insincere. She believed that he had never told the truth about his dealings with his Soviet contacts, had never implicated anyone of importance who had not already come under suspicion and, most devastatingly of all, had never changed his political opinions. It was also noticed that he had never said anything of any relevance to Hollis, although perhaps that was not so odd if Blunt's KGB-run Ring-of-Five had been kept in a watertight compartment, separate from a spy operated by the GRU.

With Mitchell cleared, and the HARRIET case shown to be a KGB disinformation ploy, Hollis was the only alternative suspect. It was a grotesque proposition, as Furnival Jones had rightly observed, compromising many of the nation's post-war secrets, yet there seemed to be no other logical explanation for MI5's numerous leaks and failures. Hesitantly, K7 began accumulating the evidence against the former Director-General.

Meanwhile, Hollis was living quietly in the country, apparently oblivious to K7's activities. He had left Leconfield House for the last time late in 1965, moving first to Wells and then to a small cottage called Crossways in the tiny village of Cadcott, near Bridgewater. Three years after his retirement he abandoned his wife of thirty-one years and married his long-time mistress and former secretary, Val Hammond. But these were matters for his family, not the Security Service. He still had three brothers: Christopher, a former Conservative Member of Parliament for Devizes; Michael, an assistant bishop; and Marcus, a former SIS officer. His son Adrian was a brilliant chess player and had become a don at Oxford.

K7's research centred on Hollis' early life. Most of the well-known, ideologically motivated moles had a good grounding in Leftist activity which could be traced with sufficient legwork. Burgess, Philby, Blunt, Maclean, Long, Watson and Cairncross had only taken steps to conceal their true political views some time after a traceable record had been left. There were membership rolls, suspicious associations, contributions to magazines, letters to family and friends, and photographs to bear testimony to their erstwhile opinions. But none of these applied to Hollis. There were few mysteries in his past. He had left Oxford early, without a degree, to travel abroad, and his career within MI5 was well documented, covering his life from 1938 to 1965. Gradually, the area of interest was narrowed down to the period between his decision to leave university and his acceptance into the Security Service.

The only information known about this critical period of his life comes from Hollis himself. He went up to Worcester College as an undergraduate in 1924, but instead of completing his final year he opted to work in the City as a clerk in order to finance a long trip abroad. He took a passage by boat to China, via Penang, and tried to earn a living as a freelance journalist. Early the following year he joined a subsidiary of the British American Tobacco Company. Apart from one period of leave in England during the summer of 1934, Hollis stayed in China until July 1936 when he returned, via Canada, to Europe for treatment for tuberculosis at a Swiss sanatorium. On 17 July 1937 he married Evelyn Swayle, the daughter of a wealthy Glastonbury solicitor. The following year he applied to join SIS but was rejected on health grounds. Instead, he was recruited into MI5.

The K7 molehunters searched into the decade between Hollis' departure from Oxford and his entry into the Security Service in order to find the tell-tale clues of a crypto-Communist, but there was no trace. The best they could come up with was the existence of a well-established Soviet spy ring based in Shanghai's expatriate, European community at the same time that Hollis was known to have lived there. In addition, it was known that one of the GRU's most accomplished agents, Ruth Kuczynski, had been active in China, Switzerland and Oxford at the very times that Hollis had lived in those places. She had been a member of Richard Sorge's celebrated network in Shanghai, and had later moved to Geneva where she had played an important part in the famous LUCY ring. Thereafter, she had moved to Oxford to live near her father and brother, both known to have been Soviet agents. She had suddenly returned to East Germany, where she now lives, following the arrest of Klaus Fuchs in 1949. In 1977 she published her memoirs, *Sonia's Rapport*, in which she gave a sanitised account of her adventures with the GRU. Her brother Jürgen followed in 1983 with his *Memoirs*, also published in East Berlin, but his story had also been censored heavily. Although there was much to link the two Kuczynskis to Klaus Fuchs, there was nothing to show that either had ever met Hollis. It was simply that both had been at the same places at the same time. This was a very fragile connection, but it was treated seriously by K7. With little else to work on, a request was made to Furnival Jones for permission to recall Hollis from retirement for interrogation.

The decision required of Furnival Jones was distasteful in the extreme. If he refused permission, as he was entitled to do because the evidence against Hollis was entirely circumstantial, he knew the molehunts would continue. After all, the final FLUENCY report had identified the three remaining indications of Soviet penetration that demanded investigation. If K7 was frustrated in its attempts to establish the truth, there would be cries of a 'cover-up'. On the other hand, the full-scale investigation of a former Director-General of the Security Service was no light matter. Apart from being unpalatable (for Hollis had originally appointed Furnival Jones as his deputy and recommended his succession to the Prime Minister), there were also the political consequences. Even if Hollis was cleared, as Mitchell had been, a leak would have been disastrous. Finally, there was also the possibility that Hollis might confess. That too would complicate an already difficult situation. It was bad enough having the Blunt case waiting to detonate like an unexploded bomb. The implications of a confession from Hollis were even more alarming, although a criminal prosecution was considered 'unthinkable'.

Faced with these considerations Furnival Jones gave his consent to an interrogation, which took place during an entire day in 1970 in the presence of the Director-General and his deputy, Anthony Simkins. Peter Wright and John Day prepared the questionnaire and listened in to Hollis' performance.

Hollis was invited to give a detailed account of his early life and his recollection was challenged on several incidents. He was vague on some matters, equivocal on others and pleaded a poor memory on several telling points. He recalled having met Agnes Smedley, a lifelong Communist activist, in Shanghai, but denied any later connection with her. He certainly had never met Ruth Kuczynski, the GRU agent. He was unable to recall the details of his meeting with Gouzenko, but he did give a full account of his post-war career. When challenged about his refusal to allow Mitchell to be interrogated, Hollis claimed to have placed the issue before the Prime Minister. And as regards his treatment of Arthur Martin, he had no regrets and there was never any question of penalising him for his devotion to duty. Martin had simply been swopped with an SIS officer who had taken his place in MI5.

To Peter Wright and John Day, the interrogation was unconvincing. Hollis had pleaded a bad memory on matters that he might reasonably be expected to remember. They thought he had been evasive and, on a couple of occasions, demonstrated an element of cunning. Furnival Jones and Simkins took the opposite view. They considered that Hollis had not shown any signs of antagonism and had been as co-operative as possible, given the somewhat uncomfortable circumstances. The only remotely

damaging admission made by Hollis was an omission early
in his career, concerning the personal file of a fellow
Oxford undergraduate and well-known Leftist. MI5 personnel are required to endorse the files of individuals
known to them if they happen to deal with them. A brief
note acknowledging the connection then remains on the
file and is a common occurrence. On just one occasion
Hollis had failed to make the necessary entry, but it was
an oversight, he insisted, and nothing more sinister.

Hollis underwent a second, shorter interview a few weeks
later when K7 had been able to check his answers and construct a second questionnaire of outstanding points. At its
conclusion he returned to his retirement home in Somerset,
leaving Furnival Jones to sort out the mess.

5

COVER-UP

Furnival Jones' dilemma about how to handle the Hollis interrogation was not made any easier by the rather strained relationship between his organisation and the Prime Minister. It is now well known that Harold Wilson had strong views on the Security Service and his criticisms were later to be articulated to two television reporters, Barrie Penrose and Roger Courtier. Shortly after his retirement in 1976, Wilson invited both BBC journalists to investigate certain developments. One of his more startling claims was that, while he had been in office, he had been the victim of an MI5 plot to destabilise his administration. It was an extraordinary allegation, but it was one founded in reality. Its origin was even more bizarre.

Rather more than a year before Wilson's election to Downing Street in October 1964, the Security Service had initiated an investigation into his background at the behest of Anatoli Golitsyn, the KGB defector. Golitsyn had made no direct charges concerning Wilson, but he did say that the KGB had planned to assassinate the leader of a European opposition party so as to pave the way for the succession of a more sympathetic, pro-Soviet replacement. Britain had not been identified as the country in question, but the unexpected death of Hugh Gaitskell in January 1963 seemed to have fitted the bill. Gaitskell had died after a short illness from an extraordinarily rare infection of the heart and kidneys. According to Golitsyn's scenario, Gaitskell's condition might have been induced artificially, perhaps concealed in food or drink. While sounding implausible, the proposition was tested and it was learned that Gaitskell had visited the Soviet Consulate in the Bayswater Road prior to his illness and had been given some refreshments while awaiting a visa. Further research had showed that Gaitskell's rare condition could have been contracted as a result of his having ingested a concentrated toxin. Such fantastic ideas may seem a trifle melodramatic, but since that time there have been several examples of troublesome anti-Soviet activists falling victim to strange illnesses. One such victim was Georgi Markov, the exiled Bulgarian dissident who was stabbed with an umbrella tip on 7 September 1978. The incident occurred near Bush House, the headquarters of the BBC's External Services, where he worked as a broadcaster. Markov was injected with a tiny metal pellet made of a platinum alloy, containing a microscopic quantity of Ricin, a deadly toxic substance which has no natural origin. According to the experts at the germ warfare research establishment at Porton Down where traces of the poison were isolated, Ricin is an artificial derivative of the castor oil seed. It is as close to an untraceable poison as can be found. Markov died in hospital, his illness a mystery. Another dissident, Vladimir Kostov, was luckier: he was attacked in a similar way in a busy Paris street, but survived the experience.

If the KGB had assassinated Gaitskell, it followed that Wilson ought to be investigated, and a preliminary review of his background indicated that at one time in the early 1950s, after his resignation as President of the Board of Trade in April 1951, he had made frequent business trips across the Iron Curtain for the timber tycoon Montague Meyer. These visits, totalling nineteen in all, became known as the 'lost weeks', because there were long periods when Wilson's movements in the Soviet Union could not be traced. On some he was known to have been accompanied by his private secretary, Mrs Marcia Williams. Accordingly, a further, deeper investigation was authorised involving surveillance on some of Wilson's closest associates, of whom not a few were considered to have strong Eastern Bloc connections. Indeed, Joseph Kagan, later ennobled by Wilson, had been born in Lithuania, and Harry Kissin's brother had actually been Trotsky's private secretary. In the event, the extraordinary suggestion that either Wilson or Williams had been disloyal was scotched by the investigators, and, as was later revealed, Wilson was in fact the victim of a Security Service conspiracy to discredit his administration.

It might be argued that this step took the Security Service far beyond reasonable limits and, in retrospect, it is a little hard to understand, but at the time MI5 was exercising its conventional independence from direct political control. The organisation's first duty is the protection of the realm and, though the decision to investigate Wilson was to cause extreme embarrassment later, it was seen at the time as a vital task which, in spite of its constitutional implications, had to be executed. The alternative – simply burying the investigation because it was too uncomfortable to pursue – was not really an option available. Deliberate suppression of any evidence implicating the highest elected official in the country would have been a greater dereliction of duty than a sensitive, undercover enquiry to establish the Prime Minister's loyalty. In any event, there seemed little likelihood of the Service ever being called to account publicly for its behaviour. In this at least those involved made a serious misjudgement. Exactly how MI5's enquiries were conducted will be examined later, as details of the story emerged.

The main preoccupation of the Security Service's mole-hunters in 1970 was to determine who had been responsible for penetrating MI5, and to ensure that its recruitment had not been tainted. The argument that, because both of the two main suspects, Mitchell and Hollis, had now retired, there was no further cause for concern was not one that held water. It had already been agreed that penetration at such a high level, involving men who had certainly influenced recruitment policy over a long period, would leave the organisation compromised. The extent, of course, was debatable, as were the culprits, but the fundamental issues

were not in question. Or were they? If both Mitchell and
Hollis had received clearances, where did that leave MI5?
Did that mean that senior management did not now believe
the FLUENCY Committee's principal conclusion, that
penetration was undeniable? Much depended on the
Director-General's attitude and that of his deputy, but
both were about to leave the office themselves. Anthony
Simkins retired in 1971 and was replaced by the Director
K Branch, Michael Hanley. When Furnival Jones went
the following year Hanley succeeded him, and Ronald
Symonds was appointed Deputy Director-General. Thus,
at the very moment when the Security Service ought to
have been coming to terms with the implications of the
Hollis interrogation, and the less than unanimous decision
to clear him, two of those holding the greatest responsibility had reached the end of their terms of office. So too
had Peter Wright who, for the past three years, had worked
as Hanley's personal assistant, supervising K Branch's
most delicate molehunting operations.

   In these circumstances it is not surprising that Hanley
sought Wright's help and asked him to remain on in the
Security Service in a part-time capacity as his special adviser on Soviet penetration of Whitehall. Wright agreed,
and arranged to spend part of the week at MI5's new
headquarters in Gower Street and the remainder at the
small stud farm in Cornwall operated by his son Bevis.
This unusual arrangement gave MI5 the continuity which
seemed threatened by the retirements of Simkins and
Furnival Jones. The passage of time since the PETERS
operation had been initiated meant that virtually none of
the participants of the early molehunts were still employed
by K Branch.

   Wright's new post in the Security Service put him in a
unique position in that he had actually served rather longer
in K Branch than any other MI5 officer, having first joined
it in April 1963 when it was still designated D Branch. Since
that time he had served under four different directors:
Malcolm Cumming, Martin Furnival Jones, Michael Hanley and, most recently, McDonald. All had played some

part in the molehunts, but none could match his extraordinary grasp of the detailed investigations carried out during the previous decade. Indeed, there were probably only two other officers left who could even begin to match Wright's knowledge, and both were in SIS. Arthur Martin had become Head of Registry and was now approaching retirement, and Stephen de Mowbray was back in action after a two-year stint overseas as the SIS Head of Station in Washington between 1966 and 1968. His return from America had coincided with Dick White's official retirement, to a new Cabinet Office post created specially for him as Intelligence Co-ordinator.

It was at this point, during the transitional year of 1972, that Martin and de Mowbray began to express anxiety about the way MI5's molehunting had been conducted. It seemed to them that there was a grave danger of the entire matter being allowed to drop. What was the official line on the Hollis interrogation? If he had been cleared, then what further action was required to trace those responsible for leaking MI5's secrets to the Soviets? These were questions that demanded answers, but none seemed to be forthcoming. The clincher was an inter-Allied counter-intelligence conference, codenamed CAZAB, held in London at which Michael Hanley, acting on Furnival Jones' authority, disclosed the existence of Operation DRAT and invited the assembled company, from America, Canada, Australia and New Zealand, to assume that Hollis had been a lifelong Soviet agent. This was a precaution taken on Wright's advice, backed by John Day, and was designed to act as a warning that cases known to Hollis may have been compromised. It was a 'worst case' assessment and was not necessarily to mean that the Security Service had reversed its official position on Hollis' innocence. It was this latter qualification which seemed so difficult to swallow, especially for those who had known the full background to the molehunts. Either Hollis was a spy, in which case the proper steps should be taken to minimise the damage he had inflicted, or he wasn't. If that were true, a further search was needed to trace the real villain.

What was profoundly unacceptable was the dual standard implied by MI5's compromise approach: we are sure Hollis is innocent but just in case he isn't . . .

It was the fudging of this vital contradiction which led de Mowbray and Martin to seek Maurice Oldfield's help. Oldfield had only become the SIS Chief in 1973, and this situation had all the makings of a sizable constitutional crisis on the gravest issue imaginable: the safety of the realm. Some of his staff were calling 'foul' on the activities of MI5, accusing the organisation of avoiding its central responsibility: the prevention of hostile penetration. Oldfield had the choice of disciplining his two officers and pulling them into line, thus leaving himself open to the charge that he had condoned what amounted to a cover-up, or backing de Mowbray. His decision, for which he was to be much criticised, was to opt for the latter course, but only in a very half-hearted way. Instead of looking into the matter personally, or insisting that FLUENCY be reconstituted, Oldfield suggested that if de Mowbray was sure of his ground he should take the matter to the Prime Minister, Harold Wilson. This he did in June 1974, but his attempt to gain a hearing before the Prime Minister failed. Instead, the Cabinet Secretary, Sir John Hunt, interviewed de Mowbray and told him that his allegations were so serious that he would consult the Prime Minister and then let him know what action was to be taken. In the event, Hunt recommended that Wilson ask his immediate predecessor, Sir Burke Trend, who had only just retired after a decade as Cabinet Secretary, to carry out a full review of PETERS and DRAT. De Mowbray left Downing Street confident that a cover-up had been averted, but not everyone shared his optimism.

The fact that Martin and de Mowbray had kept in touch, long after the winding-up of the FLUENCY Committee, has led them to be referred to as the 'Young Turks'. The term was first used by Dick White when, as we shall see, he was prompted to rebut allegations against his old mentor, Guy Liddell. In fact, there was no concerted effort to reopen DRAT. Martin and de Mowbray simply wanted to be sure that the Security Service did not shelve an embarrassment. The prospect of Burke Trend undertaking a complete review of the files was encouraging although, if anyone thought a further interrogation of Hollis might be warranted, they were disappointed. Hollis died of a stroke late in October.

Trend's enquiry, which began in July 1974, continued for almost a year. Twice a week he travelled up to Gower Street from Lincoln College, where he had been installed as Rector. He sifted through all the relevant dossiers accumulated during the molehunts of the 1960s and interviewed a selected group of officers. Although he saw Peter Wright twice, he did not interview Arthur Martin. Trend's task, of course, was not to apportion blame or identify any hidden moles. His was an administrative job to see that MI5 had pursued every possible line of enquiry and reached the proper conclusions based on the evidence available. He was there to certify that MI5's molehunts had been executed 'in a proper and thorough manner'. In short, he was appointed to ensure that there had been no cover-up, as alleged by de Mowbray. But it was not part of Trend's brief to sit as judge and jury on the case against Hollis or, for that matter, against anyone else, although that is what Wright believed his function to be. Wright assumed, when cross-examined by Trend, that he had been appointed as an independent assessor of the DRAT case, but he had not. This misunderstanding was to lead to considerable difficulties later, especially when it was finally revealed that Trend had completed his report and delivered it to the Prime Minister and his Home Secretary, Roy Jenkins. The document was to be kept strictly secret, but it was agreed, when de Mowbray asked about Trend's progress, that Jenkins should give him a briefing in which Trend's conclusions would be outlined. In short, Trend concluded that MI5 had acted entirely properly throughout the molehunts and had pursued the case against DRAT exhaustively.

While Trend was still deliberating, Wright had his own troubles. He was due to retire from the Security Service completely at the end of January 1976, but he was becoming increasingly worried about his pension. Under Civil Service rules, he was entitled to 1/80th of his final year's salary for each year of service, but on this basis, counted from his entry into the Security Service in 1955, he had only completed seventeen years in full-time employment as his work since 1972 had been part-time. There was also some question about the technical grade he had held until he had acquired officer rank in D Branch. When all the calculations were made, and the sum of £5,000 had been deducted as the amount Wright had taken in a lump sum as a commuted pension, he was to be left with just £2,000 per annum. This was a cause of great anxiety to him, especially when he learned that upon his death his wife Lois would receive only half the benefit.

Wright began to follow up the various Civil Service appeals procedures in order to have his pension increased and, in the meantime, took steps to ensure his future. The most succinct account of this period in Wright's life is given by Chapman Pincher in his autobiography, *Inside Story*, which was published in 1978, although he was careful to conceal Wright's identity. Unnamed, he is portrayed as someone who, during the course of his secret duties, had uncovered extremely damaging information about certain members of Wilson's administration:

One senior MI5 officer had become so incensed by the activities of two particular ministers that he decided it was urgently in the national interest for them to be exposed, irrespective of what his Director-General, then Sir Michael Hanley, or the Prime Minister might decree. He was prepared to name the ministers and reveal details of their activities from his knowledge of the files containing evidence against them, some of it derived from undercover surveillance.

The MI5 officer, who had steeled himself to make the disclosures, knew that his action would cause such a sensation that it would certainly end his career as a public servant even if he escaped prosecution under the Official Secrets Acts. So he approached a very senior Whitehall personality, whose name I know but I will call 'Q' to preserve his anonymity. Knowing that he would lose his pension, the officer needed some guarantee of future employment after he had made his sacrifice. He therefore asked Q, whom he knew to be sympathetic regarding the danger of left-wing activities of some ministers, if there was any way of obtaining a job in advance, perhaps in some security role, to ensure that he and his family would have some income. Q did not attempt to dissuade him.[1]

According to Pincher, the mysterious Q then went to a senior City figure in an attempt to find the MI5 officer employment. All apparently rejected the idea.

On being told this by Q the MI5 officer completely lost heart and kept both his silence and his job. Had he been sufficiently encouraged to go through with his venture, the naming of three ministers in Labour governments as serious security risks might have been enough to bring the existing government down.[2]

Eleven years after these events, Wright was called upon to give an account of his relationship with Lord Rothschild. In doing so he described how, many years earlier, he had approached Rothschild for a consultancy post as a security adviser in Rothschild's family bank, N. M. Rothschild & Sons. Thus, if Pincher's memoirs were accurate, Wright was probably the man 'prepared to sacrifice his career and risk prosecution to do what he believed to be a public service', by leaking MI5's secrets while he was still a serving member of the Security Service.

Wright's decision not to proceed with his planned disclosures may have been motivated by the lack of any alternative employment as suggested, or it could have been influenced by the continuing negotiations about his pension. If Wright was only putting £2,000 a year at risk, in return for a highly paid job in the City, his sacrifice would not have been so terribly painful to endure after all. It is also possible that there was another consideration which prevented him from 'going public' at such an early stage: his knowledge of the unauthorised, freelance efforts by certain K Branch members to destabilise Wilson's fragile majority.

In July 1974 a selected group of journalists received a Xerox copy of what purported to be a Swiss Bank Corporation statement, showing a credit balance of 163,000 Swiss Francs, in the name of Wilson's deputy leader, Ted Short MP. In those days possession of an undisclosed, overseas bank account was a serious breach of the exchange control regulations and the document was a severe embarrassment to the government. A Scotland Yard investigation eventually established that the photocopy was a skilful forgery, but why had Short been selected for what had turned out to be a technically impressive political smear? Chapman Pincher, who was one of those in receipt of the statement, had no doubt that it had been 'a KGB-inspired device to discredit the British government through one of its senior ministers',[3] but although the method could easily have come from a Soviet disinformation handbook, its execution had been MI5's responsibility.

This particular incident, one of several involving the leakage of politically sensitive information, came from within K Branch and Sir Michael Hanley was later to apologise to the Prime Minister for the behaviour of a few of his officers. Hanley assured Wilson and the Cabinet Secretary, Sir John Hunt, that disciplinary measures had been taken and that there would not be a repetition of the incidents.

In fact, Hanley was in no position to give such a sweeping undertaking because several of those with knowledge of MI5's unexploded bombs had retired, and one of the biggest bombshells of all – the concealment of Sir Anthony Blunt's confession of treachery – was already about to be detonated.

In the aftermath of Blunt's exposure there has been much speculation about the role played by the three so-called 'Young Turks', Martin, de Mowbray and Wright, but in reality none of them had the remotest idea that two journalists were under contract to write books about what Andrew Boyle termed *The Climate of Treason* and Donald McCormick, writing under the name of Richard Deacon, referred to as *The British Connection*. Both men had been researching the background to the Burgess and Maclean affair quite independently of each other, and neither had received any help from the three dissidents. All had now retired: de Mowbray to start a new family at his home in Kent, Martin to the House of Commons to work as a clerk, and Wright to build a stud farm with his son in Tasmania. But before describing how Deacon and Boyle discovered the truth about Blunt, we ought to have a brief look at the numerous books that had been published on the subject of Soviet moles.

The first book, *The Great Spy Scandal*, had been a compilation edited by another journalist, John Mather. This was a popular account, based on the newspaper stories of the time and included, in an appendix, the government White Paper of 1955. This was followed by *The Missing Macleans* by Geoffrey Hoare, a close friend of the Maclean family, which concentrated on the disappearance in Switzerland of Donald Maclean's American wife, Melinda, two years after the original defections. She eventually turned up in the Soviet Union too and left her husband to live with Philby.

The reappearance of Burgess and Maclean at a press conference in Moscow in February 1956 prompted Tom Driberg to organise a reunion with his old companion, Guy Burgess. The result of this meeting was *Guy Burgess: A Portrait with Background*. Much of the by now familiar territory was covered again, although with a degree of affection that had been lacking in earlier histories.

In January 1963 Philby made his controversial, secret confession and then disappeared, but when *Burgess and Maclean* by Anthony Purdy and Douglas Sutherland was released the following September, there was no mention of these events. Instead, the authors drew attention to Anthony Blunt's friendship with Burgess. The details of Philby's dramatic escape from Beirut (though not his acceptance of an immunity from prosecution) were revealed in the *Sunday Times* in 1968 and led to *The Philby Conspiracy* by three of the paper's leading investigative reporters, Bruce Page, Phillip Knightley and David Leitch.

This development prompted Philby to write his own version, *My Silent War*.

Philby's own notorious, and occasionally cruel, memoirs were quickly followed by *The Philby Affair* by Hugh Trevor Roper, *The Third Man* by E. H. Cookridge and *Kim Philby: The Spy I Loved* by his wife Eleanor, with help from a Beirut-based foreign correspondent, Patrick Seale. In 1972 Goronwy Rees contributed his autobiography, *A Chapter of Accidents*, in which he mentioned Blunt's attempt to dissuade him from approaching MI5 after Burgess' defection. Perhaps with the law of libel in mind, he omitted to mention Blunt's name:

I also told another friend of Guy's, who had served in MI5 during the war, and still preserved close connections with it, of what I had done. He was greatly distressed and said he would like to see me. On Monday he came down to my house in the country, and on an almost ideally beautiful English summer day, we sat beside the river and I gave him my reasons for thinking that Guy had gone to the Soviet Union; his violent anti-Americanism, his certainty that America was about to involve us all in a Third World War, most of all the fact that he may have been and perhaps still was a Soviet agent.

He pointed out, very convincingly as it seemed to me, that these were really not very good reasons for denouncing Guy to MI5.[4]

Blunt 'did not disguise his disapproval of what [Rees] was going to do'[5] thereby implicating himself, or so it had seemed to Rees who, of course, knew nothing of Blunt's confession eight years earlier. He was, nevertheless, a continuing danger to Blunt and a potential threat to MI5 if he could ever persuade anyone to take his claims of Blunt's treachery seriously.

In 1973 Patrick Seale teamed up with another journalist, Maureen McConville, and returned to the subject with *Philby: The Long Road to Moscow*. They remarked of Blunt that,

when Burgess defected with Donald Maclean to Moscow in 1951 and was revealed as a Soviet agent, the effect on such friends as

Blunt was shattering. It was not only the disclosure of treachery, but also the betrayal of complex personal values.[6]

The following year Malcolm Muggeridge, once a wartime SIS officer, aired his views on the defections in *The Infernal Grove*. Finally, in 1977, John Fisher released *Burgess and Maclean*.

In total, no fewer than twelve books had told and retold the story of what had become a nation's obsession, yet none had dared speculate on the existence of other Soviet moles, and only a couple had even made a passing reference to Blunt. The danger of an action for defamation was certainly one powerful disincentive, but in truth none of those looking into the defections ever guessed the scale of the molehunts that had continued right into the 1970s.

It was against this background that Richard Deacon, a retired Foreign Manager of the *Sunday Times*, began his own enquiries into what he called 'Russia's manipulation of British individuals and institutions'. He had already written some popular books about espionage and intelligence, including *A History of the British Secret Service* and *A History of the Russian Secret Service*, and was known to have useful sources. Soon after he had started work Deacon realised from the reactions of usually helpful contacts that he was touching a raw nerve. His experience as a veteran newspaperman told him that he was on the verge of an important coup, and gradually he centred on the possibility that either Rothschild or Blunt, or both, had been Soviet agents. His two chief suspects responded to requests for an interview in entirely different ways. Lord Rothschild invited Deacon to a lunch for two in N. M. Rothschild's private dining-room and offered the bank's strongroom as a suitable repository for the author's research; Blunt declined to meet Deacon.

On one memorable occasion, when one of his researchers mentioned Soviet penetration of the Security Service to a former senior member of MI5, the source flinched slightly and, instead of denying such a catastrophe, invited the researcher to name names. The first person named, Graham Mitchell, elicited the thoughtful, slightly tortured response, 'I have no reason to think that Graham has ever been anything but loyal; who else?' When Sir Anthony Blunt was suggested, the retired officer replied, 'Ah, well that is quite a different case.'

The dilemma facing Deacon after this confirmation that Blunt had been guilty of disloyalty was the apparent inconsistency of his status as Surveyor of the Queen's Pictures, his high standing in the academic community and his alleged treachery. The contradiction was highlighted by the award of a knighthood to Blunt in 1956, five years after he had supposedly come under suspicion as a KGB mole. As recently as 1972 he had been appointed Adviser to the Queen's Pictures and Drawings. It seemed improbable that the Security Service would allow the Queen to be embarrassed by a member of the Royal Household, and surely no Prime Minister would agree to an honour being granted to someone who, in all probability, had betrayed his country. Although Deacon was never able to find out about the circumstances of Blunt's confession in return for an immunity from prosecution, he accumulated enough hearsay material to confront him. Blunt refused all Deacon's requests for an interview and then threatened to sue for defamation. Someone who had read Deacon's manuscript had tipped off Blunt that it contained a strong inference that he had been the fourth man. When promoting *The British Connection*, Deacon's publishers pulled no punches:

Who is the 'Fourth Man' – the man behind Philby, Burgess and Maclean – the arch schemer inside the British Establishment who over a long period has betrayed his country's interests and aided the Soviet Union? The question has been asked many times. In *The British Connection* Richard Deacon seeks to supply an answer. In doing so he comes up with some surprising and even sensational discoveries. It is not so much a Fourth, as a Fifth and a Sixth and a Seventh and many more besides.[7]

But, for all the hyperbole, the threat of a prolonged legal action prevented Deacon's final text from doing anything worse than focusing on Blunt's former Marxism and his friendship with Burgess. He chose his words carefully:

It was Anthony Blunt (now Sir Anthony Blunt) who introduced Guy Burgess to the ranks of the Apostles. This brilliant young acsthete was already an influential figure outside the university as well as in it. It has been said that Burgess converted him to Marxism, but though Blunt tended toward the left this was more due to an enthusiasm for Soviet painting and left-wing literature than to a liking for Marxist dogma.[8]

Deacon went on to link Blunt with Tomas Harris, another wartime MI5 officer whom Deacon identified as having been a long-term Soviet mole. He was on safe grounds here, for Harris had been killed in a road accident in January 1964, and had indeed been considered by the molehunters at one time as a possible spy.

The world of art in the late 1930s seems to have led a number of improbable recruits into the world of Intelligence, notably Tomas Harris, the art collector, and, after he had joined the army and been evacuated from Dunkirk, Blunt himself, who was brought into MI5 through his ex-Cambridge contacts in the organisation.[9]

Deacon deliberately omitted to mention that Blunt had been recommended for employment in MI5 by Rothschild, and came as close to tying Blunt to espionage as his lawyers would let him. But, in the event, the book was never put on sale. Soon after its serialisation in the *Guardian, The British Connection* was injuncted by Professor Sir Rudolf Peierls, whom Deacon incorrectly described as having supplied the Russians with atomic secrets and as being dead. It was an appalling blunder and a libel of the gravest kind. When asked to comment by reporters Peierls replied, 'The allegation that I have been a Russian spy is as accurate as the claim that I am dead.' The book was immediately withdrawn and pulped, making the few that slipped through to the shops both rare and valuable.

Blunt was extremely relieved by the swift and unexpected demise of *The British Connection*, but he was granted only a temporary respite. Andrew Boyle was hot on his tracks, armed with information from the same source that had confirmed Blunt's guilt to Deacon's researcher, and from Goronwy Rees. Rees, of course, had not named Blunt as the former MI5 officer who had urged him not to tell MI5 of his suspicions about Burgess, but he had given this description of him:

He was the Cambridge liberal conscience at its very best, reasonable, sensible and firm in the faith that personal relations are the highest form of all human values. He reminded me of E. M. Forster's famous statement that if he had to choose between betraying his country or betraying his friend, he hoped he would have the courage to betray his country.[10]

This passage gave Boyle a chance to invent a fictitious persona, 'Maurice', after E. M. Forster's last novel of the same name, in which the homosexual hero, also an academic, uttered the maxim about betraying friends. With this ingenious device Boyle hoped to avoid a libel suit. Obviously, Blunt would know that he was the 'Maurice' character in *The Climate of Treason: Five who Spied for Russia*, but almost nobody else, apart from Rees, would be able to make the connection. He also believed that a second traitor, a scientist, had also been uncovered but let off the hook, and he named this individual 'Basil'. It was a clever ploy, but he did not anticipate an intervention by MI5.

The Security Service was alerted to Boyle's book by Blunt, who feared that Boyle had discovered his secret. A half-hearted attempt was made to persuade the publishers to let MI5 see a copy of the manuscript, but the request was rejected. The passage that was to cause so much concern was not really very accurate, but it did convey the idea that 'Maurice' had been granted some kind of immunity. It was the first time that the suggestion had been made:

Yet less than two years after the reappearance of Burgess and Maclean in Moscow, 'Maurice', the Fourth Man, belatedly called on the security authorities to confess all he knew about the past links between himself and his fellow conspirators. His motives for coming forward were mixed. Fear that Burgess might 'get in first' and reveal the worst to the world at large may well have clinched his decision to speak. No bargains were struck in advance: 'Maurice' was scarcely in any position to bargain. Nevertheless, like 'Basil' in Washington before him, he received in the utmost secrecy the equivalent of a 'Royal Pardon' for turning Queen's evidence and contritely unfolding his own secondary but guilty role in the nefarious exploits of Burgess, Maclean and, to a lesser extent, of Philby. Dick White had no authority to promise 'Maurice' unconditional favours; but those above him could and did exercise their discretion.[11]

The most obvious flaws concern timing, Blunt's motives and the involvement of Dick White. Blunt's confession was extracted, not volunteered, in 1964, not 1953. It had been obtained after the inducement of an immunity from prosecution had been offered, and had not been prompted by Blunt's alleged fear of being shopped by Burgess. But why was White's name dragged in? Was he the 'former senior executive of the British Secret Service whose spasmodic intellectual pleasure in reading certain crucial sections of the finished article may have been offset by ingrained professional reservations' thanked but not named by Boyle in his acknowledgements? He had expressed his gratitude to no fewer than ten former intelligence officers – Malcolm Muggeridge, Lord Rothschild, Goronwy Rees, David Footman, Nicholas Elliot, Felix Cowgill, E. H. Cookridge, Walter Bell, Sir Robert Mackenzie and Professor Hugh Seton-Watson – for their assistance, but had coyly neglected to name the 'former senior executive'. One possible explanation for the inclusion of White as having played a role in the decision to grant 'Maurice' a 'Royal Pardon' may have been a deliberate inaccuracy to demonstrate that he could not have vetted the final text. While Boyle had at least got the gist of the Blunt case, he was completely off-target in his claims about 'Basil', who turned out to be a distinguished physicist, Dr Wilfred Basil Mann, who had once been run against the Soviets as a CIA double agent. He indignantly dismissed Boyle's ill-founded charge that he had been the 'Fifth Man' in an intriguing rebuttal, *Was There A Fifth Man?*, published in 1982, which took Boyle's theory apart, line by line.

Publication of *The Climate of Treason* quickly led to Blunt being identified in 8 November edition of *Private Eye* as Boyle's 'Maurice' and a Parliamentary Question on the subject being tabled by Ted Leadbitter, the Labour MP for Hartlepool. The Question was due to be answered by Mrs Thatcher at Prime Minister's Question Time on Thursday, 15 November. The morning before, Blunt's solicitor, Michael Rubinstein, was telephoned by the Cabinet Office and summoned to see the Cabinet Secretary. In a brief interview Sir Robert Armstrong told Rubinstein that the Prime Minister intended to make a detailed statement about Blunt's self-confessed treachery. When the news was conveyed to Blunt, he was incredulous. How could the Security Service let him down? Why on earth was the Prime Minister so determined to expose him when there were enough inaccuracies contained in Boyle's version of events for her to prevaricate if she was so minded.

The short answer was that Mrs Thatcher had no intention of being a party to a sordid cover-up, even though the Security Service felt that a complete statement would inhibit its ability to attract similar co-operation in the future. This advice was drafted by John Jones, the Deputy Director-General who had been passed over upon Sir Michael Hanley's retirement earlier in the year. Instead, the top job had gone to an outsider from the Foreign Office, Sir Howard Smith. In 1976 he had been appointed ambassador in Moscow and, quite by coincidence, had been given his routine security briefing by Peter Wright.

Jones took the standard intelligence viewpoint that any disclosure concerning assistance alleged to have been given to the security authorities would be damaging, and that any mention of a formal immunity from prosecution would reveal a useful and as yet unknown weapon in MI5's limited armoury. What Armstrong's opinion was on this occasion can only be guessed at, but considering his long relationship with the Security Service, dating from his most recent

tenure at the Home Office as the Permanent Under-
Secretary for the past two years, and his five years at
Downing Street as the Prime Minister's Principal Private
Secretary under both Edward Heath and Harold Wilson,
it seems likely that he might have supported Jones. But
the newly elected Prime Minister's legal mind probably
foresaw problems. What would happen if Blunt sued Boyle
for defamation and perjured himself in the witness box?
Was the government expected to stand by and say nothing?
And why should an administration have to endure discomfort because of an awkward situation created by a
previous administration? And why should a self-confessed
traitor expect to receive special protection from a Cabinet
that had no direct knowledge of the original deal? The
clincher, if one were needed, was probably the fact that
Blunt had only been given an immunity from prosecution.
He had received no undertakings concerning public disclosure of his predicament. Blunt, of course, had always
believed that such a commitment was implied in the immunity he had accepted.

Mrs Thatcher made her statement to a packed House of
Commons on 15 November 1979 and gave a full account
of the circumstances surrounding Blunt's confession back
in April 1964. Her key sentence, referring to the all-
important post-war molehunts, stated:

It was considered important to gain his co-operation in the
continuing investigations by the security authorities, following
the defections of Burgess, Maclean and Philby, into Soviet penetration of the security and intelligence services and other public
services during and after the war.[12]

This was the first occasion since Edward Heath, as Lord
Privy Seal in July 1963, was obliged to make his statement
revealing Philby's defection that the public had been allowed to learn anything about the molehunts which had
so paralysed MI5. The Prime Minister's statement on Blunt
was to prove far more significant than anyone present
could have guessed.

6

OTHER CONNECTIONS

Future events in what was to become the saga of Peter Wright's struggle to publish were to involve Lord Rothschild, so his concern during the weeks after Mrs Thatcher's momentous statement ought to be looked at. The two chief protagonists in exposing Blunt, Deacon and Boyle, did not believe that Rothschild had anything to fear. He had co-operated with both authors and his help to Boyle had been openly acknowledged in *The Climate of Treason*.

At that time Rothschild was seventy years old, having retired as chairman of the family bank, of which he remained a director. He had a large house at 11 Herschel Road, Cambridge, where he lived with his second wife Teresa ('Tessa') Mayor, and a flat in St James's Place, where he spent part of the week. His career had been extraordinarily varied. After Harrow he spent four years at Trinity College, Cambridge, as a Prize Fellow, and was elected a member of the Apostles. In 1933 he had married Barbara Hutchinson, daughter of St John Hutchinson, one of the leading barristers of his day. He had inherited his title from his uncle who died in 1937, and spent the war in the Security Service, heading B1(c), the small anti-sabotage unit in which Tessa worked as his secretary. In 1945 he joined the Labour Party and the following year he married Tessa. His post-war career was spent in scientific research, much of it at Cambridge's Department of Zoology, and in 1971 he had been invited to lead the

Prime Minister Edward Heath's 'think tank', the Central Policy Review Staff, at Downing Street.

So what did such a distinguished figure feel about the public revelation that someone who had once been a close friend, and from whom he had since drifted apart, had been a Soviet spy, given the widespread knowledge that Rothschild had been close to Burgess as well as to Blunt?

His relationship with Burgess dated back to the days when he had introduced Burgess to his mother, Mrs Charles Rothschild, who had employed him as a financial adviser to give her investment tips. During the war, Rothschild leased an apartment on three floors at 5 Bentinck Street, directly above the editorial offices of a medical journal, *The Practitioner*, and Blunt and Burgess lived there for much of the war as subtenants of Tessa Mayor and Patricia Parry (now Baroness Llewelyn-Davies, the life peeress created by Harold Wilson in 1967). Mischievous stories of riotous parties had been circulated by Goronwy Rees, who said that 'civil servants, politicians, visitors to London, friends and colleagues of Guy's, popped in and out of bed and then continued some absorbing discussion'.[1] Rothschild's wartime duties sometimes took him abroad and prevented him from being in London full-time, and many of his weekends were spent at a colleague's country cottage, so he was rarely at Bentinck Street. Therefore, Rees' absurdly exaggerated tales of debauchery and the revelation of Burgess' illicit activities must have come as a total shock to the scientist.

It was the widespread knowledge of Burgess' promiscuity at Bentinck Street that seems to have rattled Rothschild, although concern about defamation limited comment. Yet strangely, it was later to be claimed by Pincher that 'people were suggesting that Rothschild himself had been a spy'.[2] He also reported Wright as stating that 'articles had been appearing in the British media suggesting that Rothschild had been a Soviet agent himself'.[3] In fact, no such articles ever appeared, and Rothschild retained Lord Goodman of Goodman, Derrick & Co., the well-known solicitors, to send warning letters to the occasional journalist seeking to research the subject. Phillip Knightley, one of the *Sunday Times* journalists who failed to obtain an interview with Rothschild when preparing his book on Philby, was on the receiving end of a sharp missive from Rothschild's lawyers.

That Rothschild had become acutely sensitive about his relationship with Blunt is understandable because he had originally recommended Blunt for recruitment into the Security Service and had introduced him to Guy Liddell. This was a matter of record within MI5 and was known to a great many of his former colleagues, some of whom had mixed feelings about Rothschild. He had a much better brain than most of his contemporaries and a mega-genius IQ level of 184, which was possibly the cause of some resentment. Apart from his intellectual prowess, there was another thing that may have unfairly isolated him from his colleagues: Rothschild was much in demand as MI5's counter-sabotage expert and was often called upon to defuse suspected booby traps. For one particular act of gallantry, dismantling a crate of explosive onions found on a cargo ship, he was awarded the George Medal. Once he was even called upon to inspect a consignment of the Prime Minister's Havana cigars to ensure they had not been tampered with. On another occasion an ingenious incendiary device actually ignited in his office in MI5's St James's Street headquarters while he was examining it.

But none of this could explain Rothschild's behaviour during the summer of 1980. What prompted him to arrange for an economy return air ticket to London to be delivered to Peter Wright's new retirement home in Tasmania, where he had been living since March 1976? (Wright cashed in the ticket and bought two round trips so that his wife Lois could accompany him.)

At the time, contrary to the claims made, there were no allegations circulating about Rothschild's conduct, and the fact that he had recommended Blunt for recruitment into MI5 was only known to what was still the closed circle of the Security Service. The first person to be accused of misconduct in relation to Blunt, based on allegations made by Goronwy Rees shortly before his death on 12 December 1979, was the late Guy Liddell. On 20 January 1980 Andrew Boyle wrote about Rees in the *Observer* and quoted him as having said that Burgess' 'main source must have been Guy Liddell with whom he and Anthony Blunt remained, of course, on very close terms. I was strongly convinced, though I had no direct proof, that Liddell was another of Burgess' predatory conquests. I know that dead men cannot answer back, but there was to my mind something sinister about Liddell's protectiveness in regard to both Blunt and Burgess.'

Boyle was not the only person peddling this view. He was joined by a retired intelligence officer, David Mure, who had written an account of the wartime strategic deception campaigns waged in the Middle East, claiming that while researching his book he had 'come across a chain of circumstances which, in my opinion, make it certain that Liddell was a Russian agent'.[4] The accusation was calculated to stir great passions.

Shy, reserved and not a little mysterious, Guy Liddell had been involved in counter-espionage work since 1919, when he joined Scotland Yard and was regarded by everyone who met him as a brilliantly intuitive professional intelligence officer. Like both his brothers, David and Cecil, who also worked for MI5, he had won the Military Cross for gallantry during the First World War. His home, 42 Cheyne Walk, was the scene of frequent, extremely popular musical soirées where he played the cello with great skill. At one time he was rated as the best amateur cellist in the country. He also had a fine collection of pictures and English pottery. However, his private life was rather less successful. His eccentric wife, Calypso Baring, had deserted him before the war and later took their four children to America, where she moved in with her half-brother, Larry Taylor. Liddell thoroughly disapproved of their bizarre relationship and made frantic legal efforts to recover his children, but failed. Many of his friends were homosexuals, but almost certainly he was not. Nevertheless, he enjoyed and preferred the company of bright young men, especially those in the Security Service. In 1953, aged sixty-one, he had left MI5 and joined the Atomic Energy Authority, where he remained at his post as chief security adviser until his death of a heart attack in 1958. He was unquestionably a very odd character, but he was never a spy as many of his friends were quick to point out. Two of his closest wartime colleagues, Malcolm Frost and Kenneth Morton-Evans, wrote letters to *The Times* in his support, and Dick White indignantly defended his memory in a public statement, an almost unprecedented act for a man in his position.

In a further attempt to confirm Liddell's innocence of the charges laid against him, the retired head of MI5's Watcher Service, Jim Skardon, gave an interview to the *Sunday Times* from his home in Torquay. He gave a spirited defence, but in the process let slip that 'incensed by the accusations against Liddell' he was 'thinking about writing his memoirs'.[5] This indiscretion brought a swift rebuke, almost by the next post, from the Security Service reminding him of his obligations.

Blunt also joined in the tirade and denounced Liddell's critics. Somewhat unexpectedly, he emerged from self-imposed seclusion in his London flat to deny that Liddell had ever had any sinister involvement with either himself or Burgess. But the matter could not be decently laid to rest because Boyle and Mure were equally sure that Liddell's connection with Burgess and Blunt was suspicious. Blunt's public statement in support of Liddell proved counter-productive, as Boyle countered that Blunt was 'hardly the most reliable witness in all the circumstances'.[6] Mure also wrote to *The Times*, on 19 February 1980, asking: 'If Blunt is wrong and Liddell was guilty of impeding the course of justice on one occasion, then surely, it is permissible to question his conduct on others?' Mure's comment was unjustified, as he was later to admit in private, and not entirely unconnected with his desire to publicise his new book, *Master of Deception*, which contained not one shred of evidence that Liddell had ever been disloyal. The only criticism levelled by Mure turned out to be limited to an easily dismissed charge of incompetence over Liddell's handling of intelligence concerning the Japanese attack on Pearl Harbor back in 1941. Mure had no first-hand knowledge of these events, and his supposition gained no credence because it was based on his faulty analysis of what prior knowledge the Allies had acquired before the Japanese raid.

The entire episode, accurately described by Dick White as 'grotesque and preposterous',[7] outraged Rothschild who had known Liddell well. He was later to describe him as 'a brilliant, sensitive and delightful man whose image, I am sorry to say, has become somewhat tarnished, with no justification, by what are nowadays called investigative reporters'. Rothschild continued, 'But of course the crushing blow about Blunt has destroyed my confidence. For whom would I put my hand in the fire? I can still name a few and among them would, undoubtedly, be Guy Liddell.'[8]

In fact, the investigative reporters Rothschild disliked had already uncovered another mole, alive and living in Rome. John Cairncross was found after a tip from Sir Jock Colville to Barrie Penrose that Blunt had not been alone. Penrose had doggedly pursued the very sketchy information about the unnamed Soviet spy and, without warning, confronted Cairncross with the allegation. Shocked by Penrose's unexpected appearance, Cairncross confirmed that he had supplied Burgess with information while working as a civil servant in the Treasury. He omitted to mention the comprehensive confession he had given Arthur Martin sixteen years earlier and played the role, not of a spy, but of someone who had been penalised for an indiscretion.

Cairncross' exposure, so close after the Prime Minister's statement on Blunt, may also have contributed to Rothschild's concern. Both men had been at Trinity College at the same time and, although they did not know each other, they had plenty of mutual friends, including Anthony Blunt who admitted to having 'talent-spotted' Cairncross for the Soviets.

Although it is impossible to judge Rothschild's state of mind at the time of these events, it is possible to imagine a somewhat lonely, albeit highly distinguished, troubled figure, who for the first time in his life feels powerless. Close friends or fellow undergraduates were under attack or had actually been revealed as traitors. Add to this the certainty that Rothschild knew a great deal more about at least one other mole, and you have a picture of a man inextricably caught up in events beyond his control. The further spy was the scientist Alister Watson.

At this stage, in the spring of 1980, Watson was aged seventy-two and living quietly in Hindhead, Surrey, with his wife Susan, having retired from his post at the National Institute of Oceanography. Watson had first learned that he was under suspicion when he was questioned by the Security Service back in 1967. What he did not know was that Rothschild had been the source of MI5's information that Watson had been a Communist when he had been up at King's College, Cambridge. That tip had led to Watson's interrogation and his removal from access to classified material at the Admiralty Research Laboratory at Teddington. Rothschild's secret help to Peter Wright over Watson, and his assistance to the molehunters when seeking to trap Philby, were both indications, perhaps even proof, of his true loyalties, but how could he gather the evidence in anticipation of a challenge to himself?

When Rothschild had introduced Flora Solomon to the Security Service in 1962, the critical event which led to Philby's confession early the following year, he had done so through Dick White who, in 1974, had stepped down from his post-retirement Cabinet job as Intelligence Co-ordinator and had moved to a small village near Arundel in Sussex. Having headed both MI5 and SIS, White had unrivalled experience of Britain's intelligence organisations and, in another situation, might have been an ideal person to supply Rothschild with the testimonial he required. But the situation Rothschild found himself in was far from normal and White was not in a position to give one. Unlike Rothschild, who had only seen wartime service, White had been a career MI5 officer, having joined in 1936. Inevitably, he had a different perspective on molehunting and may even have believed that Flora Solomon's evidence, while invaluable, was also tainted. Why had she waited so long before offering to denounce Philby? It was surely not for the lack of opportunity, for her son, Peter Benenson (the founder of Amnesty International), knew the inside of the intelligence community, having spent some years in GCHQ. Her own excuse was that she 'had not volunteered information as every public statement had pointed to [Philby's] innocence'.[9] MI5's view was that this was all the more reason for her to have stepped forward.

But even if White had been willing to help Rothschild, would he have been able to supply the right kind of first-hand knowledge of the two important cases that Rothschild believed he had cracked for MI5? After Rothschild had brought MI5 and Solomon together, the detailed statement concerning Philby had been taken down by Arthur Martin at a second interview. White had not been present. Nor had he been privy to the exact details of the Watson interrogation. If Rothschild did consider approaching White, he probably rejected the idea because White would have been less than an ideal witness. What Rothschild thought he needed was someone who had a comprehensive grasp of MI5's molehunts, together with a first-hand knowledge of Rothschild's help. Arthur Martin did not fit the bill because he had left MI5 in 1964 and Rothschild could not have known whether Martin had been privy to the Watson case three years later. The ideal candidate was Peter Wright.

If Wright was the 'dissident MI5 officer', as seems probable, then by seeking to leak politically embarrassing information from Security Service files, he had already compromised himself.

According to the accounts of what took place in August 1980 given by Chapman Pincher, 'Rothschild had turned to Wright for advice on how best to deal with the allegations, which were untrue, and to provide a document which would prove his loyalty.'[10] 'Rothschild asked Wright to prepare a statement about the secret work which Rothschild had done for MI5.'[11] Exactly how the desire for a

testimonial to Rothschild's innocence from Wright led to
a sensational best-seller, ghost-written by a retired *Daily
Express* journalist, is not immediately clear. Pincher later
stated that 'the truth is that Wright had already written
10,000 words of a book which he brought to Britain in
August 1980'[12] and that 'Rothschild's motive was to limit
the damage that he could see Wright doing if his intention
of going ahead alone went unchecked'.[13] In other words,
Wright turned up in England, his airline ticket paid for by
Rothschild, with a surprise manuscript of 10,000 words; he
then completed the testimonial for Rothschild. Pincher's
subsequent book was not to contain a single reference to
Rothschild.

None of this explains how Rothschild came to suggest
that Pincher work with Wright. Nor does it explain Wright's
contention that he had been 'drawn into an authorised operation'.[14] But before proceeding further, a word or two
should be said about the self-styled 'Man Who Was There'.

In 1980 Chapman Pincher had retired from nearly thirty
years of full-time Fleet Street journalism to a beautiful
period house in the picturesque Berkshire village of
Kintbury. Although originally trained as a scientist, 'Harry'
Pincher had made his formidable reputation primarily as
a disclosure journalist, concentrating on defence-related
political issues. He was a familiar figure to regulars at the
A L'Ecu de France restaurant in Jermyn Street, where he
wined and dined politicians and other indiscreet contacts,
and, although his politics were firmly to the Right, many
of his best sources were senior members of the Labour
Party, including George Wigg and George Brown.

Pincher's greatest coup was probably his revelation in
February 1967 of what was to become known as the D
Notice affair, although the newspaper story he wrote concerned the government's long-standing practice of inter-
cepting overseas cables and not Whitehall's system of
self-censorship. He had been approached by a disenchanted telegraphist named Robert Lawson, formerly
employed by two big communications companies, Com-

mercial Cables and Western Union, and told that the
Ministry of Defence routinely collected copies of the
companies' incoming and outgoing cable traffic and returned them forty-eight hours later. In fact, Lawson had
visited several Fleet Street papers to interest them in his
claim, but Colonel Sammy Lohan, the secretary of the D
Notice Committee, had managed to persuade the corre-
spondents concerned to drop the story. When Pincher
telephoned Lohan, who was one of his regular contacts,
he received the routine denial; but when he called the Post
Office for a comment, it was reluctantly conceded that
some overseas cables were indeed submitted to the security
authorities on a regular basis. The two statements each
contradicting the other caught Pincher's interest, and his
scoop was printed on the front page of the *Daily Express*,
sparking off a major political storm.

The cause of the row was not so much Pincher's sensational story, but the claim that it had been published in
defiance of an official request, through the D Notice system, to avoid commenting on such matters because to do
so would threaten national security. Pincher retorted that
the relevant D Notice covered the occasional interception
of communications and did refer to the general principle
of wholesale cable vetting. A government enquiry was set
up to determine whether the *Express* had breached the
D Notice convention and, having taken evidence from
Colonel Lohan, concluded that there had been a misunderstanding over a lunch given by Pincher. Lohan had left the
A L'Ecu de France believing that he had persuaded
Pincher to kill Lawson's allegations. Pincher thought he
had obtained a clearance to go ahead. The Prime Minister,
Harold Wilson, was appalled by the enquiry's handling of
the affair and issued a White Paper condemning Pincher
and the *Express*.

The net result of the affair was an enhancement of
Pincher's standing as a defence correspondent because the
substance of his story had been perfectly true. Actually,
the authorities had been reading overseas cables since 1920
and were entitled to do so under the provisions of Section

4 of the Official Secrets Act of that year, but no one had ever taken the trouble to give the issue publicity.

Pincher's fame, or notoriety, naturally extended to the Security Service. Soon after Martin Furnival Jones had been appointed Director-General, Pincher had written a story referring to his sources within MI5. Furnival Jones was infuriated by the claim which, if true, was in direct contravention of the standing rule banning MI5 staff from any contact with journalists, and ordered an investigation into Pincher's supposed links. It later turned out that apart from the occasions when the Legal Adviser, Bernard Hill, had attended official D Notice Committee briefings, no MI5 personnel had been in touch with Pincher. The only exception was an incident which had occurred back in 1961, when the correspondent had volunteered information to the Security Service about a Soviet diplomat named Anatoli Strelnikov.

Strelnikov had invited Pincher to lunch, and the journalist reported this to Lohan's predecessor at the D Notice Committee, Admiral George Thomson. He offered to cultivate the diplomat for MI5, and the offer was duly passed on by Thomson to MI5's Legal Adviser. At first Hill did nothing, but when Pincher pressed his case with Thomson by repeating his offer, Hill relayed it to the Soviet counter-espionage section of what was then D Branch. An internal debate had followed, centring on the advisability, or otherwise, of taking up Pincher. Some in the Soviet order-of-battle section had argued in favour, saying that so little was known of the Embassy's internal workings that any opportunity should be grasped to learn more. Those officers taking the opposing view had suggested that Pincher's only motive was to clear himself in case his lunches with Strelnikov had been spotted, and that once Pincher had established contact with MI5 it might prove difficult, if the need arose, to choke him off. The final, prevailing view was that Pincher should be encouraged, and a D Branch case officer was assigned the task of meeting Pincher. A couple of meetings had taken place, but Strelnikov lost interest in Pincher soon afterwards and the luncheon invitations had ceased. As predicted by the D Branch cynics, the case officer subsequently experienced some difficulty in shaking off Pincher, to whom he had unwisely given his real name.

All of these contacts had been officially authorised and the Director-General was anxious to establish that there had never been any illicit dealings with Pincher. He was assured that there had not, and anyway since 1964 the case officer who had handled Pincher had been stationed abroad, as MI5's Security Liaison Officer in Washington.

Although Pincher had few, if any, sources inside the British intelligence community, he did hear the political gossip circulating at the time. Quite apart from his direct involvement with the Ted Short letter, he received word of several rumours concerning ministerial appointments made by Harold Wilson. The accuracy of each varied considerably. One story referred to Judith Hart MP, whom Wilson promoted to the Cabinet post of Paymaster-General and who later served as Minister for Overseas Development. When notification of her appointment was referred to MI5, two traces of a 'Mrs J. Hart' were found in the files, both containing adverse information. One was Jenifer Hart, married to H. L. A. Hart, the Professor of Jurisprudence at Oxford. She had been part of the covert Communist cell, or 'Fabian-style discussion group', which had included Bernard Floud and Dennis Proctor among its membership. Shortly before the war she had worked in the Home Office, handling MI5's applications for tele-phone intercept warrants, and had also been holding meetings with rather an odd middle-European. She had recommended her future husband, Herbert, for recruit-ment by the Security Service in 1940. MI5's trace on Judith Hart MP had thrown up 'Mrs J. Hart' as having been interviewed by Peter Wright, the D Branch molehunter.

The other 'Mrs J. Hart' mentioned was Dr Tudor Hart's wife, a prominent member of the CPGB. Thus, there was the making of a newspaper story about MI5's opinion of Mrs J. Hart, although neither of the two files had any relevance to Judith Hart MP.

Pincher had also been tipped off about the allegedly discreditable circumstances in which,

A member of Wilson's government had been required to resign following representations by MI5 acting on information supplied by MI6 from foreign sources. Wilson was given evidence that the minister had placed himself in serious danger of being blackmailed by Soviet bloc intelligence. The minister then resigned in a way which covered the truth.[15]

While these stories were not based on any substantive evidence, they would have been an embarrassment to Wilson's administration, but they never appeared.

However, two other security-related episodes in which MI5 played a major investigative role were eventually made public. In July 1969 a Czech intelligence officer, Jozef Frolik, defected to the United States and named three Labour MPs as having been spies or agents of influence. The first, Sir Barnett Stross, had died in May 1967, so there was no action to be taken, but the other two, John Stonehouse MP and Will Owen MP, were both alleged to be working for the Soviet cause: Stonehouse, who was then Labour's Minister for Posts and Telecommunications, because he had been a victim of blackmail, entrapped during an official visit to Prague; Owen because he was supposed to have acted as a mercenary.

Stonehouse had been summoned to Downing Street and confronted with the allegation by the Prime Minister, but he had denied the charge and continued to hold ministerial office until the general election in 1970. Six years later, in an unrelated incident, he was convicted on eighteen charges of fraud and theft, and imprisoned. Owen, on the other hand, was interviewed by Special Branch and later had been charged with offences under the Official Secrets Act. Although he had been acquitted at the Old Bailey in May 1970, Owen subsequently made a full statement, including an admission of his guilt, to MI5 in a secret interview conducted in the presence of his nominee, Leo Abse MP.

Both Stonehouse and Owen were to become headline

news and, although Peter Wright knew of their investigation, there is nothing to show that he leaked information about them to Pincher, or anyone else. That Pincher received details of Jozef Frolik's debriefing has already been admitted, for (Sir) Stephen Hastings MP, himself a former SIS officer, was able to use parts of it, supplied in confidence by Pincher, in a Parliamentary Question designed to embarrass Wilson in 1976.

According to Pincher's own account, his first involvement with Peter Wright came in August 1980 when he received an unexpected call from Lord Rothschild, with whom he was acquainted socially:

Lord Rothschild did not know I was at home but he telephoned me in Berkshire. He was lucky to find me because my wife and I were preparing to spend the evening trout fishing. In cryptic language Lord Rothschild told me that a man, who was obviously a former Secret Service officer, wished to see me. Such opportunities are so rare that I immediately accepted and met the man later that evening at Lord Rothschild's home in Cambridge. He turned out to be Peter Wright.[16]

Pincher is emphatic that he had not met Wright before that momentous evening. 'I had never heard of Wright or discussed his book with Rothschild before I met Wright during that visit,'[17] he has asserted. But that claim does not entirely square with the account he had given in 1978, in *Inside Story*, which obviously contains references to Wright as a 'dissident MI5 officer' and gives a full description of Operation SATYR, on which it is known that Wright worked as team leader. Furthermore, the name of Wright's father, Maurice, actually appears in the book, apparently gratuitously, in connection with a matter that 'is still rightly covered by the Official Secrets Act'.[18]

While denying any previous contact with Wright, Pincher has confirmed that Wright 'knew a lot about me because he investigated some of my Defence Ministry sources and he agreed that I would be suitable'.[19] But suitable for what? Surely not the preparation of Wright's testimonial to Rothschild's innocence of having been a

Soviet spy? What both men had in mind, for perhaps different reasons, was a sequel to *Inside Story* in which Pincher could make more of the sensational revelations for which he had become famous.

The idea of a book detailing Wright's molehunting activities was not quite as straightforward as it might have appeared to sound initially. The first obstacle was the fact that Wright had only recently retired from the Security Service. While this was superficially attractive from the point of view of the reliability of the information contained in the book, it also presented a sizable problem in terms of actually getting the material published in defiance of the Official Secrets Act. Naturally, there is no limitation on MI5 officers writing fiction, as has been demonstrated by the novelists John Bingham (now Lord Clanmorris), his daughter Charlotte and John Dickson Carr, all of whom were once employed by the Security Service. But there was no precedent for a recently retired MI5 officer taking to his typewriter to reveal sensitive information. However, there had been several books written by former MI5 officers which, to a greater or lesser extent, had mentioned their work, albeit chiefly in a wartime context. By 1980 just four had been published. As long ago as 1948 the then Director-General, Sir Percy Sillitoe, obtained permission from the Permanent Under-Secretary at the Home Office, Sir Frank Newsam, to write his own memoirs, *Cloak without Dagger*. An internal rumpus had followed when Sillitoe assigned his own personal assistant, Russell Lee, to help prepare the manuscript. Newsam eventually gave Sillitoe a formal consent, in the form of a letter, releasing him from his obligation of confidentiality, on the authority of the Home Secretary, Sir David Maxwell-Fyfe.

In 1953 Sillitoe retired from MI5 to run a sweetshop in Eastbourne and when, the next year, *Cloak without Dagger* was approaching publication, Sillitoe's successor, Sir Dick White, raised an objection, and a large part of the chapters dealing with the Security Service was deleted. Sillitoe was furious but, out of office, there was little he could do. After some argument the shortened version was released in 1955 and, to prove that it was no back-door disclosure, it contained a foreword contributed by Clement Attlee who, as Prime Minister in 1946, had appointed Sillitoe to run MI5.

Six years later, in 1961, the drama critic Stephen Watts had written his autobiography, *Moonlight on a Lake in Bond Street*, and, perhaps encouraged by the absence of any action against Watts, Derek Tangye, MI5's wartime press liaison officer, wrote his autobiography, *The Way to Minack*, seven years later.

None of these three books could be described as even remotely controversial, but they did set something of a precedent and paved the way for *The Double Cross System in the War of 1939 to 1945* by J. C. Masterman. Sir John Masterman was a well-known Oxford academic, who had been brought into the Security Service late in 1940 to co-ordinate the work of an inter-Service committee which was attempting to run double agents against the enemy. It had been a sensitive post and, though not a professional intelligence officer, Masterman had soon grasped the essentials of manipulating the Nazi intelligence apparatus and had earned the respect of both MI5 and SIS. More importantly, the work of his group, known as the Twenty Committee (or XX Committee, after the Roman numerals), had proved hugely successful and had made a vital contribution to the deception campaign mounted by the Allies to prevent the Abwehr from discovering the secrets of the D-Day landings. At the end of the war Masterman, like several other key officers, had been invited to record aspects of their work for MI5's archives. As a trained historian, Masterman had found the task easy, if not a little frustrating because of the knowledge that his report was unlikely ever to gain wide circulation. As a precaution, but without permission, he had retained a copy of it. In 1954, while Sillitoe was locked in combat with Dick White, Masterman requested permission to publish the report, but was turned down. He tried again in 1961, but Roger Hollis, who was by then MI5's Director-General, had been implacably opposed to its release.

Undeterred, Masterman made a further approach in October 1967 when Hollis had gone into retirement. He went to see Burke Trend, the Cabinet Secretary, and Dick White, who had once been his pupil at Christ Church. Both had seemed mildly sympathetic, so early in January 1968 he obtained an interview with MI5's new Director-General, Sir Martin Furnival Jones, and gained the impression that the principle of public disclosure had been won. But just to be on the safe side he made alternative arrangements, which included the search for an American publisher, out of the jurisdiction of the British courts. He then leaked his plan to Furnival Jones via MI5's Director of Personnel, John Marriott, who had served as the XX Committee's secretary during the war but had already expressed his disapproval of Masterman's desire to publish. To apply further pressure, Masterman also warned Dick White of the existence of a willing publisher in the United States, through an old friend, Ian Fleming's brother, Peter. This was done against the advice of his legal adviser, Christopher Harmer, who was himself a former MI5 case officer experienced in handling wartime double agents. By this stage Masterman had been engaged in a polite battle with Whitehall's bureaucrats for nearly fifteen years and had been driven to the conclusion that an unorthodox *fait accompli* was the only satisfactory method of obtaining anyone's attention.

However unconventional, the ploy certainly speeded matters up, because in June 1969 Masterman was invited to attend a meeting at the Cabinet Office where he could put his case to Burke Trend and the Permanent Under-Secretary at the Home Office, Sir Philip Allen. At its conclusion, Trend and Allen agreed to brief their respective political masters and inform Masterman of the outcome. In April the following year Allen told Masterman that permission to publish would not be forthcoming. The verdict had gone against him, allegedly, on inter-departmental and administrative, not on security, grounds. Reluctantly, Masterman went on to the offensive and, after some initial hesitation on the part of various American publishing houses, obtained a contract from the Yale University Press. Once the contract was signed, Masterman wrote a letter explaining his intention to publish abroad to Sir Philip Allen, and sent a copy to Furnival Jones. He also requested confirmation that his report was a classified document no longer.

The response was immediate. Sir Alec Douglas Home, another of his pupils at Oxford who was now Foreign Secretary, summoned Masterman to lunch and then escorted him to the Home Secretary, Reginald Maudling. Together Maudling and Douglas Home explained that the matter was now in the hands of the Attorney-General, Sir Peter Rawlinson, who would decide on what legal action, if any, should be taken to prevent publication and perhaps bring a criminal prosecution.

In the event, Masterman succeeded in obtaining permission to publish his report, with the government taking half the royalties. As he said later, 'I cannot know what Alec did to protect me. . . .'[20] After further skilful negotiations by Christopher Harmer, a few passages were deleted from the original typescript and *The Double Cross System* was published the following year, in 1972, and became a best-seller.

Looking back three years later on this unique episode in his autobiography, *On the Chariot Wheel*, Masterman recalled:

I realised how strange it was that I, who all my life had been a supporter of the Establishment, should become, at eighty, a successful rebel. Perhaps, contrary to the accepted view, the old are more ruthless than the young. They have little time to spare and become impatient. But the strongest feeling was simply this. Sometimes in life you feel that there is something which you must do and in which you must trust your own judgement and not that of any other person. Some call it conscience and some plain obstinacy.[21]

Masterman's breach of protocol, not to say the Official Secrets Act, was a remarkable milestone because, unlike Sillitoe, Watts or Tangye, he had reproduced what was largely an original Security Service document. This was demonstrated by the copyright imprint on every copy which bore the words 'Crown copyright reserved'.

The only other example of an official MI5 document being released to the public in book form involved Lord Rothschild. In 1977 he had published a collection of essays entitled *Meditations of a Broomstick*, and among them was a short account of his act of bravery in 1944 for which he had been decorated with the George Medal. In fact, it was the transcript of his running commentary given over a field telephone while dismantling the booby-trapped box of onions, and had been quoted in the citation of his award. Thus, when in 1980 Rothschild became involved in Wright's book, there had only been four occasions when MI5 personnel had put their own names to books and Rothschild had first-hand knowledge of one of them.

That is not to say, though, that the Security Service was necessarily averse to books being written on the subject of espionage and intelligence. Back in 1948 two MI5 officers collaborated, with official approval, on the preparation of *Handbook for Spies*, the autobiography of a self-confessed GRU agent, Alexander Foote, who had worked for the Soviets in Switzerland during the war, operating a clandestine radio transmitter. Two of his Security Service case officers, Michael Serpell and Courtney Young, had been assigned the task of alerting the British public to the existence of a world-wide Russian spy network. Their names never appeared in the text; nor did Jim Skardon's when he was instructed to collaborate with Alan Moorehead on *The Traitors*, a 1952 study of the atomic spies, Allan Nunn May, Klaus Fuchs and Bruno Pontecorvo. On that occasion the Director-General's motive had been the desire to generate some good publicity after the humiliating press coverage of the Burgess and Maclean defections.

Apart from the exceptions mentioned above, the Security Service had been really quite adept at preventing publication of embarrassing literature. Two interesting post-war cases stand out. The first centred on the wartime activities of a safe-cracker named Eddie Chapman, who had been parachuted into Cambridgeshire in 1942 as a German spy. He had promptly volunteered his services to MI5 as a double agent and, after many adventures, survived the war. In March 1946 he teamed up with a journalist to write his story, but instead of getting a cheque from a French newspaper, *Etoile du Soir*, as he intended, he was prosecuted under the Official Secrets Act for his indiscretion. A second attempt in 1952 also failed and resulted in an entire edition of the *News of the World* being withdrawn from sale.

Another less successful effort to restrict comment about the work of the Security Service took place early in 1963 when a newspaper correspondent, John Bulloch, wrote *MI5: The Origin and History of the British Counter-Espionage Service*. Based largely on a manuscript prepared by Lady Kell, the widow of the first Director-General, the book had been typeset and bound when the Home Secretary summoned Bulloch and told him that certain alterations would be required. The offending passages were deleted, but not before he had obtained Henry Brooke's agreement to pay for all the extra work required in unpicking the bound copies, extracting the relevant pages and then rebinding them. *MI5* was then released in March 1963.

The reluctance of the British intelligence community to commit anything to print is not a new phenomenon. Up until recent events, the most celebrated case of suppressing a book was the trial in 1932 of Sir Compton Mackenzie, author of *Greek Memories*. This was the second volume of a trilogy of memoirs in which Mackenzie had recorded his intelligence work in Greece during the First World War. On the day of publication an injunction was obtained to prevent distribution of the book and Mackenzie was charged with offences under the Official Secrets Act. The subsequent trial at the Old Bailey was an acute embarrassment to both MI5 and SIS, especially when it emerged that the prosecution objected to the mention of Sir Eric Holt-Wilson's name in the book. Holt-Wilson was MI5's Deputy Director-General and a personal friend of Mac-

kenzie's, who had already given his personal approval to
the book. Mackenzie pleaded guilty to the charges and
was fined £100 with £100 costs. An expurgated version of
Greek Memories was eventually released in 1938 and
only a handful of rare first editions are known to exist.
The copy in the British Library can only be read with the
permission of 'Room 055, Old War Office Building', the
Security Service's cover postal location, and to date no
one has successfully obtained it. Mackenzie's indignation
at his treatment prompted him to write *Water on the Brain*,
a wickedly entertaining satire on the British intelligence
establishment.

In the post-war era the Secret Intelligence Service only
gave its blessing to one publication, an internal handbook
on Soviet subversion written by Robert Carew-Hunt. Entitled *The Theory and Practice of Communism*, Carew-
Hunt was granted permission to publish it commercially
through Geoffrey Bles in 1950. As regards the suppression
of books, SIS have fared rather better than MI5. Apart
from the obvious examples of Malcolm Muggeridge,
Graham Greene and Kim Philby, very few SIS officers
have ever written about their own, first-hand experiences.
Neither Hugh Trevor Roper nor Alec Waugh, both good
writers on other matters, have been tempted to give first-
hand accounts of their own activities while employed by
SIS. In fact, just two cases stand out.

The first was *The Quiet Canadian*, a biography of Sir
William Stephenson completed in 1962 by Dr H.
Montgomery Hyde, a former member of Stephenson's
staff at British Security Co-ordination in 1944. A prolific
author as well as having been the Unionist Member of
Parliament for Belfast, Hyde had sought and received
permission to name the mysterious Chief of the wartime
SIS, Sir Stewart Menzies. This sensational disclosure
caused uproar at the time, but Hyde emerged unscathed.
A decade later Stephenson's second biography, *A Man
Called Intrepid*, was written by a Canadian journalist,
William Stevenson, and a rumour reached London that his
project was to be based on secret archival material of the

kind that Masterman had been invited to write at the end of the war. This news caused Dick White, then Intelligence Co-ordinator to the Cabinet, to demand from Sir William Stephenson any official documents he may have retained. Furious telegrams were exchanged between the Cabinet Office and Stephenson's home in Bermuda, but the elderly spymaster resolutely refused to surrender his old files.

In another embarrassing fiasco, this time in 1966, a former career SIS officer named Leslie Nicholson wrote his memoirs, *British Agent*, under the pseudonym John Whitwell. Nicholson had been obliged to leave SIS because of his wife's illness and, in an interesting parallel reminiscent of Peter Wright's position, had been locked in argument with his former employers over his lack of a decent pension. Nicholson had moved to America, beyond the reach of the British courts, and *British Agent* was published without any deletions. Indeed, it even contained two contributions from wartime SIS colleagues: an introduction from Malcolm Muggeridge and the following endorsement from Captain Henry Kerby, the Conservative MP for West Sussex:

This is a piece of publishing history. For the first time ever, a former senior member of the service which officially does not exist tells the true facts of life as a secret agent. For security reasons the author has adopted an assumed name, but he is an old friend of mine and I can vouch for the valuable work which he carried out for Britain in his highly skilled and dangerous, and in many ways thankless, missions. The glut of fiction written on this theme has tended to make the work of such men into the realm of the fairy tale. But this book is no fairy tale. I am delighted that at last a factual account is to be published, for I believe that the public are entitled to know something of the realities of this splendid service – after all, they pay for it.[22]

This, then, was the contradictory, not to say confused, situation in which Wright's proposed book was discussed. The options were limited by the precedents already mentioned. While the Security Service had certainly tolerated the relatively short, inoffensive, autobiographical passages written by Sillitoe, Watts, Tangye and Rothschild, it would be unlikely to sit back and let a post-war official tell all. Furthermore, no publisher would risk handling material known to have come from an authentic, privileged source. The only way to avoid an Official Secrets Act prosecution would be to publish under a false name and to conceal the book's origin, or simply to supply the information to an established author.

The latter course offered the best chance of success, as had been so ably demonstrated by Deacon and Boyle. In order to suppress *The Climate of Treason*, the Security Service's hard-pressed Legal Adviser had been confronted with two, equally unpalatable alternatives requiring either criminal or civil actions. The first was the option of a criminal prosecution under Section 2 of the Official Secrets Act. Contrary to popular belief, everyone in the United Kingdom is subject to the Act, whether or not they have signed it. The ritual of having individuals sign the document is intended simply to draw the signatory's attention to the Act's provisions and penalties. Anyone convicted of an offence after having signed the Act could reasonably expect a stiffer sentence because they could hardly claim ignorance in mitigation. In Boyle's case, espionage on behalf of a foreign power was hardly viable, thus ruling out Section 1 and leaving the catchall Section 2 which has proved unpopular with juries when used against *bona-fide* journalists and historians.

MI5's other remedy lay in civil litigation alleging breach of confidence. This is not formalised in statute, but is what might be termed judge-made law and allows an employer protection against the loss of trade secrets through the action of servants. Thus, when applied to the Coca-Cola Corporation, one of its employees could not betray its secret formula. In the event of serious wrong-doing, there is an overriding argument of national interest to protect whistle-blowers. However, exactly what is, or is not, in the public interest is left to the judge to decide.

This civil option has become MI5's favoured method of embargoing offending material, because the very little case law on the issue is entirely favourable to the plaintiff. The most memorable confrontation alleging breach of confidence occurred when the Crown sought to prevent publication of the late Richard Crossman's Cabinet diaries because they had been recorded in defiance of the convention concerning confidential Cabinet discussions. The defence was allowed to publish, but only after an overriding principle of national security had been conceded. Thus, anyone wishing to challenge MI5's claim on what was, or was not, a matter of national security ought to anticipate an extremely long court battle against a plaintiff backed by almost unlimited resources.

Getting back to *The Climate of Treason*, breach of confidence proceedings would require the plaintiff to prove that Boyle had been in receipt of specific items of information from named individuals not authorised to disclose them. Of the named people thanked by Boyle for having assisted his research, only Lord Rothschild had been privy to the secret of Blunt's confession but, given MI5's intimate knowledge of the case, he could hardly have been considered a possible source. If the Security Service Legal Adviser could have identified the unnamed 'former senior executive' as Boyle's source, and he had somehow been persuaded to give evidence, there might have been the merest shadow of a basis of a case. But such a scenario was unlikely in the extreme. And if the case ever got to court, the defence could simply point out that the information relating to Blunt was so inaccurate that it could never have come from an insider.

When it came to the crunch MI5 made no attempt to prevent publication of *The Climate of Treason* because there were no grounds to do so, criminal or civil. In the months after publication, when Wright, Rothschild and Pincher were considering how to proceed, Boyle's easy experience must have been a factor.

If Pincher were to write the book based on Wright's information, all that needed to be settled were the financial arrangements.

At the moment that these delicate discussions were

broached, Lord Rothschild apparently left the room so
that the other two men could thrash out the minutiae of
the deal. Pincher recalled that,

left alone with him, Wright explained that he was in desperate
need of £5,000 to save his stud farm from bankruptcy. He told
me about the 10,000 words written but would not let me see them
at that stage. Instead I was shown a list of traitors with which he
proposed to deal. It included Hollis. Wright and Wright alone
suggested that I should write a book on information he would
provide, and that we should share the proceeds.[23]

On the vital question as to whose idea it was that Pincher
and Wright should work together on a book, Pincher is a
little inconsistent. On this occasion it was 'Wright and
Wright alone', but within a fortnight of having made the
above statement Pincher's memory had changed and it had
become Rothschild's suggestion, but for the most laudable
of motives:

Wright came to the meeting armed with 10,000 words of his book
and showed them to Lord Rothschild. Realising Wright was
determined to complete the book and despairing of any action
by MI5 to stop him, Rothschild suggested Wright should get me
to do it.[24]

If Rothschild truly was in a state of despair, as alleged, at
the prospect of Wright completing his book, it seems odd
that Pincher should have been introduced on to the scene.
If despair is a fair description of Rothschild's state of mind,
why did he not lift the telephone and denounce Wright to
MI5? Indeed, Rothschild had apparently been in touch
with Sir Michael Hanley on Wright's behalf for the past
three years:

In 1977 Wright wrote to his friend Lord Rothschild, also a former
MI5 officer, complaining about his meagre pension and saying
he was thinking of writing a book about the Soviet penetration
of the secret services. Rothschild was already corresponding with
the Director-General of MI5, Sir Michael Hanley, to improve
Wright's £2,000 a year pension. Sensing the danger of an embit-

Beaconshaw, Donald Maclean's home outside Tatsfield in Kent. All the telephone instruments were surreptitiously fitted with listening devices, but Maclean was warned that he was under surveillance. MI5 learned of his escape in May 1951 too late to prevent it.

5 Bentinck Street: Lord Rothschild rented the upper part of this house to his future wife, Tessa Mayor, and her friend Patricia Parry. They, in turn, sublet rooms to Guy Burgess and Anthony Blunt. The parties held here during the war became legendary.

A unique photograph of Igor (left) and Svetlana Gouzenko outside a Toronto court. The Soviet defector spent his retirement suing authors and newspapers and took elaborate measures to prevent his picture from being taken. On this occasion he failed.

Sir Roger Hollis, Director-General of the Security Service from 1956 to 1965, who became the subject of an intensive molehunt when it was realized that MI5 had been penetrated at a very high level by the KGB.

6 Campden Hill Square, the home of Sir Roger Hollis while he was Director-General. It was also the venue for the secret meetings held while his Deputy D-G, Graham Mitchell, was the subject of a molehunt.

Anthony Blunt, the wartime MI5 officer and Soviet spy who was persuaded to confess by Arthur Martin in April 1964, and subsequently underwent a lengthy debriefing by Peter Wright. Blunt's information led the molehunters to believe that their own organization had been penetrated at a high level.

Barncote, Graham Mitchell's home near Chobham Common, which was 'wired for sound' when the Deputy D-G came under suspicion of being a Soviet mole.

Leconfield House, the post-war headquarters of the Security Service. Graham Mitchell's office was next door to the Director-General's on the fifth floor, overlooking South Audley Street. A tiny spy camera was inserted through the ceiling so that the molehunters on the floor above could monitor his activities.

33 South Audley Street, the 'wired accommodation' in Mayfair where Graham Mitchell and Sir Roger Hollis underwent a detailed interrogation at the hands of MI5's molehunters.

Dr Alister Watson, the Admiralty scientist who underwent three weeks of interrogation in 1967 after he had been identified by Anthony Blunt as a Soviet mole, recruited at Cambridge University.

The top-secret Admiralty Research Establishment at Teddington, where Alister Watson worked on highly classified nuclear submarine projects until MI5 discovered he had been meeting KGB case officers.

Above left. On Easter Sunday 1983 Michael Bettaney offered to spy for the KGB *rezident* in London, Arkadi Gouk, not realizing that Gouk's deputy, Oleg Gordievsky, was a mole who had worked for Britain's Secret Intelligence Service for more than a decade. Thanks to a tip from Gordievsky, Bettaney was arrested before he could inflict lasting damage. The incident convinced Peter Wright that MI5 was still seriously flawed and open to hostile penetration.

Above right. Lord Rothschild, the former MI5 officer and friend of Guy Burgess and Anthony Blunt.

Harry Chapman Pincher, the veteran Fleet Street journalist who co-authored *Their Trade is Treachery* with Peter Wright after having been introduced to the MI5 molehunter by Lord Rothschild.

The Cabinet Secretary, Sir Robert Armstrong, in an angry confrontation with a Fleet Street photographer while on his way to Australia, where he was to give evidence in the legal action brought to suppress Peter Wright's book.

Peter and Lois Wright on their way to court in Sydney, accompanied by Paul Greengrass (second left) of Granada Television and Heinemann's London solicitor, David Hooper (left).

tered MI5 officer with a load of saleable secrets stewing in near poverty in Tasmania, safe from the Official Secrets Act, Rothschild twice warned Hanley about the book.[25]

Presumably with Wright back in England, actually in Rothschild's country home, the Security Service could have had an ideal opportunity to show Wright the error of his ways, or at least be offered some good, practical reasons why he should refrain from carrying out his threat, as already conveyed by Rothschild, to detonate a few of MI5's unexploded bombs. But the meeting was to remain a secret, with each of the three participants having their own reasons for keeping it in that condition.

Pincher later took the view that Wright's principal interest had been in generating some cash and not in the exposure of Hollis as a Soviet spy. This was also the basis of Wright's post-retirement relationship with Rothschild, whom he had known since they were first introduced to one another in 1958. By Wright's own admission, Lord Rothschild set up a Swiss bank account for him and prepared a dummy company, registered offshore, to receive half the royalties and conceal Wright's involvement in the project. In fact, the consultancy firm destined to receive half the book's income employed only one consultant, Peter Wright.

But Wright's own version of these events is strikingly different to Pincher's, although he concedes that Rothschild originally invited him

to come to London to discuss the impact of the Blunt disclosures, disclosures with which I was not involved in any way. The approach came totally out of the blue. When I arrived Lord Rothschild explained that he had recently met Mrs Thatcher and she was inexperienced in intelligence matters. We discussed the Hollis affair as we had many times before. I expressed concern that the true facts of the Hollis case be placed in front of her, and showed Lord Rothschild a paper I had begun to write on the subject. I asked him if he would be prepared to use his influence to place the document in Mrs Thatcher's hands. Lord Rothschild said this would not work, as Mrs Thatcher would feel obliged to

refer any official approach direct to MI5. He told me the best
way to procure a proper investigation of the Hollis affair was to
write a book. He told me that the book would have to be written
by someone else and he suggested Harry Pincher. He telephoned
Mr Pincher and shortly afterwards he appeared. I had the distinct
impression this meeting had been prearranged.[26]

This account differs from Pincher's in several respects, not
the least of which is the emphasis Wright places on Hollis.
Pincher claimed that 'it was Wright who introduced the
subject of Sir Roger Hollis with Rothschild who had little
interest in it'.[27] Furthermore, when Pincher read the 10,000
words written by Wright, 'they contained no mention of
Hollis. He had not reached the time of the Hollis case in
his book.'[28] Pincher is insistent that 'it was Wright, not
Rothschild, who suggested that I should write his book for
him in return for 50 per cent of the royalties. He told me
about the 10,000 words he had written and later gave them
to me when I visited his home in Tasmania.'[29]

   The visit to Wright's twenty-three hectare smallholding
just outside the village of Sygnet in Tasmania began on 19
October and lasted two weeks. It was 'an Aladdin's cave'
of MI5 secrets, and there were a few that contradicted
Pincher's previously stated views on several earlier
intelligence-related incidents. As Wright expounded his
theories about Operation DRAT, Pincher must have recalled what he had already stated on the subject. On
1 August 1977 he had written this article in the *Daily
Express*:

The *Observer* published an attack on MI5 suggesting that the
fourth man in the Philby affair had been a high-ranking MI5
officer. . . . My enquiries with officers involved in the Philby
affair convinced me that this story was untrue and that the heads
of MI5 and MI6 feared that they were being subjected to a smear
campaign of the kind which has damaged the CIA to the great
delight of Russia's KGB.

By the time he came to write *Inside Story*, which was
published the following year, Pincher had reversed his

position and had made a brief reference to Hollis, without naming him: 'At least one suspect spy was detected in MI5 itself during Wilson's premiership. He, too, was quietly removed by being induced to resign.'[30] By the time the paperback edition of *Inside Story* had been released, Pincher had obviously acquired more information, because he had been in a position to expand his earlier passage and name Hollis:

Early in Wilson's first premiership there was strong suspicion about the loyalty of the director general of MI5, the late Sir Roger Hollis. Evidence has accrued from Iron Curtain defectors suggesting that Hollis, who by that time was in retirement, might himself have been a defector-in-place, but a long and searching enquiry failed to produce proof.[31]

Wright's impressive depth of knowledge forced Pincher to change his mind about the circumstances of Philby's escape in 1963. When dealing with the matter in *Inside Story* he had commented that, 'the conclusion that the British authorities wanted to frighten Philby into defecting to the safety of the Soviet Union is inescapable'.[32] Wright's disclosure of Philby's immunity from prosecution put Philby's hasty departure into an entirely different context, and no doubt Pincher must have gasped at the implications of what he was now being told. At long last, at the end of his career, he had stumbled across a source that undermined all his previous observations about MI5 and its brilliant efficiency.

Undeterred by what he had learned, and carrying Wright's draft manuscript, Pincher returned to England armed with more than enough material to construct a two-page synopsis. This he offered to Sidgwick & Jackson, the publishers of *Inside Story*, and for whom he was already collaborating on a book with Harold Wilson's secretary, Marcia Williams (Lady Falkender), on the subject of Soviet influence over the British trades union movement. That project, entitled *The Infiltrators*, was put on the back burner while a new contract was agreed for *Their Trade is Treachery*, a title once used by the Security Service in

1964 for a handbook of cautionary tales distributed to businessmen planning to visit the Soviet Union. By 14 November Pincher was optimistic about their chances of obtaining a contract and, signing himself 'Henry', wrote to Wright who, in their prearranged studfarming code, was to be called 'Philip': 'All your information about your stud arrived safely. . . . I am confident that I can produce some quick sales.'[33] On 10 December he sent a further progress report, using the same code: 'I ran into problems with the publication of the brochure. These now seem to be resolved and, barring any last minute hitch, I should have a contract.'[34] On 12 December 1980 Pincher signed a contract with Sidgwick & Jackson, the two proprietors in the document identified only as Summerpage Limited, a £100 off-the-shelf company controlled by Pincher and his wife, and Wright's offshore outfit. The first half of the advance of royalties, amounting to £30,000, had been transferred, via Switzerland, to Wright in Tasmania. As yet the Security Service had no knowledge of these events, but on 18 December 1980 the issue was raised in a letter to the Director-General of the Security Service, Sir Howard Smith. The contents of the letter have not been revealed, but the fact that Pincher's two-page synopsis was attached demonstrates that someone, most probably in Sidgwick & Jackson, had handed a copy to MI5. Pincher, of course, was ignorant of this development and continued to work on the project until he was ready to deliver a complete manuscript, which he did at the end of January 1981. One copy was shown to the editor of the *Daily Mail*, Sir David English, who had negotiated the purchase of its newspaper serial rights in December for £35,000, and another was sent to be typeset. However, as soon as the typeset page proofs were ready, in mid-February 1981, a complete set was handed to the Security Service and distributed, in confidence, to various interested parties, including the Cabinet Office. This occurred a full six weeks before *Their Trade is Treachery's* scheduled publication date at the end of March 1981.

The page proofs were read by the Cabinet Secretary,

Sir Robert Armstrong, and a conference was called to decide what advice should be given to the government. Could the book be suppressed? Could Pincher be prosecuted? Was either option desirable? These were the questions pondered by Armstrong, the newly appointed Director-General of the Security Service, John Jones, and Bernard Hill's successor as MI5's Legal Adviser.

A little is known of their deliberations because of evidence later given in court by Sir Robert Armstrong, but it is not difficult to reconstruct the various matters which must have received their consideration. Firstly, there was the matter of MI5's clandestine source for the synopsis and page proofs of *Their Trade is Treachery*. Both items were strictly illegal in that they were either unauthorised photocopies or stolen originals, and this effectively prevented the government's law officers from being consulted. Presumably neither of the two contractual parties directly concerned, Sidgwick & Jackson on the one hand and Pincher (with Wright's offshore company) on the other, gave their consent to this manoeuvre, so the action taken by the government would, to some extent, be dictated by a desire not to compromise the illicit source. In consequence, neither the Attorney-General, Sir Michael Havers, nor the Treasury Solicitor, (Sir) Michael Kerry, were consulted at this early stage.

Quite who this source might have been is a matter for speculation. No one has owned up, but the field must be a narrow one. In the course of his evasive replies during the Australian court case, Sir Robert Armstrong indicated that the material had been volunteered by a trusted individual who had demanded complete anonymity. Accordingly, his (or her) identity has never been disclosed.

Whatever the source of the page proofs, intensive, secret discussions were held with the Prime Minister and the Home Secretary, William Whitelaw, to determine whether there was a basis for restraining the book. That these meetings took place at all tends to discredit Wright's later claim that he had been 'drawn into an authorised, but deniable operation which would enable the Hollis affair and other MI5 scandals to be placed in the public domain as a result of an apparently inspired leak'.[35]

It was a major part of Wright's subsequent defence in court that Lord Rothschild's connection with the project was proof of an unofficial, deniable sanction. After all, was not Lord Rothschild a confidant of the Prime Minister, and had she not recently met him? In fact, Mrs Thatcher hardly knew Rothschild and, at the time of his meeting with Wright the previous August, she had met him only once, at a private dinner party held on 11 July at the Cheyne Walk home of Nuala Allason, the ex-wife of a Tory MP. Those present at the dinner included Lady Avon, widow of the late Prime Minister, Lord Dacre (formerly Hugh Trevor Roper), Lord Goodman, Lord Charteris and Sir Isaiah Berlin.

By early March 1981, before the release of the first extracts of *Their Trade is Treachery* in the *Daily Mail*, the decision had been made against taking legal action to prevent publication. A preliminary, joint examination of the page proofs by MI5 and SIS had not identified firmly a single source for the material, although it must have been obvious to anyone with a knowledge of MI5's molehunts, or even the background to the Trend Report, that either Wright, Martin or de Mowbray must have leaked the material to Pincher. The author himself gave no clue to having ghostwritten Wright's book and in his foreword claimed to have spent years researching the subject: 'Researchers looking for source references will find few here, for in the main this book deals with prime source material, collected over the years from people who insisted on remaining anonymous in their lifetime.'[36] In the absence of a self-incriminating admission from Pincher, and the lack of legal proof, there was no chance of the authorities obtaining an injunction citing breach of confidence. If Lord Rothschild had twice warned Sir Michael Hanley that Wright intended to use a book as a blackmail weapon, as Pincher was to allege, Sir Howard Smith, his successor, made no mention of any such warnings.

There was probably a *prima-facie* case to be made for

an offence under Section 2 of the Official Secrets Act, but such a move must have been judged counter-productive, especially as the authorities had yet to obtain legally a copy of the book, which was still under an embargo. On 23 March, three days before publication, two copies were requested by Sir Robert Armstrong in a telephone call to Sidgwick & Jackson. After consulting the author, the publishers responded with a condition: they asked for a written undertaking that no attempt would be made to stop publication if they supplied copies. Armstrong replied the same day and gave the undertaking requested. In it the Cabinet Secretary stated:

I can understand your need and wish to protect the confidentiality of the book until publication date. I can assure you that, if you are able to comply with my request, that confidentiality will be strictly observed, that the copies will not go outside this office and the Prime Minister's office.

His stated reason for requesting advance copies of the book was so that the Prime Minister could read it before making a statement to the House of Commons. In fact, the real reason was the desire to cover the fact that MI5 had already been in possession of the page proofs for a little over six weeks.

7

'THEIR TRADE IS TREACHERY'

Even before the book had been delivered to the shops, thanks to the headlines of the *Daily Mail*, faithfully copied (by arrangement) in *The Times, Their Trade is Treachery* had become a national issue. Sir Roger Hollis had been suspected as a spy, barked the front pages. Important figures in the establishment had been traitors. Whitehall had been engaged in an unprecedented cover-up to hide the truth from the public. Such ideas sell newspapers and Sir David English's investment in Pincher was amply rewarded. Syndication around the world ensured that his sensational, exclusive *exposé* was relayed to millions.

The book's central theme was simply that Hollis had been suspected of having been a Soviet spy, and that Pincher had 'known about the cover-up of the Hollis situation for several years' (although on this latter point readers of his *Daily Express* column would have had a different recollection). According to Pincher, the suspicions against Hollis had been endorsed by no less a personage than Lord Trend, but the scandal had been covered up in order to avoid embarrassment. Pincher revealed that,

after a three-week study, Lord Trend concluded that there was a strong *prima-facie* case that MI5 had been deeply penetrated over many years by someone who was not Blunt. He named

Hollis as the likeliest suspect, the circumstantial evidence against him being so weighty as to demand an explanation. In his view, Hollis had not cleared himself during his interrogation. His answers to searching questions had been unconvincing and his memory had been at fault only when it had suited him. Further, the evidence showed that Hollis had consistently frustrated attempts by loyal MI5 officers to investigate the obvious penetrations of their service.[1]

As a summary of Trend's report, this was a travesty. Far from spending a superficial three weeks skimming the files, Trend had taken the better part of a year to complete his detailed study. However, Wright had never seen Trend's finished report, so he had only been able to convey to Pincher the gist of what he believed Trend had said. Pincher had paraphrased it even further, leaving himself open to the charge of having distorted Trend's opinion.

For the six weeks before the Prime Minister's statement on 26 March 1981, MI5 and SIS had been scrutinising the page proofs of *Their Trade is Treachery* and had come to some interesting conclusions. That much of the book had been an 'inside job' was immediately obvious, because the heart of it was really a series of potted biographies of Soviet spy suspects which contained information that could only have been extracted from MI5's molehunting files. With the sole exception of John Cairncross, whose case was described in some detail, most of the individuals named as having endured investigation were dead. Among them were Dick Ellis, Sir Andrew Cohen, Tom Driberg, Bernard Floud, Tomás Harris, Herbert Norman, Paddy Costello, Phoebe Pool, Tom Wylie and, of course, Hollis himself. Clearly this was to protect the author from libel actions.

There was, however, a second group of people, all of whom had been interviewed by the molehunters, whom Pincher dared not name for fear of legal action. Instead, he included enough peripheral information to make clear that he knew their identities, but the significance of each was lost in the deliberately obscure references. Thus, Flora

Solomon was a 'Jewish woman normally resident in London';[2] Graham Mitchell was only referred to by his code-name, 'Peters', of which he was unaware; Michael Straight was simply 'a middle-aged American belonging to a rich and famous family';[3] Leo Long had enjoyed 'access to valuable secrets during the war but now works for a commercial company';[4] Alister Watson was 'a defence scientist in a most sensitive position'.[5] There were also more obscure references in the text to Sir Dennis Proctor ('having retired from the public service he retired abroad'[6]), Sir Edward Playfair and Jenifer Hart ('a woman who later managed to insinuate herself into a highly sensitive position in the Home Office'[7]). Clearly, Pincher had tapped into a vein of detailed knowledge about MI5's molehunting, but only a handful of molehunters knew to whom he was referring. Shrewdly, he also left a trail of false clues as to who had spoken out of turn.

When the first detailed analysis of *Their Trade is Treachery* was completed, there were several puzzling aspects which still had to be explained. Mixed in among the gems of solid fact were some extraordinary blunders. If the final manuscript or even the page proofs had been run past Pincher's chief source, he would surely have spotted them. For example, two points in particular were noticed about the treatment of Hollis. Pincher seemed unsure of the exact year in which he had joined MI5 and gave two quite different dates, two years apart. He also said that 'Hollis became acting head of Section F',[8] then that 'Hollis was still in charge of Section F',[9] and finally he referred to 'Directorate F which was then being run by Hollis'.[10] In fact, there was never a 'Section F' or an 'F Directorate' in MI5. A small mistake, but certainly one that showed through its repetition that the author had only the vaguest background knowledge of the wartime structure and responsibilities of the Security Service. Hollis had worked in F Division, which had subsequently been redesignated F Branch. It had never been known as 'Section F'.

Pincher's chronology was also out of sequence, for he thought that Blunt's confession had prompted the

PETERS enquiry. In fact, the investigation into Graham Mitchell had begun slightly more than a year before Blunt's decision to co-operate. There were other, less serious errors that would not have been made by anyone with an inside knowledge of MI5. For example, Harold Gibson was described as having been a pre-war MI5 officer. In fact, he was a career SIS officer, who was only ever based in London for a five-year period from 1951. All the rest of his service, from 1919 until his suicide in Rome in 1960, had been spent in Constantinople (1919–21), Bucharest (1922–30), Riga (1930–3), Prague (1933–9), Istanbul (1941–4), Prague (1945–8), Berlin (1948–51) and Rome (1955–60).

That the author himself must have recognised the short-comings of his first edition is demonstrated by the extra-ordinary *volte-face* he made on a wartime issue, that of the deliberate leaking of Bletchley's secrets to Moscow via a Soviet network in Switzerland. In his first edition he says he 'can find no evidence for this',[11] but by the second edition he had 'secured confirmation of this from secret intelligence sources'.[12]

The quality of information in *Their Trade is Treachery* seemed to vary from the most positive of MI5's deductions to the most inaccurate speculation which had already appeared in *Inside Story*. Far from assisting those charged with ident-ifying Pincher's sources, the test only seemed to confuse matters because the author had taken steps to deliberately conceal the fact that he was really ghost-writing someone else's book. For instance, when Pincher introduced his chapter on Anthony Blunt, he spoke of how, 'after long and difficult research, I have been able to piece together the major parts of Blunt's confessions . . .'.[13]

Several of the episodes described by Pincher indicated that he had spoken to Arthur Martin. The book included accounts of meetings and confrontations containing the kind of authenticating detail that only he could have known about. Indeed, the very first sentence of the book describes an incident which had occurred early in 1980, soon after Blunt's public exposure, when Martin had approached

Jonathan Aitken MP with additional information. At that time Martin had just left his post-retirement job as a clerk in the House of Commons, but he had decided to give a fuller account of MI5's molehunts to a Member of Parliament. He had chosen Aitken because of the latter's well-known interest in the subject (in 1971 he had written *Officially Secret*, following his acquittal on a charge of having breached the Official Secrets Act). Aitken had written to the Prime Minister on 31 January expressing his concern about Martin's private revelations, but Mrs Thatcher had given him a non-committal reply, stating that she was fully aware of the situation. The significance of Pincher mentioning this private correspondence was to implicate Martin as his source. Perhaps Martin, having been frustrated by the lack of action, had taken matters into his own hands and leaked the same information to Pincher. In what appeared to be confirmation of contact with Martin, Pincher wrote about the circumstances in which Martin had been gratuitously sacked from MI5 by Hollis: 'The officer assumed then that Hollis had realised that he suspected him and therefore wanted rid of him. This is still his view.'[14]

Pincher could only know that a particular opinion was 'still his view' by having talked to Martin. This seemed odd, because it was known that Pincher had approached Martin for information and that Martin had rebuffed him. During January 1981 Pincher had written letters to several former members of the FLUENCY Committee, seeking permission for an 'off-the-record' interview. By then both Arthur Martin and another officer had long-since retired from SIS and had moved to Gloucestershire. Each had reported receiving Pincher's letter and had been commended for their refusal to see him. His knowledge of FLUENCY's activities, as recorded in the four brief references to it in *Their Trade is Treachery's* first edition, is therefore weak. This is demonstrated by his comment that the committee acquired FLUENCY 'for want of a better name'. In fact, the word was the next on a list of suitable cryptonyms drawn up by the Joint Intelligence Committee.

By the publication of the book's paperback edition, the number of references to FLUENCY had grown to more than a dozen.

In the case of one counter-intelligence officer, who was briefly one of SIS's representatives on FLUENCY, the circumstances had been more difficult. His daughter was married to Pincher's closest neighbour in Kintbury, and Pincher persistently had asked her to pass on requests to her father. The officer declined Pincher's invitations. In the absence of definite proof against any of the three best suspects, the Prime Minister was advised that neither MI5 nor SIS could be sure which ex-officer was responsible for supplying Pincher with information. Nevertheless, they could offer a catalogue of errors in the text which tended to indicate that the author had relied on a single source, and had been either unable or unwilling to check the accuracy of the final version with the source. In reality, Pincher had failed to give Wright a copy of the final draft, perhaps because he knew that Wright would be bound to disapprove of his chosen method of presentation. Pincher must have anticipated that Wright would become enraged with the comment that, 'It is not my purpose in this book to urge that such an enquiry should be made.'[15] In his conclusions, summarised in the ultimate chapter, entitled 'Should there be an enquiry?', the author states:

In my opinion, and in that of experienced security officers whom I have consulted, any enquiry except by people with personal knowledge of security and intelligence operations would be of little use in evaluating the efficiency and loyalty of the security services.[16]

This, of course, was diametrically opposed to the view held by Wright that any kind of enquiry into MI5's management of the molehunts was needed as a matter of urgency.

One of those who had been entrusted with photocopies of the purloined page proofs was Sir Martin Furnival Jones, who was invited up to London to give his judgement on Pincher. He said, 'I do not think it is fair and it is very

unbalanced. It distorts the facts and confuses the issues.'
Another person invited to comment was Lord Trend who,
knowing the secrecy surrounding his report, must have
been surprised to learn that his role was about to be made
public. In her statement to the House of Commons the
Prime Minister described some of Pincher's material as
'inaccurate and distorted' and gave a brief account of the
background to the Hollis molehunt:

The case for investigating Sir Roger Hollis was based on certain
leads that suggested, but did not prove, that there had been a
Russian intelligence service agent at a relatively senior level in
British counter-intelligence in the last years of the war. None of
these leads identified Sir Roger Hollis, or pointed specifically or
solely in his direction. Each of them could also be taken as
pointing to Philby or Blunt. But Sir Roger Hollis was among
those that fitted some of them, and he was therefore investigated.
The investigation took place after Sir Roger Hollis' retirement
from the Security Service. It did not conclusively prove his
innocence. Indeed, it is very often impossible to prove innocence.
That is why in our law, the burden of proof is placed upon
those who seek to establish guilt and not on those who defend
innocence. But no evidence was found that incriminated him,
and the conclusion reached at the end of the investigation was
that he had not been an agent of the Russian intelligence
service.[17]

The Prime Minister then explained how this verdict had
been challenged and how Lord Trend had been commissioned to review matters:

He reviewed the investigations of the case and found that they
had been carried out exhaustively and objectively. He was
satisfied that nothing had been covered up. He agreed that none
of the relevant leads identified Sir Roger Hollis as an agent of
the Russian intelligence service, and that each of them could be
explained by reference to Philby or Blunt. Lord Trend did not
refer, as the book says he did, to 'the possibility that Hollis might
have recruited unidentified Soviet agents in MI5'. Again, he said
no such thing. Lord Trend, with whom I have discussed the
matter, agreed with those who, although it was impossible to

prove the negative, concluded that Sir Roger Hollis had not been an agent of the Russian intelligence service.[18]

After the Prime Minister had made her scathing remarks about Pincher's accuracy, she took the opportunity to announce that the Security Commission had been instructed to advise on future precautions to prevent hostile penetration, but what she did not announce to Parliament was a secret investigation into Pincher's sources.

Ninety minutes after Mrs Thatcher sat down, Pincher opened a press conference at the Waldorf Hotel in London to say that she had been 'enormously and badly misled'[19] by her advisers. He singled out the suggestion that the evidence of penetration could have been 'taken as pointing to Philby or Blunt' as entirely misguided, but, in the limited context of wartime leaks as proposed by Volkov and Gouzenko, the statement was entirely accurate. From Tasmania Wright was later to describe the Prime Minister's remarks as 'a masterly piece of Whitehall deception'[20] because, as he knew only too well, the very first clues to Soviet penetration, such as Philby's confession, had taken place long after the war, and many years after Philby and Blunt had been excluded from access to secrets. The molehunts had not been based on wartime allegations. The molehunts had been initiated some twenty years later, but had found corroborating evidence from the two Soviet defectors in 1945. There were other areas for criticism, including the claim that Hollis had been investigated after his retirement. Admittedly the DRAT enquiry had taken place post-1965, but that was to ignore the PETERS operation, and the firm knowledge in 1963 that either Hollis or Mitchell, or both, had been spies.

Pincher was obviously shaken at being branded inaccurate, distorted and wrong, so much so that he made an offer that was overlooked at the time:

If Mrs Thatcher needs a first-hand briefing from someone who was really involved up to the hilt all the time and knows the story backwards, I can suggest someone for her. He is a man who, more than anybody else, knows all the details of this matter. So,

either the Security Commission could question that gentleman,
or I have reason to believe that he would be quite happy to see
Mrs Thatcher himself.[21]

Pincher remained convinced of his scoop and refused to
take back one word, in spite of considerable pressure. The
Prime Minister had effectively cleared Hollis and there
were plenty of people, including Sir Dick White and Sir
Martin Furnival Jones, willing to make statements in support of their late colleague. The Hollis family received
considerable sympathy and Lady Hollis was taken from
her cottage to a Security Service safe-house for a rest until
the storm died down.

While the press and the public were sorting out the
claims and counterclaims, a further detailed study of *Their
Trade is Treachery* was undertaken jointly by MI5 and SIS,
and both Stephen de Mowbray and Arthur Martin were
interviewed. They were the only two members of the
FLUENCY Committee named by Pincher, but both men
denied ever having seen Pincher, which was true. Each
suspected Peter Wright's hand in the book, but they had
no proof to offer, apart from the deliberate omission of
his name from the text where there was a reference to the
FLUENCY Committee's chairman. Why had Wright been
left out? And why had Rothschild's name been excluded?
This was very strange, because Rothschild had played a
major part in the molehunts and had been interviewed on
several occasions. It was assumed that Pincher knew of
Rothschild's involvement, because the author had referred
to a shadowy 'visitor from England' who had met Flora
Solomon in Israel and passed on her damning testimony
about Philby to MI5. There was also an obscure allusion
to some adverse information about Watson, the Admiralty
scientist. In total, there ought to have been at least three
separate references to Rothschild, taking into account his
assistance over Solomon and Watson, and his interrogations, but there were none. At the time little importance
was attached to these omissions. In 1982 Pincher almost
completely rewrote *Their Trade is Treachery* for the paper-

back edition. In that version the 'Jewish woman normally resident in London' was named as Flora Solomon, yet Lord Rothschild continued to be the anonymous 'visitor from England'.[22] Why had Pincher not taken the opportunity to explain the entire episode in full, naming everyone involved? Why was Lord Rothschild singled out for special treatment? His act of introducing Mrs Solomon to Dick White was entirely praiseworthy and was one of the items he had apparently been so anxious to put on the public record to establish his innocence, so perhaps something had happened to make him change his mind.

Now it is known that Rothschild originally put Pincher and Wright together, one is left to wonder whether Rothschild was entirely satisfied with the outcome. Far from quelling damaging speculation about the extent of Soviet penetration of Whitehall, Pincher had fuelled it by veiled remarks about traitors in high places. Hints to the identities of the 'prominent Englishman, knighted for various services', the 'senior Civil Servant in the Home Office', and 'another senior Civil Servant . . . denied a knighthood'[23] were surely designed to inspire a further molehunt by Fleet Street. Yet this was exactly what Rothschild is reported as wishing to avoid.

In the months that followed publication, SIS obtained conclusive proof that Pincher had flown to Tasmania in October the previous year, and a line-by-line analysis of his book showed that Wright had been his chief source. According to some, it was the purchase of Pincher's airline tickets that betrayed Wright. In any event, the conclusion was announced at a special weekend conference called to discuss the implications at SIS's training-centre.

Among those who were not privy to the exposure of Wright as Pincher's source was Anthony Blunt, still living quietly at his flat in Portsea Hall, Bayswater. Enraged by what he believed to be a thoroughly mischievous portrayal of the help he had given to MI5, he unexpectedly agreed, when asked, to co-operate with me as I was then engaged in the final stages of three years' research into the wartime history of the Security Service. The first of a series of meet-

ings took place on 27 May, and thereafter I double-checked
the substance of his information with Peter Wright, speaking
over the telephone from Tasmania. Naturally, he gave no
clue that he had co-authored *Their Trade is Treachery*, and,
indeed, he was highly critical of Pincher.

During the course of these conversations with Wright,
when other matters inevitably arose, he mentioned his
intention to write a complete summary of his own experiences of his molehunting activities, in order to set the
record straight once and for all. When this news reached
the Security Service, it caused much anxiety and, on 20
July 1981, John Allen, MI5's Director of Establishments,
sent Wright a warning:

I am not sure how seriously to take your remark to [Nigel] West
that you would 'be writing an accurate history of what happened
but that it would not be published in my lifetime'. But, to avoid
any uncertainty, I must tell you that your obligation not to
make such a record, whether for publication or not, remains
unchanged. I have little doubt that the authorities here would
respond to a breach of your obligations by invoking any available
remedy under civil as well as criminal law.[24]

This astonishing letter was written and posted some considerable time after Wright had been identified as Pincher's
unnamed partner, but was intended to keep that knowledge from Wright himself.

Wright obviously did not take MI5's warning very
seriously, because he was later to complete a 637-page
typescript entitled *The Spycatcher*, which was destined to
become the subject of a prolonged legal action. In the
meantime, Pincher and Wright continued to correspond,
and at one stage there was a proposal for a further collabor-
ative effort, entitled *The Atlantic Connection*. However,
the public furore created in the days before the publication
of *Their Trade is Treachery* had been swiftly extinguished
by the Prime Minister's statement. Lady Hollis' only comment was to say that 'it had been a very painful episode
indeed. The very possibility he may have been a Russian
agent never occurred to me. I have never doubted that he

was innocent.'[25] There were other statements of support for Hollis, including one from Graham Greene who, at Philby's request, had written the foreword to the spy's 1968 autobiography, *My Silent War*.

Pincher himself remained silent until 21 July 1981, by which time, evidently, he had been able to exchange messages with Wright. On that day the *Daily Mail* published a further article by Pincher in which he was able to give a more accurate account of the Trend Report and to disclose the circumstances of Stephen de Mowbray's visit to Sir John Hunt in 1974. He also corrected his original erroneous claim that Trend had written his report 'after a three-week study'. Having consulted Wright, he conceded that Trend had spent 'two days a week for several months browsing among the relevant files at MI5 headquarters in Curzon Street'.[26] While it was true that Trend had spent 'almost a year' assessing the evidence, he did so from MI5's headquarters in Gower Street, not the Security Service's better-known administrative and technical offices in Curzon Street.

Pincher was unbowed by Mrs Thatcher's criticism and said that he 'had been able to consult people who have read the report';[27] he gave a strong hint that he had been in touch with Stephen de Mowbray, but in fact he had not. According to Pincher,

In 1975 de Mowbray was seen by Hunt and briefed on Trend's findings. He declined to accept them, arguing that Trend had done no more than follow the convenient departmental line previously taken by the heads of MI5 and the Secret Service.[28]

A clue to Pincher's true source for his additional information can be found in his remark that, 'Trend took a value judgement, deciding that while he could not be certain that Hollis had not been a spy, he should not be given the benefit of the doubt.'[29] The wording is almost identical to a statement made by Peter Wright during his *World in Action* television interview three years later.

Pincher's article was designed to be a detailed rebuttal of the Prime Minister's statement, and the four-month delay in publishing it was probably accounted for by the elaborate precautions both he and Wright were still taking to conceal Wright's role as *Their Trade is Treachery's* co-author. Meanwhile, there were further developments.

The first revelations concerned the identity of Michael Straight, the American who had originally told Arthur Martin about his recruitment by Blunt and had provided the key testimony that, combined with the immunity from prosecution, had persuaded Blunt to confess. Blunt had given his version of Straight's intervention during his secret interviews with me, and the substance of it appeared in my book, *MI5: British Security Service Operations 1909–45*, which was published in October 1981 and prompted the exposure of more suspected moles, including three former members of the Apostles, and there were even more in store. On 1 November 1981 Leo Long made a public statement in which he admitted to having supplied Blunt with secrets during the war. A week later Alister Watson issued a formal denial that he had ever been a Soviet spy, insisting that the confession he had given MI5 in 1967 had been extracted under duress after weeks of intensive interrogation and 'he was so confused he was saying things he did not really mean'.[30] On 29 November Edward Scott, another Cambridge graduate, but not linked to Blunt in spite of having shared an office with Guy Burgess for three years, confirmed that he too had been in contact with Soviet Bloc agents following his return from Prague where he had been appointed the British chargé d'affaires in 1959. He had later retired from the Foreign Office, having given MI5 an account of his dealings with Czech intelligence.

While the media weighed up the implications of this latest evidence of treachery in high places, the Canadian government released some of the embargoed transcripts of Gouzenko's evidence before the Royal Commission in 1946, and Gouzenko himself came forward to comment on them. Suddenly, his remarks about the two ELLIs took on a new significance and he gave *The Times* an entirely new version of the episode:

In late 1942 in the cipher room of the military intelligence headquarters in Moscow, Lieutenant Lev Lubimov, the clerk sitting next to him who was an old friend from before the war, surreptitiously passed him a six- or seven-line telegram from London which he had just decoded. The gist of the message, he said, was that ELLI's controller in Britain had made contact with him using a *dubok* [hiding-place] for messages in a crack in a tombstone. 'It was in the telegram that he was in MI5. It was unusual, the fact that he was in MI5, so he pushed it over to me,' Mr Gouzenko said. Lubimov told Mr Gouzenko that ELLI 'had something Russian in his background'. The information preyed on Mr Gouzenko's mind so that on September 5, 1945, when he sought sanctuary with the Canadian authorities, he asked his wife Svetlana to memorise the ELLI story and tell the Royal Canadian Mounted Police if he was seized by the Russians.[31]

This latest story was quite different from previous versions in several important respects. In his statement of May 1952, Gouzenko had not been able to remember the date of the telegram. Now he knew it was 'in late 1942'. Secondly, ELLI had been 'in MI5' specifically, rather than 'British Counter-intelligence' as he had first alleged. This point is critical, especially as Mrs Thatcher had stated that his allegation had 'suggested, but did not prove, that there had been a Russian intelligence service agent at a relatively senior level in British counter-intelligence in the last days of the war'. Perhaps equally significant was Gouzenko's assertion that his defection had been prompted by the burden of his knowledge. This latter claim was completely novel, for he had not mentioned this as his motive to the Royal Commission, or put it forward as a reason in his autobiography which is devoid of any reference to ELLIE (*sic*) apart from those concerned with Kay Willsher. Nor, for that matter, had Svetlana in her book, *Before Igor*. In previous statements Gouzenko had attributed his decision to defect to the fact that he had completed his tour of duty in Ottawa and had been notified of his imminent return to Moscow. On 10 October 1945 Gouzenko had given the RCMP a political reason for his defection:

Convinced that such double-faced politics of the Soviet Government towards the democratic countries do not conform with the interests of the Russian people and endanger the security of civilisation, I decided to break away from the Soviet regime and to announce my decision openly.[32]

In his book published in 1948 Gouzenko had confirmed the ideological nature of his conversion and had said that 'instead of convincing myself that doctrines instilled by the Soviet Union were still sound, I had found my thoughts drifting toward the democratic way of life'.[33] He also described how he had tried to ensure his family's safety by taking two vital telegrams from the cipher room at the Embassy as a preliminary to his eventual defection, 'one from Moscow requesting information on the atomic bomb, the other a report from Zabotin to Moscow on Fred Rose's election'.[34] Of all the compromising documents and information at his disposal, Gouzenko had selected these two to act as his meal-ticket, a bargaining chip to guarantee a good reception.

'These are purely precautionary,' I explained. 'If anything goes wrong I will still have these two telegrams to show the Canadian authorities. If anything happens to me then you can take them to the authorities yourself and ask protection.' Anna took the telegrams into the kitchen pantry and placed them on a shelf. Besides them she put a box of matches for use in case the telegrams had to be burned in a hurry.[35]

Once again, there is no mention of ELLI, either in the context of having been so important that Svetlana had to memorise the details, or of the knowledge of ELLI's existence having been the catalyst for his defection. In fact, it would seem that if anything had pushed Gouzenko to switch sides, it was Colonel Zabotin's suggestion, in August 1945, that, because the clerk who had been sent out as Gouzenko's replacement had almost finished his training, the Gouzenkos ought to plan to return to Moscow early in October when accommodation had been found for them on a ship.

Although it could not be said during his lifetime, an objective review of Gouzenko's numerous allegations fit the pattern of 'defector syndrome', the desire for publicity and the embroidery of claims to gain attention. One person intimately involved with Gouzenko was Peter Dwyer, the SIS officer who first reported his defection to London. He retired from SIS late in 1949 and went to Ottawa to head Canada's fledgling signals intelligence organisation, the so-called Communications Branch of the National Research Council. He died of a stroke on New Year's Eve, 1972, so he was unable to assist MI5's molehunters, but he is reported as having said that, 'Apart from Nunn May, Gouzenko gave us crap.'[36]

Peter Wright, who had great faith in Gouzenko (although he never met him), later countered this view by producing a VENONA decrypt, dated soon after the defection, which had been intercepted between Moscow and London and which revealed that permission had been granted to the GRU to discuss KGB information about Gouzenko's defection as supplied by STANLEY, the KGB's cryptonym for Philby.[37] Obviously, Philby had been keeping his KGB contact in London up to date with Gouzenko's revelations, and Moscow was confirming the reliability of Philby's messages. Wright interpreted this somewhat obscure signal to mean that Gouzenko's tip about ELLI was genuine, but there is another explanation. As Peter Dwyer had commented, the most damaging spy betrayed by Gouzenko had been Allan Nunn May, the atomic physicist from Trinity Hall, Cambridge, and, as a result, a major surveillance operation lasting five months was mounted by MI5 to keep him under observation. Among the documents removed from the Soviet Embassy by Gouzenko had been one dated 31 July 1945 from Colonel Zabotin to Moscow, for onward transmission to London, indicating how, where and when Nunn May, codenamed ALEK, was to be contacted upon his return to London:

We have worked out the conditions of a meeting with ALEK in London. ALEK will work in King's College, Strand. It will be

possible to find him there through the telephone book. Meetings:
October 7.17.27 on the street in front of the British Museum. The
time: 11 o'clock in the evening. Identification sign: A newspaper
under the left arm. Password: Best regards to MIKEL. He cannot
remain in Canada. At the beginning of September he must fly to
London. Before his departure he will go to the Uranium Plant
in the Petawawa district where he will be for about two weeks.
He promised, if possible, to meet us before his departure. He
said that he must come next year for a month to Canada. We
handed over 500 dollars to him.[38]

This plan was vetoed by Moscow, who replied on 22
August, and a new one suggested more comprehensive
instructions for the rendezvous with Nunn May:

The arrangements worked out for the meeting are not satisfactory. I am informing you of new ones.
   1. Place: In front of the British Museum in London, on
Great Russell Street, at the opposite side of the street about
Museum Street, from the side of Tottenham Court Road repeat
Tottenham Court Road. ALEK walks from the Tottenham
Court Road, the contact man from the opposite side,
Southampton Row.
   2. Time: As indicated by you, however, it would be more
expedient to carry out the meeting at 20 o'clock, if it should be
convenient to ALEK, as at 23 o'clock it is too dark. As for the
time, agree about it with ALEK and communicate the decision
to me. In case the meeting should not take place in October, the
time and day will be repeated in the following months.
   3. Identification signs: ALEK will have under his left arm
newspaper 'Times', the contact man will have in his left hand the
magazine 'Picture Post'.
   4. The Password: The contact man: 'What is the shortest way
to the Strand?'
   ALEK: 'Well, come along. I am going that way.'
   In the beginning of the business conversation ALEK says 'Best
regards to MIKEL'.
   Report on transmitting the conditions to ALEK.[39]

Dwyer had conveyed these details to MI5 and the watchers
had been posted along Great Russell Street on all the
appointed dates, but Nunn May had failed to turn up.

Had he been tipped off? If so, by whom? One possible explanation, which undermined Wright's view, was that Philby had been informed that MI5 intended to catch Nunn May in the act of meeting his new Soviet case officer, and that Philby had dutifully passed along a warning, just as he was to do for Maclean five years later. Indeed, Nunn May and Maclean briefly had been contemporaries together, just for a year, at the same Cambridge college. This might have been an added incentive for Philby to have taken a special interest in the investigation. Perhaps this was the true reason for Nunn May's non-appearance, and the true meaning of GCHQ's decrypt. In other words, Wright's trump card, the KGB's telegram, might have been an emergency signal for ALEK, not ELLI, in the event of which the case for ELLI is diminished further.

Gouzenko's interview in *The Times* in October 1981 served to reopen the Hollis saga, with Chapman Pincher claiming, in a *Daily Mail* article entitled 'I was right', that 'the evidence Gouzenko gave in 1946 confirms the claims I made'.[40] In reality Gouzenko's latest offering actually served to reduce his credibility. Additional action was required to put an end to what had now become the Hollis affair, so in an unprecedented move Sir Martin Furnival Jones and his former Deputy Director-General, Anthony Simkins, wrote a joint letter to *The Times*:

Up to the time we retired in the early seventies there was not a shred of evidence that Sir Roger Hollis had been disloyal at any time or in any way, let alone evidence that he was a spy (report, October 16). Moreover, throughout his career his positive contribution to security was outstandingly valuable and his wartime record makes ludicrous any suggestion that he might have been sympathetic to the USSR. We both worked closely with him for many years and were intimately concerned with the investigation of his background and his subsequent interrogation. We are wholly convinced of his innocence.[41]

Far from silencing Pincher, this unequivocal letter of support prompted a swift reply from the author, who latched on to the word interrogation and drew a distinction between a friendly interview and a hostile interrogation. This was further evidence vindicating the claims he had made in *Their Trade is Treachery*, and was 'the first official confirmation'[42] that Hollis had undergone the latter. On the matter of lack of evidence, Pincher dismissed Furnival Jones' letter by pointing out that there was plenty of evidence against Hollis, but not of the legally admissible variety.

At this point Pincher appears to have got back in touch with Wright for further help, for by mid-December he had acquired further information and was in a position to name John Day in *The Times* as the MI5 officer from K7 who had conducted Hollis' interrogation. In both his hardback and paperback editions, Pincher had only referred to him as 'an ex-Marine Commando'.[43] Pincher said he was now convinced that Mrs Thatcher's statement to the House of Commons had been 'an Establishment concoction intended to bury the horrific Hollis Affair and anything connected with it'.[44] Her description of his book as inaccurate and distorted was 'a smear'.

One item of information released to Pincher by Wright at this time, which he used to bolster his theory that Mrs Thatcher had been deliberately misled by the Security Service, was the disclosure that in May 1974 Sir Michael Hanley had called an inter-Allied counter-intelligence conference in London and recommended those present to assume that Hollis had not been cleared.

Quite apart from Pincher's continuing clandestine contact with Wright, he was at this stage constantly on the look-out for new evidence, and his search prompted him to take a certain Mrs Joanna Phipps out to lunch, now better known as Joan Miller, authoress of *One Girl's War*. During the war Mrs Phipps had worked for Maxwell Knight, one of MI5's most brilliant and eccentric case officers. She had first-hand knowledge of Knight's handling of Tom Driberg as an agent inside the CPGB and confirmed one of the more sensational but peripheral claims made in *Their Trade is Treachery*.

Pincher's latest article in support of his contention that

'it is far from impossible that proof might still emerge' brought this response from Sir Charles Cunningham, the Permanent Under-Secretary at the Home Office who had negotiated Blunt's immunity from prosecution with Hollis and the Attorney-General:

Sir Roger Hollis can no longer defend himself: nor can his widow and son, whose distress must be very great, any effective means of doing so. I believe that the dead, no less than the living, are entitled to the presumption of innocence until guilt is proved. In support of that presumption, may I be allowed just to say that during the decade in which I knew Sir Roger Hollis well I had at no time any reason to doubt his integrity or to regard him as other than a loyal, zealous and dedicated public servant.[45]

If Sir Charles believed this would bring the Hollis affair to a discreet conclusion, he was mistaken, for the Hollis family had decided to embark on their own research through the medium of a close neighbour in Oxford of Hollis' son, Adrian.

Adrian's friend was Dr Anthony Glees, a lecturer in the department of government at Brunel University, who was then researching a book on the subject of governments in exile during the Second World War. One of his more controversial theories was that the post-war standing of the Social Democratic Party in Germany had been deliberately undermined by Philby and Blunt, acting in concert. When this idea was published, in the *Listener*[46] in October 1981, it caused Blunt to protest that, while he had been guilty of many things, the division of Germany was certainly not one of them. He explained that his duties in the Security Service had never brought him into contact with the governments in exile, as suggested, and therefore he had never been in a position to influence Allied policy. He insisted that Glees' main contention, that 'Philby in MI6 and Blunt in MI5 were in a position to control the flow of information on which British policy was based',[47] was unfounded, and thereby sparked off a brief and unusual academic debate.

This minor episode was Glees' first encounter with the intelligence world, but when the Hollis family showed him a collection of hundreds of letters written by Sir Roger while he had been in China before the war, Glees was convinced that they shed important light on his activities at the very time that the molehunters believed he may have been recruited or reactivated by the GRU. As Pincher had already stated, 'If Hollis was a Russian spy the odds are that he was recruited before he wormed his way into MI5.' The letters had been recovered from a box found after the death of the first Lady Hollis in 1980, and had been addressed to his mother, the wife of the Bishop of Taunton. If he had associated with such Comintern activists as Agnes Smedley or Ruth Kuczynski, he certainly gave no clue in his correspondence which concentrates on his desire to play golf again, the need for old school ties and an almost xenophobic dislike of those around him. Writing from Dairen he remarked:

This hotel is filling up with Japanese, blousy Russians and a sprinkling of rather un-Aryan looking Germans. Completely unexciting. . . . There is a large colony of Russians here who go down to the beach every day to sunbathe in the most attenuated costumes. They are flamboyant, bright-red with raw patches and not very beautiful. . . . As for the Japanese, they'll move us out of China unless something is done to stop them. . . . I am so sick of these filthy little people.[48]

As for the journey back to Europe from China while on leave in 1934, Hollis had some interesting observations to make about Moscow. It was his first (and only) visit to the Soviet Union, but the molehunters had placed some importance on it because of Gouzenko's claim that there had been something Russian in ELLI's background:

. . . and now for the journey on the trans-Siberian express of which I could tell you little before as the Russians have a way of reading letters and criticism is not encouraged. Berlin struck me as a wonderful city but I didn't like the militaristic Hitlerism which one finds everywhere. Uniforms, strutting self-importance and fantastic salutations on all sides. The poor civilian is very small beer . . . the next day we arrived in Moscow where we were met by a representative of Intourist in a very luxurious

Lincoln car with a charming young lady as a guide. The Kremlin looked fine – from the outside. Lenin's tomb looked rather like a high-class public lavatory without any dignity or artistic merit. I have never seen anything which depressed me so unutterably as Moscow. It is a huge drab slum, people ill-dressed in the most deplorable ready-mades, though not in rags I admit.[49]

When all the Hollis letters had been sorted through and put into chronological order, they gave a fascinating insight in Sir Roger's eight years in China between 1928 and 1936 and made it possible to reconstruct his movements. They also demonstrated that he was not short of cash. In November 1935 he wrote home asking for 'a statement of my shares': 'They're not quoted in *The Times* so I can't gloat over all the money I'm making. I think I'll invest a little over here. We don't spend much for there's nothing to spend it on.'[50] If Hollis was recruited into the GRU while he was up at Oxford or later while he was in China, there is no clue to it in his papers. Glees believes they 'totally destroy Pincher's main accusation against Hollis' and if the future Director-General really did undergo a grooming process for his later, covert mission as a mole, he managed to conceal it really very well, as is illustrated by this revealing comment made in a letter to his fiancée late in 1936:

Hidden away in me I have always had a passionate loyalty to the monarchy and to the ideal and duties of the English gentleman. All my time abroad has strengthened that because I've seen how much other people do respect our code.[51]

In April 1981, two days after the first of these letters were made public by Dr Glees in an article in *The Times*, Pincher was back on the attack, pointing out that if Hollis had been recruited as a mole the topic would hardly be expected to be found in his letters to his mother. And as for pointing out Moscow's shortcomings, that was a recurring feature of letters from both Burgess and Maclean in their later years. Pincher went on to defend his position by remarking, with what was to turn out to be unusual candour:

Like my previous critics, Dr Glees gives the impression that *Their Trade is Treachery* is the product of private enquiries into Hollis' life by me. In fact, as the book clearly states, it is a record of the evidence and allegations mounted against Hollis by his own colleagues in MI5 assisted by others from MI6.[52]

This was a detectable change in tack from Pincher's previous confidence when he had asserted that he 'had known about the cover-up of the Hollis situation for several years',[53] and that since then he 'had confirmed details of most of the evidence against him, together with the sinister events and the strange aspects of Hollis' behaviour which eventually led to his dramatic interrogation'. This statement leaves little room for doubt about Pincher's certainty, yet a year later the author had evidently changed his view:

While I believe that the Fluency Committee and Section 7 were correct in their conviction that MI5 had been penetrated for many years at a high level by a pro-Soviet agent long after Blunt and Philby had left the scene I have not said that Hollis was a spy. I agree with those of his former colleagues who believe he is the prime suspect, but I regard the case as unproven either way.[54]

After a lengthy study of the Hollis papers Dr Glees concluded that 'to depict Hollis as a convinced Marxist is both unhistorical and utterly absurd'.[55] Apart from his connection with Adrian Hollis, there is no reason to believe that Glees was prejudiced either way before embarking on his project which, incidentally, was never followed up by the molehunters. Indeed, until Adrian Hollis volunteered his father's papers to Glees, MI5 had no idea that this key evidence even existed.

In spite of the considerable work undertaken by Dr Glees, there still remained the possibility that Hollis was 'the most ingenious liar of the twentieth century',[56] as he concedes, or that Hollis was induced into co-operating with the Soviets and was never an ideologically motivated spy. Hollis had described himself in a letter in 1936 as a 'staunch Conservative', and no amount of research into his political allegiances has uncovered the tell-tale reversal in opinion which marked the careers of Blunt, Burgess, Philby, Maclean *et al.*, who were unable to conceal a long track record of membership of or at least support for the CPGB at some stage. Subsequent research into Hollis had only produced a university friendship with Claud Cockburn, the well-known Marxist writer, and nothing stronger than a brief acquaintance in Shanghai with Agnes Smedley. If politics were ruled out, as the Hollis papers seemed to indicate, had Hollis been coerced into helping the Soviets?

Hollis had entered into a long-standing affair with his secretary, Val Hammond, as early as 1947, so blackmail is one option, although the liaison was such an open secret within the Security Service that it is difficult to know how the information could have been used against him. Certainly he was never a homosexual, and his relative lack of a substantial fortune was a condition that was altered when he married Evelyn Swayne in July 1937.

Neither Peter Wright nor the K7 molehunters had known anything about the Hollis papers and their discovery (and their authentication) was a turning-point. If Hollis had not been ideologically motivated, he would have been unique among his particular generation of spies recruited by the Soviets during their most intensive period of activity, in the late 1930s. Furthermore, agents acting under duress invariably seize at an opportunity to make a confession, whereas it is a common characteristic of the classic mole to resist interrogation; if Hollis was guilty, that was what he would have done in 1970.

The molehunters themselves were never in any doubt that their quarry was a skilled operator, having sabotaged so many of MI5's operations over such a very long period, without ever having left a worthwhile trace for the investigators to follow up. If, as seemed increasingly likely, bearing in mind the unreliability of Gouzenko and the testimony of Hollis' own correspondence from China, that Hollis was not MI5's supermole, then the argument for reopening the PETERS enquiry had suddenly become overwhelming. The problem facing those anxious to estab-

lish the truth was how to do so without bringing the
Security Service into further disrepute.

It will be recalled that at this critical stage the identities
of the members of the FLUENCY Committee were still
not in the public domain. The two molehunters identified
in *Their Trade is Treachery* were Arthur Martin and
Stephen de Mowbray. In their retirement they had both
kept in touch with Anatoli Golitsyn, and had edited his
magnum opus on Soviet disinformation entitled *New Lies
for Old*. Unfortunately, they had experienced considerable
difficulty in finding a publisher for the book but, in anticipation, they had already obtained permission to write an
introduction and put their names to it, without actually
revealing any details of their involvement with the defector. De Mowbray's name, or his role as an SIS officer
and molehunter, had never been disclosed until Pincher
mentioned him, just once, in *Their Trade is Treachery*.
Martin, on the other hand, had been compromised as long
ago as 1968 by Kim Philby in *My Silent War*, when he is
referred to as having attended Philby's interrogation at the
hands of 'Buster' Milmo in 1951. John Day had been
exposed by Pincher in a *Times* article in December 1981.
Of the remaining eighteen molehunters directly concerned
with PETERS and DRAT, not one had been identified.
The names of Ian Carrel and John Day had actually been
deleted, at the request of the Security Service, from the
original manuscript of *MI5. British Security Service Operations 1909–45*, which had been published in October.

One consequence of *Their Trade is Treachery* was the
exchange of information between the various officers who,
at different times, had been privy to aspects of the molehunts. The widespread belief that Martin, de Mowbray
and Wright had somehow acted together as 'Young Turks'
was completely unfounded. Wright had taken care to avoid
contact with his former colleagues, and in his capacity as
FLUENCY's chairman was in a better position than most
to have an overview of the molehunts. He had also spent
longer than anyone else concentrating on the narrow field
of Soviet penetration of the British establishment and so

was well placed to keep Pincher supplied with information, but he did not know the full picture. In fact, when some of the retired molehunters read *Their Trade is Treachery*, they realised the appallingly simple truth: that MI5 had failed to identify the person or persons responsible for betraying its secrets during the 1950s, right up until Philby's defection in 1963. Not surprisingly, some decided to take action to find the culprit.

That there truly had been high-level penetration of the Security Service was unpalatable but undeniable. Many officers in MI5 and SIS had known that various secret investigations had occurred at different times, but only a handful of insiders were ever allowed to discover the extraordinary scope of the molehunts. When, after his resignation, Harold Wilson had inadvertently mentioned some internal MI5 scandal involving a Soviet spy, few had taken him seriously. Chapman Pincher's book had not only served to alert the public to what Peter Wright perceived as a continuing problem, it had also enabled individual MI5 officers who had been bound by their code of strict silence to compare notes. Opinions varied, but one common theme of these discussions was that there was a very good chance that the original suspect, Graham Mitchell, may have outwitted them all. The question remaining was, how could he be persuaded to confess if he had already been interrogated and officially cleared, and if the office was so obviously anxious to shelve the entire matter. One possible solution was the preparation in secret of a highly detailed dossier so that he could be confronted and offered the opportunity to confess in return for a solemn undertaking that no word of his admission would be released until after his death, which, according to an officer assigned to keep a casual eye on him, was probably imminent. The unorthodox method chosen was to be *A Matter of Trust*.

8

'A MATTER OF TRUST'

Before examining the weight of evidence against Mitchell, one should be reminded of the overwhelming proof that MI5 had experienced high-level Soviet penetration. Even discounting the wartime evidence of Gouzenko and Volkov, which, as the Prime Minister had correctly pointed out, could have referred to others within British counter-intelligence, there were the large number of double-agent operations against the Soviet Union which had floundered; the index of Security Service documents bearing post-war dates that had been seen by Golitsyn; Wright's technical report which was known to have been circulated in Moscow; the warnings delivered to Nunn May, Cairncross, Maclean and Prybl which had enabled them to avoid, or delay, interrogation; the extraordinary circumstances of Philby's incomplete confession in 1963. Apart from these specifics, there were the broader issues of MI5's record of failure, over a long period, to attract defectors and its apparent inability to catch any Soviet spies. On top of all this was the construction of a plausible, if not slightly paranoid, theory that virtually all of the Security Service's supposed successes, such as the arrest of Gordon Lonsdale and John Vassall, had been little more than the KGB's deliberate discards or decoys.

That MI5 had been manipulated by a skilled, top-level spy was the uncomfortable conclusion reached by no fewer than sixteen of the twenty-one molehunters called in to investigate, and their verdict had been confirmed by no fewer than three separate enquiries. The disposing of Hollis as a suspect did not invalidate the argument. It simply underlined the need to extend the search elsewhere, or to re-evaluate the evidence that had already accumulated.

As we have seen, Mitchell had been eliminated as a result of his impressive performance under interrogation in 1967. Since that date, tabs had been kept on him by office personnel who occasionally travelled down to Chobham to see him. In later life he developed a drinking problem but, as far as anyone could tell, he was not under any obvious stress. The crucial question was whether his clearance had been justified or comprehensive, or whether there was additional information that had not been available to his inquisitors.

One person intimately involved in the PETERS operation, who had not been privy to the details of Mitchell's interrogation, was Arthur Martin. He had always been uneasy about Mitchell's clearance because there were aspects of the case which suggested that, at a very early stage, Mitchell had realised he was under scrutiny. Both men had once been on a long, routine tour of inspection, visiting MI5's Security Liaison Officers in Africa. Although Mitchell had few office friends, he and Martin got along well, and thereafter the Deputy Director-General had invited Martin into his office for chats about work. These were informal, friendly occasions, which took place at irregular intervals. Soon after Operation PETERS had begun, Mitchell had become withdrawn and had seemed ill at ease when the two men were obliged to meet. There were no further cosy chats. Martin suspected that Mitchell had detected the molehunt on his own or had received a warning, either accidentally or by design, from Hollis.

If Mitchell had been the mole, it would not have been too difficult for him to hoodwink his interrogators in 1967. By that time he had been retired for some four years and had had plenty of time to prepare himself or even to consult with others on a suitable line of defence. Whatever the truth, it was certainly the case that when PETERS was first initiated, none of those involved had any reservations about his guilt. It was only much later that the doubts had crept in, and Operation DRAT had been started. What had made the case seem so convincing?

Firstly, Mitchell possessed an outstanding intellect, far surpassing Hollis'. While Hollis had only a mediocre record of academic achievement, Mitchell had been an Exhibitioner at Winchester and had completed his degree course at Oxford. During the period when Hollis was travelling around China, Mitchell had been working as a journalist in London. Records of his employment were lost during the war when the *Illustrated London News*' archives were bombed. His only credited contribution was an obscure article in the 12 October 1935 edition entitled, 'What Was Known by Abyssinia in the Seventeenth Century – A Detailed Account in a Geography of 1670'. His political views at the time are reflected by his work for the Conservative Research Department, then headed by Sir Joseph Ball. It is interesting to note that at this critical, pre-war moment several future moles were making determined efforts to establish the respectability of their political credentials. Coincidentally, Guy Burgess had offered his services as an assistant to the right-wing Tory MP, Jack Macnamara, and Philby had joined the Anglo–German Fellowship. Given Sir Joseph Ball's long connections with the British intelligence community (he was to be appointed Lord Swinton's deputy on the top-secret Security Executive in 1940), the Research Department would have been a useful environment in which a prospective mole could burrow deep. Like Hollis, Mitchell was unfit for active military duty, and his link with Ball ensured him a place in intelligence.

Mitchell's wartime experience was entirely in F Division, working in F3 which monitored the activities of the extreme Right, complementing Hollis' surveillance of the CPGB in F2. His post-war career was in both F and C Divisions, where he became Director, and then the elite D Division which he headed until his promotion, in 1956, to the post of Deputy Director-General. Mitchell's directorship of the counter-espionage division, a post never held by Hollis, was arguably the one of most interest to the Russians; it is certainly a characteristic of successive Soviet agents that they have made persistent attempts to gain access to a position where they could acquire really sensitive information and inflict real damage. Because of the strict enforcement of the 'need to know' rule and the compartmentalisation of the Security Service into separate, watertight units, the Director D is one of the very few officers with a complete over-view of the organisation's anti-Soviet operations. It is, therefore, considered to be a key target for penetration. During Mitchell's three-year tenure in D Division (which was redesignated D Branch during his term of office), not a single Soviet spy was identified or caught in England. For those sceptical that such a crucial post could ever be occupied by a Soviet spy, the cases of Philby, who headed SIS's anti-Soviet section, and Heinz Felfe, who headed West Germany's counter-espionage department, are two obvious examples. There are numerous others. Indeed, it could be said that with the KGB's unrivalled post-war record of success in placing its agents in exceptionally valuable positions, it would be remarkable if at least one Director D had not been a hostile spy.

When summing up Mitchell's career, and seeking areas where he had performed well, Dick White selected the introduction of Positive Vetting (PV) as an outstanding mark in his favour:

In the late 1940s and early 1950s Mitchell played a leading part in the construction of anti-penetration devices, designed to keep the KGB out of Whitehall, and was one of the chief architects of positive vetting for officials in sensitive posts. With senior civil servants in the Treasury and the Cabinet Office, he was instrumental in ensuring that Britain's cold war security purge avoided the excesses of McCarthyism and the aim was that there should be no public pillorying of those transferred to non-sensitive work or asked to resign.[1]

This assessment focusing on one of the high points of Mitchell's career is open to criticism as virtually every important spy since the introduction of Positive Vetting has undergone the screening process and sailed through to get a clearance without any trouble. Blake, Vassall, Britten, Allen, Bossard, Prime and Bettaney, to name a few of the more notorious examples, were also submitted to Mitchell's system and were granted access to the nation's secrets. If the PV programme was rated a success, one wonders what might have happened if someone ill-disposed had played a part in its creation.

Far from being a success, the PV process has been dogged by problems and has been the subject of several official enquiries which have broadened its scope. When originally introduced, it was intended as a method of preventing Fascists and Communists from gaining access to secrets. Following the defections of Burgess and Maclean, it was widened to allow background field enquiries to be made on individuals so as to eliminate those suffering from the 'personality defects' of drunkenness, indebtedness and homosexuality that might make vetting candidates susceptible to blackmail. At a later stage, the further criteria of relatives living in Eastern Bloc countries was added.

From its inception the PV system was handicapped by the lack of trained staff to undertake the background checks required and to conduct the interviews with individual candidates. John Vassall, a blatant homosexual who ostentatiously lived beyond his means, was never spotted as a security risk and received a clearance for access to classified material. This was because the interviewing officer, a retired colonial police officer, had practically no relevant experience or training and had been impressed by Vassall's membership of the Bath Club. Incredibly, neither the interviews nor the field enquiries were carried out by the Security Service because Mitchell had recommended that MI5 was too secret to be exposed to the public. Instead, responsibility for all the legwork was handed to a small staff in the Procurement Executive of the Ministry of Defence. Apart from comparing the names of candidates to those listed in the indices kept by MI5's Registry, the Security Service played no part in the PV arrangements. Furthermore, the organisation itself was exempted from having to endure PV checks because details of its own personnel were top secret. This, then, was the brainchild of Graham Mitchell which was supposed to protect the realm from hostile penetration.

In terms of access to information concerning MI5 operations that backfired, Mitchell had advance knowledge of the date on which Donald Maclean was to be interrogated, and knew that Vladimir Petrov had agreed to defect. He had also known about MI5's plan to trap the Czech military attaché, Colonel Oldrich Prybl, in the act of meeting a contact. In 1958 D Branch had received a tip from the FBI suggesting that Prybl was known to be in touch with an aeronautical engineer based at Shoreham in Sussex. The information had come from a cipher clerk named Tisler, who had defected from the Czech Embassy in Washington. Intensive surveillance on Prybl failed to catch him meeting his agent, so his source, Brian Linney, was confronted by the police. He immediately confessed to having sold secrets to the Czechs and implicated Prybl, but the military attaché was never detained. An internal review of the investigation indicated that Prybl had somehow been alerted to MI5's interest in him. Suspicion fell on the watchers, but the source of the leak had never been traced and had remained on file as one further operation compromised by a high-level mole. Once again, Mitchell was found to have had the right access.

The incident that had sparked off Operation PETERS had been Philby's phoney confession delivered to Nicholas Elliott in Beirut in January 1963, which constituted the clearest evidence of a leak. Mitchell had been the first suspect and, once Hollis had been cleared, he moved back into the spotlight. Mitchell, of course, had become closely involved in the investigation of Philby as the Director of D Branch, yet he was one of the very few officers who attempted to defend him. Uniquely, he took Philby's side right up until the latter's eventual defection and had been directly and solely responsible for drafting the Burgess and Maclean White Paper which was released on 23 September

1955 during Parliament's long summer recess. It will be recalled that at that time Mitchell's only superiors were Roger Hollis, the Deputy Director-General, and Sir Dick White, who had just received a knighthood.

The White Paper was widely criticised and, as will be shown, it has not stood the test of time. Quite apart from Mitchell's blunder over which Cambridge college Maclean had attended, the document reflected Mitchell's well-known scepticism about the reliability of defectors. It was inaccurate, downright untrue in places, defensive in tone, and was deliberately vague on important issues while offering a mass of irrelevant detail on less vital matters, such as the subsequent disappearance of Melinda Maclean. Far from suggesting the involvement of a third man, Mitchell placed emphasis on Burgess and Maclean themselves and subtly denigrated the evidence of Petrov who, of course, was a senior KGB officer, as was his wife.

In view of the suspicions held against Maclean and of the conspiratorial manner of his flight, it was assumed, but it could not be proved, that his destination and that of his companion must have been the Soviet Union or some other territory behind the Iron Curtain. Now Vladimir Petrov, the former Third Secretary of the Soviet Embassy in Canberra who sought political asylum on 3rd April 1954, has provided confirmation of this. Petrov himself was not directly concerned in the case and his information was obtained from conversation with one of his colleagues in Soviet service in Australia. Petrov states that both Maclean and Burgess were recruited as spies for the Soviet Government while students at the University, with the intention that they should carry out their espionage tasks in the Foreign Office, and that in 1951, by means unknown to him, one or other of the two men became aware that their activities were under investigation. This was reported by them to the Soviet Intelligence Service who then organised their escape and removal to the Soviet Union. Petrov has the impression that the escape route included Czechoslovakia and that it involved an aeroplane flight into that country.[2]

The exact route taken by the two absconding officials was of no consequence whatever, but the evidence of 'Petrov' (note that he was not given the courtesy of a 'Mr', unlike

everyone else mentioned, apart from Burgess and
Maclean) was not only important, but it was known to be
true. It had been verified by the evidence volunteered by
Goronwy Rees four years earlier.

Mitchell's attitude to Vladimir Petrov is inexplicable.
The Petrovs were the most senior KGB officials ever to
have defected, and their escape was the conclusion of a
long operation conducted with great skill by the Australian
Security and Intelligence Organisation to tempt them to
switch sides. It was a brilliant *coup* and both produced a
wealth of valuable information, including dozens of secret
documents stolen from the Embassy. In intelligence terms
Vladimir Petrov's stature is infinitely greater than Gouzenko's, who had been a mere cipher clerk with virtually
no first-hand knowledge of individual Soviet agents. Both
Petrovs were in a position to name names and they did.
The part of Vladimir's debriefing relevant to Burgess and
Maclean had come from his friend Filipp Kislitsyn,
the Second Secretary in Canberra who had served in the
KGB's London *Rezidentura* in 1951 at the time of the
escapes, and had even had a hand in Melinda Maclean's
vanishing act in Switzerland in September 1953.

The critical sentence that 'one or other of the two
men had become aware that their activities were under
investigation' and that 'this was reported by them to the
Soviet Intelligence Service' was entirely untrue. MI5 knew
that Maclean had been tipped off by Burgess, and had a
suspicion that Philby had been responsible for the leak. In
fact, neither Burgess nor Maclean was known to have had
any contact with the Soviets. In reality, the vital message
ordering Maclean to escape had been given to Burgess by
Blunt, acting as a cut-out, but this was not known for some
time to come. The White Paper had this to say on the
possibility of a tip-off from an insider:

It is now clear that in spite of the precautions taken by the
authorities Maclean must have become aware, at some time
before his disappearance, that he was under investigation. One
explanation may be that he observed that he was no longer

receiving certain types of secret papers. It is also possible that he
detected that he was under observation. Or he may have been
warned. Searching inquiries involving individual interrogations
were made into this last possibility. Insufficient evidence was
obtainable to form a definite conclusion or to warrant prosecution.

Maclean's absence did not become known to the authorities
until the morning of Monday, 28th May.

This was an extremely misleading account of what had
taken place, not least because Maclean had been spotted
leaving for France three days earlier, on Friday evening at
Southampton. As regards the evidence against Philby, it
had been sufficient to have him sacked from SIS following
the semi-judicial hearing conducted by Milmo. None of
those present at that time had any doubt of his guilt
and they had all reached a firm, definite conclusion. The
question of a criminal prosecution was rather different,
but the Director of Public Prosecutions who usually makes
such decisions was never consulted. If he had been, he
might have decided that there was little chance of obtaining
a conviction, but the Attorney-General might have thought
that, in the circumstances, and in view of the public
interest, a case ought to have been brought even if it was
bound to fail.

Publication of the White Paper had led to the debate in
which Philby was publicly cleared by the Foreign Secretary,
Harold Macmillan, on Mitchell's advice. Once again, the
opportunity was taken to discredit the idea of a 'so-called
third man, if indeed there was one'.[3]

The press savaged the White Paper as a cover-up, which
is exactly what it was. The charge is illustrated by Mitchell's
lame defence of MI5's two main failures. Firstly, the un-
avoidable admission that the watchers had not kept
Maclean under surveillance:

The watch on Maclean was made difficult by the need to ensure
that he did not become aware that he was under observation.
This watch was primarily aimed at collecting, if possible, further
information and not at preventing an escape. In imposing it a

calculated risk had to be taken that he might become aware of it and might take flight. It was inadvisable to increase this risk by extending the surveillance to his home in an isolated part of the country and he was therefore watched in London only.[4]

MI5 was obliged to make this embarrassing disclosure about the Watcher Service leaving Maclean at Charing Cross railway station because it had already been stated that Maclean had been under suspicion, along with one or two others, since 'mid-April'. It was, therefore, a little difficult to explain how Maclean had managed to drive to Southampton and get on a cross-Channel ferry without being challenged. The excuse of not wishing to compromise the watchers is improbably feeble, especially when it is now known that Maclean was about to undergo a hostile interrogation that would have left him in no doubt about the nature of the allegations against him.

Given half a chance, no doubt even this awkward fact would have been concealed, but there was no avoiding the truth that Maclean was already the chief suspect at the time of his defection. From the White Paper it would seem that MI5's main concern was to save itself from charges of incompetence rather than the protection of the precious VENONA source which had implicated Maclean.

MI5's second appalling error was its laxity in not taking Maclean in for questioning immediately the Foreign Secretary, Herbert Morrison, had given his consent on the morning of Friday, 25 May. The White Paper makes no mention of MI5's firm intention to question Maclean the following Monday morning, and implies that Morrison had given a broad permission with a date to be fixed sometime in 'mid-June':

In reaching this decision it had to be borne in mind that such questioning might produce no confession or voluntary statement from Maclean sufficient to support a prosecution but might serve only to alert him and to reveal the nature and the extent of the suspicion against him. In that event he would have been free to make arrangements to leave the country and the authorities would have had no legal power to stop him. Everything therefore depended on the interview and the security authorities were anxious to be as fully prepared as was humanly possible. They were also anxious that Maclean's house at Tatsfield, Kent, should be searched and this was an additional reason for delaying the proposed interview until mid-June when Mrs Maclean who was then pregnant was expected to be away from home.[5]

This part of the White Paper is patently false as was known by all the MI5 officers who had intended to prepare themselves over the weekend for the confrontation on Monday morning. As has already been seen, the Director-General, Sir Dick White, may have had his own reasons for wishing to prevent the full details of MI5's bungling to be kept under wraps, but even thirty years later it does seem amazing that this actually happened.

In fact, the White Paper can be shown to be either misleading or untrue on seventeen separate matters, which must be something of a record for such a brief government document running only to twenty-eight paragraphs (see Appendix 1).

Some of the more ridiculous statements, such as the absurd idea that Maclean could not be followed by MI5's watchers into 'an isolated part of the country' like Kent, were intended plainly to save the Security Service from embarrassment. In fact, the watchers were perfectly capable of posting inconspicuous pickets along Maclean's regular route home to monitor his progress, but no such action was taken. There was no mention of it in the White Paper, but telephone engineers had adapted both his home and office telephones so that they picked up all conversations in both places. There was, of course, no intention of waiting until 'mid-June' before interrogating Maclean. He was due to be questioned on Monday morning, but his escape had been noticed on Friday evening, and the telephone call from the alert immigration officer in Southampton who spotted Maclean had been logged at Leconfield House soon after midnight. He also reported that the ferry, the SS *Falaise*, was not scheduled to dock in St Malo until mid-morning the following day, allowing

MI5 plenty of time to prevent the defections. The call was received by the Night Duty Officer and passed through to the case officers who, by chance, were still in the building conferring about the impending interrogation. We now know that the Security Service was caught ill-prepared by this development and bungled its last opportunity to prevent Maclean from reaching Moscow.

The White Paper noted that Maclean was supposed to have been on duty at the Foreign Office on Saturday morning, but had obtained permission to be absent. This ought to have alerted someone, but it did not. Nevertheless, it is manifestly untrue that 'Maclean's absence caused no remark until the following Monday morning'. He had actually been spotted two days earlier, on the docks.

Similarly, the White Paper implied that the French authorities had been 'asked to trace the whereabouts of the fugitives and if possible to intercept them'. This was not quite true. Nor was the claim that this request had been made 'immediately the flight was known'. In the event, the French were only asked to assist some days after MI5 knew the two men had disappeared, and only because word of the mysterious disappearance had reached the press. No formal statement relating to the disappearance was issued until 7 June, thirteen days after the event, a measure of MI5's willingness to conceal the affair from ministers and the public.

Another point which escaped attention was the implication that Burgess as well as Maclean had been under surveillance. The White Paper stated unequivocally that 'Maclean and Burgess made good their escape from this country when the security authorities were on their track'. Once again, this was another deliberate falsehood as Burgess did not come under suspicion until after his defection.

Mitchell's reservations about the Petrovs, as reflected in the White Paper's text, were completely unfounded, and by the time the White Paper had been drafted they had completed a combined testimony of 104 hours before Australia's Royal Commission on Espionage in Sydney. They had given an impressive performance, and Michael

Thwaites, the ASIO case officer who supervised the operation for two and a half years before Petrov made his final
move, has recently confirmed that 'the British described
Petrov as the most senior Soviet Intelligence defector since
1937'.[6] As the KGB's *resident* in Australia, Petrov had
an unrivalled grasp of his organisation's networks, and
because his wife had been a KGB cipher clerk she could
fill in the gaps in his knowledge. Her duties had required
her to read many of the coded messages sent by other
members of the Embassy's staff. Together they had provided damning evidence of Soviet espionage, and had
given useful information concerning Burgess and Maclean
and their post-war controller, Yuri Modin:

While he was in England Kislytsin never saw either Burgess or
Maclean; but he knew the Soviet official who was in contact with
Burgess and who used to return to the Embassy with muddy
clothes after his meetings, which evidently took place at some
obscure and dirty rendezvous. Kislytsin was in London from 1945
until 1948 when he was recalled to Moscow.[7]

Petrov also told of an emergency conference called in
Moscow by Colonel Raina, the KGB officer in command
of the entire operation, 'to discuss the possibility of getting
these important agents out of danger to the safety of Soviet
territory',[8] which suggested that the entire affair was not
a last-minute, chaotic dash for freedom, but a plan carefully
orchestrated by the KGB's top brass from Moscow with
enough time for signals to be exchanged between London
and Moscow. Apart from Goronwy Rees, Petrov had
been MI5's best source of information about Burgess and
Maclean, yet Mitchell chose to play it down.
  The White Paper's final paragraph was possibly the most
remarkable of all, considering the amount of completely
bogus material contained in the document. It rebuked
MPs, the press and the public for having criticised ministerial reticence on the subject:

Espionage is carried out in secret. Counter-espionage equally
depends for its success upon the maximum secrecy of its methods.

Nor is it desirable at any moment to let the other side know how much has been discovered or guess at what means have been used to discover it. Nor should they be allowed to know all the steps that have been taken to improve security. These considerations still apply and must be the basic criterion for judging what should or should not be published.[9]

This odd demand for continued secrecy was entirely inappropriate in the circumstances, in which ministers, as well as the public, were being hoodwinked on a gigantic scale to cover up massive ineptitude. The ploy to prevent further discussion, if this is what this passage was intended to be, failed, and a debate was held in the House of Commons the following month. It was during these proceedings that Macmillan, acting upon Mitchell's advice, gave his public statement exonerating Philby of any involvement in the Burgess and Maclean defections. In the context of the White Paper, which was billed as a report into 'the disappearance of two former Foreign Office officials', MI5's reluctance to disclose details or brief ministers was a disgrace. After all, Burgess and Maclean, and presumably the KGB, knew the full details. They also knew about MI5's precious methods, as they were to show the following year at a press conference when they complained about the bugging device in Maclean's home telephone! There was no intelligence advantage to be gained by pretending that Burgess had also been kept under observation. Its only purpose was to save some embarrassment and keep up the absurd pretence that MI5 operated within the law. Peter Wright's more recent admissions that he had undertaken 'hundreds' of illegal acts throws the White Paper's belaboured point into sharp, if not ridiculous, relief. There were plenty of pretexts on which Maclean could have been prevented from leaving the country if the Security Service had realised his intention to escape in time. The evidence described as 'insufficient' to justify an arrest was the series of VENONA decrypts which positively identified Maclean as the spy codenamed HOMER. Identical evidence had been used to extract a confession from Klaus Fuchs just two years earlier, and in that episode precautions had been taken to avoid disclosing the nature of the information which had incriminated him. There was no reason to suppose that a similar exercise might not work again. In fact, considering the fragile state of Maclean's mind, only months after having experienced a nervous breakdown, he would have presented an ideal subject for arrest. After all, the decision to make him submit to a hostile interrogation had already been taken.

The professed reluctance of the authorities to conduct a search of Maclean's house also reads a trifle thin, bearing in mind that 'deniable' surreptitious entries were not altogether a novelty, whatever the claims to the contrary. Indeed, how had the bugging devices in Maclean's home been placed in position, if not by subterfuge?

Re-reading the White Paper thirty years later, when so much of it can be seen to be patently false, one can detect two motives on the part of its author: firstly, the reluctance of MI5, like any bureaucratic organisation, to admit to a blunder. This is entirely understandable, although the nature of the deception practised can hardly be explained or justified in these terms. Of the three MI5 officers responsible for delivering the White Paper, only Roger Hollis, the Deputy Director-General, deserves to escape criticism entirely, as he had played no part in the original investigation and was therefore not familiar with the details.

The second issue raised concerns the obvious desire to suggest that Burgess and Maclean had acted without the intervention of a third conspirator, and somehow had tumbled to the fact that they (sic) were under surveillance. The author knew that Philby had been sacked from SIS because of his probable involvement and, thanks to Rees, that Blunt was a strong suspect as a further mole. Yet Mitchell clearly wished to suppress that aspect and only attributed the source of the long-term nature of the pair's espionage to a disparaged defector. To have given Petrov his proper due, and perhaps a few details of his true role as the KGB's *rezident*, would have boosted his credibility and that, evidently, was not considered desirable. Instead,

he remained a lowly Third Secretary with the obvious
implication that he could not be expected to have had
access to anything more important than office gossip, so his
testimony should be treated with caution. As for Evdokia
Petrov, a KGB officer in her own right, no mention whatsoever was made of her.

Why did Mitchell concoct a document filled with so high
a potential for damage? Once the face-saving material had
been edited out, there was still a perceptible intelligence
significance to the notorious twenty-eight paragraphs. He
had drafted the report, and this was one of the vital issues
the molehunters wished to put to him in 1982. He must
have known that the White Paper had all the worst characteristics of a booby-trapped unexploded bomb, waiting to
go off the moment anyone started to tinker with it. Certainly, undue haste could not be a reason for its intrinsically
flawed nature: Mitchell had had more than four years in
which to check the facts.

The occasions on which Security Service documents are
declassified and made available to the public are rare in
the extreme. Most official papers bearing any notation
from MI5 are 'weeded' by Whitehall before they ever get
released. The opportunities to challenge an MI5 officer
with direct evidence, from the public record, of incompetence or worse are rarer still. The Burgess and Maclean
White Paper represented a unique chance, and one apparently overlooked by previous molehunters. It was believed
by some, perhaps over-optimistically, that a confrontation
with Mitchell might elicit a confession, especially if his
inquisitor was armed with a comprehensive dossier, in the
guise of an apparently impartial history which highlighted
his own participation in MI5's catalogue of post-war disas-
ters. In addition, the book would disclose certain damaging
passages from the original two Symonds Reports, and give
enough information about Operation PETERS to prove
to Mitchell that there was a serious case for him to answer.
The molehunters were also keen to know why he had
sought early retirement, why he had belittled information
supplied by *bona-fide* defectors like Petrov and Golitsyn,

why he had scrapped MI5's continuing analysis of GCHQ's treasured VENONA material, and numerous other points.

There was little to be lost by such a venture, but the potential gain was inestimable. If Mitchell took the bait, he could make a private confession which would not be disclosed until after his death, thus avoiding the public humiliation endured by Anthony Blunt, Leo Long, Alister Watson, John Cairncross *et al*. This expedient would also neatly sidestep any direct involvement with the authorities. The incentive to make such an admission was judged to be considerable, especially if, as a professional, he knew that he was close to death and had outlived his usefulness. If, on the other hand, Mitchell had never been a mole, he might be prompted to give his views on DRAT and perhaps shed new light on the matter. Either way there was an argument for proceeding with the project which was code-named WORST CASE, with the book itself carrying the provisional title *A Matter of Trust*.

The major hitch encountered by this unorthodox mole-hunt was the Security Service itself, which, by late 1982, was under the leadership of Howard Smith's successor, John Jones. By that time MI5 had become aware of Peter Wright's intention to write a book but had gained the impression, erroneously as it turned out, that John Allen's tough letter had achieved the desired result, in much the same way that Jim Skardon had been discouraged from writing his memoirs. Jones' main preoccupation was a paperback edition of *Their Trade is Treachery*, in which Chapman Pincher had identified PETERS as Graham Mitchell and had virtually rewritten all the chapters of his book's first edition. Much of this inevitably concerned Lord Trend's report, because this was one area of weakness which had been so heavily criticised by the Prime Minister the previous year. Wright's name, of course, appears no-where, but Pincher did confirm that he had never met Arthur Martin who, thanks to the clues in the original text, had been challenged by MI5 with having been Pincher's accomplice: 'I can say in all honesty that I have never met or spoken with this man,'[10] stated Pincher, somewhat belatedly. On the central issue of whether or not Pincher believed Hollis to have been a spy, he said he was

not impressed by the final decision of Lord Trend virtually to exonerate Hollis or by the government's decision to accept that verdict as final. The evidence that there was a high-level 'mole' in MI5 not only during the war but up to the middle 1960s seems more compelling to me the more that I study it. Trend's decision that this evidence did not incriminate Hollis does not dispose of it. If Hollis was not guilty, then who was? It would seem to be unlikely now, because of the passage of time and people, that there will ever be a satisfactory answer to this question.[11]

This answer indicates a considerable shift from Pincher's original standpoint, especially on the substance of Lord Trend's conclusions, but there is still the inference that there was a mole at work in MI5 'up to the middle 1960s' which is a clear allusion to Hollis who retired in 1965. Yet none of the molehunters ever produced any evidence of leaks after the PETERS operation had been initiated in the first part of 1963.

Another key issue expanded by Pincher in his new edition was the claim about the elusive ELLI attributed to Gouzenko. Since the publication of the first edition, which Gouzenko must have found most gratifying, he had emerged from hiding and telephoned the author to recall how, in Moscow during the war, he

had a desk in what had been the ballroom of a pre-revolutionary mansion. There were about forty of us at a time working in three shifts. I sat next to my friend Lieut. Lubimov and one day he passed me a telegram from the Soviet Embassy in London. He said it came from a spy right inside British Counter-intelligence in England. The spy's codename in the secret radio traffic between London and Moscow was 'Elli'.[12]

A comparison with Pincher's first edition, when he had not yet spoken to Gouzenko but had only Wright's interpretation on which to rely, reveals a crucial difference in one key respect. In his first version Pincher had stated that 'Igor Gouzenko had alleged there was a major Soviet spy inside MI5'.[13] But he had not. Now, at the end of his life, Gouzenko had reverted back to his original allegation, that ELLI had been a mole inside 'British Counter-intelligence'. The variation between 'MI5' and 'British Counter-intelligence' is of exceptional importance because, at the time Gouzenko was referring to, SIS possessed a counter-intelligence section, designated Section V. Thus, Gouzenko's claim could have referred to SIS not MI5, and at least one self-confessed mole, Kim Philby, had worked there at the relevant period. By reporting Gouzenko's words accurately, Pincher had inadvertently undermined Wright's entire thesis about ELLI being specifically in MI5. This is of critical importance, because Philby has also confirmed that he borrowed SIS's Soviet Russia source books from the Registry in much the same way that Gouzenko alleged ELLI had. In other words, ELLI might well have been a known spy, such as Philby, and not an as yet undiscovered mole.

This explanation would appear to ignore the internal dichotomy within the Soviet Union's intelligence apparatus. Since Gouzenko had been a Red Army cipher clerk, handling GRU signals, surely ELLI must have been working for military intelligence? Philby, Blunt, Cairncross and Long were known to have been run by the KGB and its forerunner, the NKVD. This division would seem to rule out the proposition that ELLI could have been run by the KGB, yet both Gouzenko and Petrov testified that such cases were not uncommon because of successive attempts to streamline Moscow's overseas intelligence-gathering operations and to centralise the arrangements for their control. Petrov had actually participated in one such ill-fated scheme and recalled the episode for his ASIO debriefers:

The idea was to get together in one building, under the direct control of the Soviet Government, all departments and Sections dealing with secret foreign intelligence. . . . In other words, the Foreign Section of the NKVD was removed, and put in the same box as its only competitor, Military Intelligence.[14]

Gouzenko had also been caught up in one of the periodic reorganisations of the Soviet intelligence structure and had described a major shake-up that had occurred in March 1943 to coincide with the official dissolution of the Comintern. One result had been that 'Military Intelligence took over the old chores of the Comintern', so it was very likely that, for a time at least, a KGB agent might find himself under a GRU umbrella, or have his messages handled by a GRU communications channel.

In the event that ELLI truly existed, and there is no obvious reason for Gouzenko to have manufactured the claim in 1945, there is a strong probability that he was actually referring to Philby. The description of 'British Counter-intelligence' fitted Philby, and it was only much later that Gouzenko started talking about 'MI5', before switching back to 'British Counter-intelligence' when discussing the matter with Pincher in 1982. In short, Gouzenko was absolutely right to have insisted that there had been a spy in British counter-intelligence in 1942 or 1943. There had been at least two, for even Blunt could have been considered a possible candidate for ELLI. Certainly, he fulfilled the stated qualification of having been able to draw Soviet files out of MI5's Registry. For a short period, not long after Blunt's entry into the Security Service, Guy Liddell had assigned him the task of reviewing the effectiveness of the Watcher Service and recommending ways of selecting priority targets for surveillance so MI5's limited resources could be deployed to greatest effect. This study required Blunt to read the files of those placed under observation and included a selection of Soviet diplomatic files. Thus, ELLI might have been Blunt, but was most probably Philby.

It was while John Jones was wrestling with the implications of Pincher's new edition, and the author's evident determination to prove that the Security Service's advice to the Prime Minister had been misleading, that word reached MI5 of the independent, freelance plan to confront Mitchell with what amounted to a damning record of his post-war career.

That such a document had been compiled was highly secret, but, because it was intended for eventual publication, I had officially informed the secretary of the Ministry of Defence's D Notice Committee of its existence in a letter dated 27 September. Ten days later Rear-Admiral W. N. Ash acknowledged having been notified and agreed to scrutinise it. In fact, he was never to do so because, in the meantime, the Security Service had acquired its own copy.

That Jones had obtained an illicit photocopy of *A Matter of Trust* became clear on 12 October 1982, when James Nursaw, the Home Office's Principal Legal Adviser, applied to Mr Justice Henry Russell in the High Court for an *ex parte* injunction preventing publication of the manuscript. Acting on behalf of the Attorney-General, Sir Michael Havers, Nursaw requested the interim injunction on the grounds that *A Matter of Trust* breached 'a duty of confidentiality owed to the Crown'. The judge heard the application in chambers and agreed to issue a court order the following afternoon on condition that Nursaw lodged an affidavit with the court confirming the substance of the application. In the affidavit, which is the only document on the public record concerning these proceedings, it was stated that the book 'contains previously unpublished information classified as "secret" and identifies, *inter alios*, present members of the Security Service who have not previously been identified in any publication'. It was also confirmed that,

there are many references in the manuscript to incidents, operations and investigations which are said to have taken place since the end of the Second World War which can only have been related . . . by past (or present) members of the Security Service. Some of these references relate to incidents, operations, investigations, and other matters which have not been made public.

The fact that a High Court order had been applied for and granted did not become known until the following day, when the Deputy Treasury Solicitor, John Bailey, attempted to serve it.

Intensive negotiations followed which, by agreement, were confidential, although there was no secrecy concerning the participation of those involved representing the Plaintiff, who were the Security Service's Legal Adviser, the Treasury Solicitor (Sir) Michael Kerry, and his deputy, John Bailey. At the conclusion of the series of meetings held, a further application to the High Court was made on 19 November 1982 at which another judge, Sir Harry Woolf, discharged the order made the previous month and granted a consent order allowing the publication of a sanitised version of *A Matter of Trust*. This was released soon afterwards, on 10 December, but it failed to achieve its principal objective: a conclusion to the molehunts.

Numerous deletions had been made to the original text including, ironically, the name of Peter Wright, whose identity, the Security Service insisted, was still a secret. When informed that Wright proposed to publish his own account of MI5's molehunts, the Treasury Solicitor expressed astonishment and insisted that such an eventuality was impossible. After further debate it was agreed that Wright should only be referred to as 'Peter W' in the authorised version of *A Matter of Trust*.

Exactly how much Graham Mitchell knew about these developments is unknown. He had certainly recognised himself as the 'Peters' of *Their Trade is Treachery* and had acknowledged that to Chapman Pincher, who confirmed having received a letter from him in his paperback edition. Mitchell had also been in touch with me since 14 January 1982, but he was not to be confronted with extracts from *A Matter of Trust* until the end of the year, by which time he had moved from Chobham Common to Sherrington, near Newport Pagnell. On that occasion he expressed surprise at the very comprehensive nature of the evidence against him and confirmed the authenticity of certain events which demonstrated that the dossier was 'an inside job'. Beyond that, he declined to comment, pleading ill-health.

In spite of the cuts that had been made, the overwhelming majority of which concerned issues not directly related to Operation PETERS, *A Matter of Trust* was intended to convey my opinion that both Hollis and Mitchell had been suspected of having been moles, but of the two it was Hollis who was innocent. According to the lawyer who read the book before publication to advise on any defamatory material contained in it, 'The reader is left with the clear impression that Mitchell was both suspected of being and was a spy for the Russians. . . . In my view it would be unrealistic not to regard a libel action by Mitchell as a real risk.' Accordingly, half a million pounds' worth of libel insurance was bought from Lloyds as a precaution. Because Mitchell had been given the opportunity to read the allegations before publication he had every chance to prevent its release, or even bring a legal action afterwards, claiming damages. In the event he did neither, and the libel insurance was never used. This should not necessarily be interpreted as any kind of incriminating admission, as he may have had various reasons for wishing to forget the entire affair, but his failure to act inevitably led to increased speculation. There is a short but impressive list of MI5 officers who have issued, or threatened to issue, writs for libel. Sir Dick White achieved a large cheque for charity when a newspaper mixed him up with Dick Ellis, a self-confessed traitor who had sold SIS's secrets to the Nazis before the war. Arthur Martin and Anthony Simkins were also to sue after defamatory comments, of a much less serious nature, had been published. Both took immediate action and obtained public apologies, costs and 'substantial' damages. Even Anthony Blunt, confused with a wartime officer who used the same *nom de guerre* by the *Sunday Telegraph*, extracted a retraction. In contrast, Mitchell did nothing.

Concern about the risk of libel did, however, inhibit comment on the role played by Lord Rothschild in securing Flora Solomon's testimony against Philby. Notwithstanding Lord Rothschild's creditable intervention, Pincher who, as we have seen, had had some dealings with him, decided against elaborating on his anonymous role in *Their Trade is Treachery's* paperback. Once again, with calculated circumspection, Rothschild is simply referred to as 'another visitor from England'.[15] But in *A Matter of Trust* Flora Solomon and Dick White were named and Lord Rothschild was discreetly referred to as 'a former wartime MI5 officer'. He had 'immediately recognised the gravity of her evidence and introduced her to Dick White, the Chief of MI6. Mrs Solomon provided damning testimony against Philby and White decided that the evidence should be given to his former colleagues in MI5.'[16] The publicity surrounding the Attorney-General's unprecedented move against *A Matter of Trust*, and then its sudden release, was watched with interest by Pincher, who at this time was still exchanging letters with Wright. In one dated 27 January 1983, Pincher mentioned having spent New Year's Day shooting with Sir Michael Havers. Pincher suggested that, 'over a cup of soup on a pheasant shoot', they had talked about the recent court case and they had speculated about the identity of one former MI5 officer thought to have been involved. In fact, Pincher's conjecture on that occasion was somewhat off the mark. Exactly how long Pincher and Wright remained in touch is not known, but it is evident that there were increasingly acrimonious arguments about Wright's half-share of the royalties to their book, which was supposed to be paid by the publishers straight into his dummy company. Pincher explained that the money was coming from Sidgwick & Jackson, not him, and once wrote, 'I've never had anything to do with the payments save for expediting them. Under the arrangement made by our friend everything has to be split 50–50 otherwise there would be insuperable tax problems.'[17]

In a letter dated 3 March 1983, Pincher suggested a further joint project entitled *The Atlantic Connection*, which he proposed to sell to *Reader's Digest* in New York, but the idea fell through and Pincher undertook to burn their correspondence.

I told Wright that I would destroy his letters because I thought it was too risky to keep them. Some were too hot to include in my book. However, after the book came out, I kept most of his other letters and still have them today. They would be very embarrassing for him if I made them public but I am not going to indulge in the same tactics. . . .[18]

The Wright – Pincher collaboration seems to have ended sometime in 1984 when Wright demanded a half of the profits from Pincher's new paperback, *Too Secret Too Long*. Pincher had refused, and has said that, 'Wright could not expect to be paid twice for the same material.'[19] Pincher insists that, 'Wright had no involvement in my 1984 book *Too Secret Too Long* which was about the need for external supervision of the secret services and was written after our relationship ceased.'[20] Wright obviously felt aggrieved at Pincher's refusal to pay up and also may have disapproved of his co-author's repeated view that there was no need for an enquiry into the Hollis affair, but that there was for some form of oversight committee to keep an eye on MI5. Certainly, these sentiments were not shared by Wright, whose stated aim had been the appointment of an independent body to take a second look at the molehunts.

A Matter of Trust's main achievement was to put into context the allegations made about various suspected moles who were still alive, including Jenifer Hart, Sir Dennis Proctor, Alister Watson and Leo Long. This was done with the help of Michael Straight, Anthony Blunt and John Cairncross, who had assisted the project by meeting me. In the months to follow Straight and Flora Solomon were to write books describing their roles, and Jenifer Hart was to appear in a BBC television interview in July 1983.

The only action for defamation to result from *A Matter of Trust*, albeit indirectly, was an extraordinary story, printed in the *Sunday Telegraph* on 23 January 1983 and written by the paper's Crime Correspondent Christopher House under the headline 'Blunt File Reopened'. Arthur Martin was not named by the newspaper, but two further articles, including one on 31 January entitled 'House of Ex-Agent Raided', alleged that a house in Chelsea belonging to a 'former MI5 agent who is still alive and in his sixties'[21] and had played a role in the extraction of Blunt's confession, had been searched and papers had been seized. Martin and Wright were the only two officers who fitted the description in relation to Blunt, but Wright had been in Tasmania for the past six years. Martin himself owned a flat in Lyall Mews West and issued a writ for libel claiming that, despite the absence of his name, the paper clearly meant him. The story was a complete fabrication, and Martin received a large cash award, part of which he used to throw a party.

Another consequence of *A Matter of Trust*'s publication was the interest of a Granada Television programme in making a documentary recording the history of the mole-hunts of the 1960s and 1970s. Two producers from the *World in Action* team, John Ware and Paul Greengrass, were assigned to the project and the latter flew to Tasmania to meet Wright for a background briefing. Although Wright was willing to supply information, he was not prepared to be interviewed on film, and Greengrass returned to London with Wright's promise to give Granada's invitation further consideration. At a subsequent meeting it was agreed that Granada would guarantee to protect Wright's pension and indemnify his legal costs if any action was taken against him. Even then, he hesitated, but on Easter Sunday 1983 a middle-ranking MI5 officer slipped an anonymous letter through the letterbox of the KGB *rezident* in London and set in motion a chain of events that was to cause Wright to appear in a television interview, to collaborate on a new book with Paul Greengrass, and to transform the Hollis affair into the Peter Wright affair.

9

THE WRIGHT AFFAIR

Just after midnight on Easter Sunday Michael Bettaney walked up to the front door of 42 Holland Park and delivered a letter addressed to Arkadi Vasilyevich Gouk, a Second Secretary at the Soviet Embassy. Bettaney's letter, which was unsigned, gave details of the recent expulsions of three Soviet diplomats named Colonel Gennadcy Primakov, Igor Titov and Sergei Ivanov. It was an attempt to establish that the anonymous author was exactly what he claimed to be: a member of MI5's K Branch, the Soviet counter-espionage division.

Bettaney was then thirty-three years old and had been transferred into the Security Service's elite K Branch the previous December. His work in MI5 had given him access to an assessment of the Soviet order-of-battle in Britain, and in particular to one document which had identified Gouk as the ranking KGB officer in London. Bettaney's proposition was simple: he wished to supply Gouk with top-secret information from inside MI5. As to his reasons, Bettaney stated that he was ideologically motivated, having become disenchanted with the work he was obliged to undertake. Some uncomfortable experiences during a two-year tour of operational duty in Belfast had undermined his commitment to MI5. Bettaney's letter gave precise instructions as to how Gouk should keep in contact with him. His acceptance of the offer should be indicated by the insertion of a coloured drawing-pin into a particular wooden banister on a staircase in Piccadilly underground station within three weeks.

Thereafter, on 7 May, Bettaney said he would tape a roll of film to the top of the lavatory cistern in the Academy 1 cinema's gent's toilets in Oxford Street. A piece of blue tape inside a nearby telephone box would be the signal to indicate that the film had been deposited.

Much to Bettaney's surprise Gouk failed to respond, so he made a second approach at midnight on Sunday, 12 June. This time Bettaney enclosed a copy of K Branch's most up-to-date assessment of the Soviet order-of-battle in London, together with a new set of signals and dead-letter drops, but there was still no response from the Soviet. Finally, in desperation, Bettaney made one last bid on 10 July suggesting that he would call Gouk at home early the following Friday morning. The form of words used by Gouk would indicate whether he intended to take up Bettaney's offer. When Bettaney telephoned, Gouk failed to answer. Frustrated, Bettaney decided to take his annual leave in Vienna and try afresh at the Soviet Embassy there.

Bettaney had been mystified by Gouk's failure to react and never guessed the reason was that the *rezident*'s deputy, Oleg Gordievsky, had been working as an agent for SIS for the past twelve years. Gordievsky had been recruited back in 1971, when he had been working under press attaché cover in Copenhagen. Since that time, Gordievsky had been in constant contact with SIS. When Gouk confided Bettaney's proposal to his deputy, Gordievsky had reported the matter to his SIS case officer and had advised the *rezident* that the anonymous letters were a blatant provocation designed to entrap the KGB officer in a compromising situation. Gouk had also consulted Moscow, but the answer had been the same: don't risk being jeopardised by such an obvious *agent provocateur*. Gouk took the advice.

Following Gordievsky's tip, SIS embarked on a highly secret molehunt to trace the would-be spy in MI5 and, after a search lasting less than a month, Bettaney was identified as Gouk's anonymous informant. He was placed

under discreet surveillance and was arrested on the first
day of his leave, Friday, 16 September, by Detective
Superintendent Peter Westcott. With a certain flavour of
Burgess and Maclean faintly perceptible, he had booked
a flight to Austria for the following Monday. When his
house at 5 Victoria Road, Coulsdon, was searched, it was
found to be packed with secret documents purloined from
K Branch's offices in Gower Street. Apparently, Bettaney
had taken the chance offered to him while alone, when
standing in as Night Duty Officer, to photograph sensitive
papers and other classified material he thought would
interest the KGB. When challenged by the Special Branch
officers who had detained him, Bettaney told them of
the many hiding-places in his house where secret papers,
exposed films and his manuscript notes, written from memory, were concealed. He then made a full confession and
admitted that he had offered himself to the Russians for
political motives. He was completely unrepentant.

Bettaney had no idea of Gordievsky's dual role, a fact
that was to remain a closely guarded secret until September
1985, when the KGB officer was finally obliged to make
good his escape and defect.

Bettaney had not completed the entry procedure and the
three-year probationary period required by the Security
Service until September 1978, by which time Wright had
moved to Australia. So they never served together, but
the case was to have a profound effect on Wright. Bettaney
had not sprung from the privileged background common
to so many of the ideological converts of the 1930s. He
had come from a working-class home, had attended state
schools and had been recommended for recruitment while
completing his none-too-distinguished education at Pem-
broke College, Oxford, where he had gained a second in
English. He had undergone the normal routine of two
preliminary interviews, followed by two Personnel Branch
interviews, and the Positive Vetting procedure which demanded no fewer than eight referees. His last hurdle had
been the final appointments board, chaired by Michael
Hanley, which had consisted of Ronald Symonds and

two other MI5 Directors. Having passed all these tests in September 1975, Bettaney had attended a brief induction course and joined F Branch to spend two months learning about the CPGB and a little of MI5's history. This was followed by the usual five-month series of lectures at the Security Service training-centre in Berkeley Street, Mayfair. In June 1976, in spite of his expressed reluctance, he had been posted to Northern Ireland, where he had been slightly injured in a car-bomb attack. On another occasion he had been obliged to hide while his informant was knee-capped by the Provisional IRA in the room next door. He had returned to London in September 1978 for a two-year posting to MI5's new counter-terrorism section studying German, French and Italian extremist groups. He then did a spell running a course in counter-terrorism at the training-centre before moving to K Branch at the end of December 1982. In short, he was an example of the classic, new breed of career intelligence officer that was supposed to supplant the last of the 'Malaya Mafia' and the wartime intake which, some believed, had handicapped the performance of the post-war Security Service. Wright was one of those who held this view and, in theory at least, personnel in the Bettaney mould, from humble origins and with the benefit of stringent background checks, would represent obstacles to those contemplating penetration.

In reality, the position was quite different. Bettaney had a record of low intellectual and academic achievement, but he was enthusiastic about joining MI5. This last qualification was shared by few of his contemporaries. The high-flyers had received better offers of employment with good prospects of satisfying their ambitions. All the Security Service could deliver was an appallingly tedious future that, as likely as not, would be spent desk-bound, in an extraordinarily rigid, disciplined environment, shuffling files. If the reward for three years of reading turgid Leftist propaganda merited such devotion, more of Bettaney's university friends might have been tempted to join, but the job was invariably a big disappointment to most and the turnover of staff with three years' experience was testimony to the attrition rate of boredom. In this unique atmosphere of low achievement, Bettaney was promoted into K Branch and passed two PV enquiries, which are routinely conducted every five years. What makes this all the more remarkable was Bettaney's criminal conviction in 1970 for deception (using an invalid railway ticket), in October 1982 for being drunk and, again the very next week, for fare dodging when travelling in to Victoria to work. Only two of these convictions were known to MI5's Personnel Branch. The third would probably have been spotted when Bettaney was due for his next scheduled PV, in January 1986, but the fact remains that someone with a confirmed drinking problem, under treatment by MI5's office doctor for an alcohol dependency requiring a bottle of whisky a day, should never have been considered a candidate for duty in K Branch.

If this were not enough, Bettaney had a reputation for boorish, drunken behaviour and had been the subject of several complaints by his colleagues. He had even been heard to boast at office parties that he had switched sides. 'Come and see me in my dacha when I retire,'[1] he used to say. Bettaney only received mild reprimands for what was seen as nothing more serious than eccentricity displayed by a lonely, insular young man, who 'was noted for a somewhat bizarre sense of humour'.

This criticism was to be endorsed by the Security Commission which took evidence from the Director-General, Sir John Jones, and found it to be unjustifiably complacent. The Commission, headed by Lord Bridge, consisted of Sir Michael Palliser, the former head of the Diplomatic Service, Air Chief Marshal Sir Alastair Steedman, and Lord Allen of Abbeydale (formerly Sir Philip Allen). Of the four, only Lord Allen had any direct, supervisory experience of MI5. Between 1966 and 1972 he had been Permanent Under-Secretary at the Home Office and had there liaised directly with the then Director-General, Sir Martin Furnival Jones, who had once given evidence, *incognito*, to the Franks Committee on the Official Secrets Act. In contrast, John Lewis Jones came from much the same kind of background as Bettaney (he was the son of a Welsh miner) and gave a very poor performance under cross-examination, as is clear from the portion of the Commission's Report eventually made public in May 1985. It highlighted a series of managerial shortcomings within MI5 and numerous in-built, structural defects, as well as a staggering lack of physical security precautions. The Commission only sat on eighteen occasions ('in most cases for full days'[2]) and in that time heard sixty witnesses. Among them were two retired MI5 officers, who would only agree to appear on condition that their identities were not disclosed to the Security Service. Considering the speed with which the Commission completed its task, one is tempted to speculate what it might have said if more time had been available to delve a little deeper, but its brief had been strictly limited to the narrow issues raised by Bettaney's treachery.

The Security Commission put forward a cover story (or maybe was deceived into accepting one) in order to conceal Gordievsky's involvement. A plausible explanation had to be given for MI5's success in spotting Bettaney before he had been able to inflict lasting damage, without implicating Gordievsky who, following Gouk's expulsion, had been promoted to the post of KGB *rezident* in London. Accordingly, an 'operational failure', of the kind MI5 was well familiar with, was manufactured. The Commission related how,

In early 1983 the Security Service had been alerted by an apparent operational failure to the possibility that there might have been a leak of information concerning a counter-espionage matter. In early July 1983 suspicions that Bettaney might have been responsible for the leak were raised by his asking questions about sensitive matters, completely unrelated to his work, of colleagues who were aware of the apparent operational failure.[3]

The convenient cover of vigilant colleagues who had in the past neglected to mention instances of Bettaney's drunken behaviour, but had initiated a molehunt by reporting him

'asking questions', neatly concealed Gordievsky's tip relayed by SIS.

The final Report singled Jones out for much of the
adverse comment, and his career, which had taken in the
successive posts of Security Liaison Officer Hong Kong,
Assistant Director F Branch, Head of Registry and Director A Branch, ended, somewhat ignominiously, with his
retirement later the same year. Instead of being replaced
by Jones' Deputy Director-General, the Prime Minister
appointed her own nominee and trouble-shooter, Sir Antony Duff.

From his remote vantage-point in southern Tasmania,
Wright also professed to be deeply shocked by the attitudes
articulated by MI5's defenders. Among them, of course,
was his own co-author, Chapman Pincher, who had remarked in *Their Trade is Treachery*:

I can find no evidence of the presence of spies at any high level
in the security services, but there may be a case for an inquiry
by some group which could reassure the community that 'moles'
no longer exist at any level.[4]

Wright may also have recalled Pincher's memorable conclusion that, 'To anyone who has the genuine interests of
MI5 and the Secret Service at heart, as I hope I have,
there are basic objections to an outside inquiry of any
kind.'[5]

On 16 April 1984 Bettaney was convicted of ten offences
against the Official Secrets Acts and was sentenced to a
total of twenty-three years' imprisonment, to be served as
a Category A prisoner, but kept in isolation from other
inmates at Coldingley Prison, near Woking in Surrey. The
few details of the case revealed to the public during the
trial, which was held largely *in camera* at the Old Bailey,
so alarmed Wright that he was stirred into giving his
consent to a filmed interview with Paul Greengrass of
Granada Television.

Wright's resolution to 'go public', having done so much
to prevent his role as Pincher's co-author from being

discovered, may have been made a little easier by a similar decision made by two other, recently resigned members of MI5. The first clue that the Security Service was still far from leakproof came in a three-part feature on MI5 published in the *Guardian* immediately after Bettaney's conviction. As the Security Commission commented,

although they contain much distortion and inaccuracy [they] display a sufficient degree of inside knowledge of the Security Service's organisation and operations as to found an almost irresistible inference that Bettaney himself must have been the ultimate source of much of the information on which the authors of the article relied.[6]

The Commission believed that because some of the evidence given at the trial *in camera* had been leaked to newspapers, the same source must have been used as a conduit for Bettaney to supply embarrassing information. Of particular concern were the source codenames AZURE, CINNAMON and STILL LIFE, the internal cryptonyms used for intelligence derived from three different, and highly sensitive, types of technical surveillance. The *Guardian* articles caused much concern and highlighted the importance of isolating Bettaney from anyone with access to the outside world, but in fact the information had not come from either him or his legal advisers, as MI5 suspected.

One person who attended the sessions of the trial open to the public was Bettaney's former secretary, Miranda Ingram. She heard the Lord Chief Justice, Lord Lane, describe Bettaney as 'puerile and self-opinionated' and wrote an article in his defence in *New Society*. In it she emphasised the political nature of Bettaney's crime and what she believed might have been a motivating factor for his treachery:

In the prevailing right-wing atmosphere an officer who dissents from the official line does not feel encouraged to voice his concern. He feels that to do so would be futile, or, unfortunately, that it would be detrimental to his career.[7]

Miranda Ingram's article earned her a sharp rebuke from
her former employers, but no further, formal action was
taken against her. Nor was anything done when Cathy
Massiter, who had previously served in F Branch, wrote a
letter to *New Society* in her support:

It seems particularly necessary to recognise that Michael Bettaney
is not some kind of exceptional anomaly who got in because of
the failure of recruitment/vetting procedures, but is to a large
extent a product of the security service itself. Though his reactions
were extreme, the conflicts and dissatisfactions which provoked
them are far from rare.[8]

Once again the Security Service recommended against
action being taken against Cathy Massiter.

Armed with these two precedents, and a subsequent
television interview with Massiter in March 1985, provoca-
tively entitled *MI5's Official Secrets*, on the subject of F
Branch's surveillance of what were deemed to be potential
subversives, Wright took the plunge. His hour-long interview was broadcast on 16 July 1984, with only one slight
amendment requested by the Independent Broadcasting
Authority on security grounds: the number on the front
door of the safe-house in South Audley Street where Hollis
and Mitchell had been interrogated was altered. The *World
in Action* production team had anticipated some kind of
government intervention to stop the transmission but, contrary to expectations, none was forthcoming. In fact, the
Security Service had received advance notice of the programme, but had opted to adopt a softly-softly approach.
Had it been realised that Paul Greengrass was the persuasive spirit behind Granada's film, or that he had entered
into a contractual arrangement with the *Observer*, the
outcome might have been different. John Jones expressed
the view that the mid-summer broadcast would be easily
overshadowed by the Security Commission and any allegations linked to Bettaney could be answered by its Report.

Wright's television appearance concentrated on the allegations against Hollis, and the retired molehunter stated

that 'intelligence-wise, it was ninety-nine per cent certain' that Hollis was guilty. When pressed about the very circumstantial nature of the evidence, Wright agreed that 'smoking gun evidence' was extremely rare in such cases. He confirmed that Ronald Symonds' enquiries had been deliberately obstructed by Hollis because 'he was anxious that Mitchell should not be found innocent because he was the next suspect', and that John Day 'had come to the conclusion that Hollis was a spy'. Wright described the overwhelming evidence of long-term Soviet penetration of the Security Service and outlined the clues he had found in the testimony of Gouzenko, Volkov, Golitsyn and GCHQ's secret VENONA source. Much of the material was familiar to readers of *Their Trade is Treachery* and *A Matter of Trust*, but it was the fact that Wright was giving a first-hand account of these events that attracted so much attention and criticism. *The Times* quoted 'one very senior counter-intelligence officer' as saying: 'I am not a vindictive person but this is a serious crime. I think that serious crimes ought to be prosecuted.' The film, spiced by the revelation that thirty-one left-wing Labour MPs had been identified as covert supporters of the CPGB after Operation PARTY PIECE in 1955, caused a furore.

The response to Wright's disclosures was immediate. Alister Watson's stepson condemned him for having alleged that Watson had been 'an even more dangerous spy than Philby', and Sir William Hayter protested that his friend Sir Dennis Proctor had never made a 'partial confession' to anything. Charles Elton pointed out that Hollis had been the Director-General at the time when the Portland spy ring had been smashed and insisted that suspicions were 'unlikely to fester in the minds of members of a service which can boast of repeated triumphs against Communist intelligence services during the last thirty years'. Elton's former colleague in D Branch, Arthur Martin, was not so sure and stated that, 'it was the evidence of continued penetration of the service after Blunt retired in 1945 which carried complete conviction among those working on the case'. The text of his important contribution is reproduced in full in Appendix 2.

Further fuel was added to the controversy when Wright produced a closely typed, 150–page dossier entitled *The Security of the United Kingdom against the Assault of the Russian Intelligence Service*, and announced that he wished to give evidence to the Security Commission:

I decided in the end that I had to speak out because the service had lost its way. It has been deeply compromised by Soviet penetration. I know that, because I spent most of my life investigating it. Even now the service has failed to protect itself adequately against future penetration, and the Bettaney case has shown just how easy it is . . .

I want to go before the Security Commission or any other suitable form of enquiry to argue my case, and I am not going to give up until they listen to me.[9]

I want to give evidence to the Security Commission. I know they are considering the Bettaney case at present and what I have in my dossier may help them in their task. I have spent many years trying to get this looked into. I did this while I was in the service and since. Now I am prepared to go public.[10]

Wright's only problem with giving evidence to the Commission was his understandable reluctance to risk arrest and prosecution by returning to London to appear in person. Certainly, no guarantee of immunity appeared likely to be given, and whenever the idea was canvassed in high political circles, it was turned down. Instead, he sent a copy of his memorandum to Sir Anthony Kershaw, the distinguished and much respected chairman of the all-party Commons Select Committee on Foreign Affairs.

The whole reason why I am doing this – which is thoroughly illegal – is to get the dossier to people who will listen. I don't mind if they cut up rough and prosecute me. I am willing to argue my case against any judge they care to produce.[11]

Sir Anthony read it over the last weekend in July and, having found it 'alarming reading',[12] handed it over the following Monday to the Cabinet Secretary, Sir Robert Armstrong.

Wright's memorandum consisted largely of a catalogue of the molehunts of the 1950s and 1960s, and listed all those who had been investigated. As the names quickly became known, attention focused on seven in particular: Sir Edward Playfair, a former Permanent Under-Secretary of the Ministry of Defence; the writers John Lehmann and Cedric Belfrage; Andrew King, a retired SIS officer; James MacGibbon, the publisher; the late Sir George Clutton, a former ambassador and Foreign Office adviser to SIS; and Sir Stuart Hampshire. All except Belfrage, who had worked for British Security Co-ordination in New York during the war but had moved to Mexico after having been named as the organiser of a Communist cell during the McCarthy hearings, had been confronted with the allegations against them and had been interrogated by MI5. Sir Edward Playfair, a close friend of both Burgess and Blunt, insisted that he had never been a spy although he did remember having been interviewed by MI5 because he 'had known a lot of Communists'.[13] The Old Etonian, John Lehmann, was one, but he had resisted the approach made to him by a Soviet agent in Vienna in 1934 and had given Jim Skardon a detailed account of the incident. 'I am surprised this should burst out now,'[14] he said.

James MacGibbon, whose publishing partnership with Robert Kee had bought the rights to Kim Philby's *My Silent War*, was another who recalled that he had been questioned three times by MI5: 'I never made any secret of the fact that I was in the Communist Party. That doesn't make me a spy. It would have been a disgrace not to have been in the mid-Thirties.'[15] Andrew King was in a similar position. He had joined SIS before the war and had declared his previous membership of the CPGB while an undergraduate at Cambridge. Unfortunately, the record of this had been lost and he was obliged to undergo several interrogations shortly before his retirement in 1967.

Of particular interest was Sir Stuart Hampshire, the Oxford academic who had been unjustifiably denounced by Goronwy Rees and Anthony Blunt. In 1966 he had undertaken a very secret review of GCHQ's operations so the Cabinet Office could reassure the Prime Minister, Harold Wilson, that the government was getting a worthwhile return on its expensive investment. Wright claimed that MI5 had not been consulted before Hampshire had been selected to look at GCHQ, and maintained he had been a security risk for that reason. Hampshire firmly rejected the allegation, but confirmed having been interviewed by MI5. He also spoke of an encounter with Burgess:

He may have said something about working for peace, but I'm pretty sure he didn't mention the Comintern. I thought it was just Guy going on. It was only in retrospect that I thought it might have been something more sinister. At the time, it was impossible to think that Guy might have been a spy; he was always drunk. I always took it that Anthony Blunt could not have been dangerous because he was an overt Marxist. The idea that one might have gone round to MI5 years later is absurd.[16]

The names in Wright's memorandum were those who had already undergone investigation of one kind or another, but it was the author's contention that in fact only a dozen or so individuals had been positively identified as moles. It was his belief that up to 200 remained to be discovered. Wright pinned all his hopes on Sir Anthony Kershaw, whose initial reactions must have seemed encouraging. He had already gone on the record stating his opposition to Wright's arrest: 'I would disagree with Mr Wright's arrest as soon as he lands. It is clear that a breach of the law has occurred. One must balance that with the advantage to the public if these rumours are able to be scotched.'[17] On Wright himself, Sir Anthony said, 'My impression is that Wright is a very expert person and trustworthy. He is working from memory rather than documents by and large. What he says in the first quarter of his book stands up very well.'[18]

Sir Anthony recognised, as soon as he received Wright's document, that it would 'have to be evaluated not just by the Prime Minister, but by those with the relevant knowledge'.[19] At one moment it was even being suggested that a Royal Commission headed by someone of the stature of Lord Franks would be appointed to review matters, but the idea was stillborn. Instead, it was not until February 1985 that it emerged that the Foreign Affairs Select Committee had shelved Wright's paper and Sir Anthony Kershaw had been persuaded that no useful purpose would be served by setting up a body to re-examine what had now become Wright's charges against Hollis: 'It cannot be proved and it cannot be disproved but I don't think there is any point in a further enquiry.'[20]

Wright, for one, was not surprised by this announcement. In fact, he had anticipated it by collaborating with Paul Greengrass on an expanded manuscript entitled *The Spycatcher*.

As soon as news reached London, via the newspapers in February 1986, that Wright had completed a book, the Attorney-General instructed a local firm in Sydney to threaten him with an injunction. However, it soon became clear that Wright had already signed a publishing contract with William Heinemann's Australian subsidiary. John Bailey, who had by now succeeded Sir Michael Kerry as Treasury Solicitor, initially tried to bring pressure to bear on the parent company in London, until it was realised that the Australian subsidiary was independent. A restraining order issued in the High Court in London would be completely worthless in Sydney. He was, therefore, forced to carry out his threat and apply for a temporary court order in the jurisdiction of New South Wales. With the help of a twenty-page affidavit signed by the Cabinet Secretary, the injunction was granted, pending a full trial. Having achieved this, no corresponding order was sought in London because neither Bailey nor MI5 had any evidence of an intention to release any of Wright's book in London.

Sir Robert Armstrong's first affidavit was filed in court before he had even read the manuscript of *The Spycatcher*, but it was a comprehensive document anyway, drawn up by MI5's Legal Adviser, offering an outline of Wright's career in the Security Service and stressing that the principle of confidentiality should be upheld to deter others from breaking their obligations, and to maintain the organisation's ability to protect its information. In short, an injunction was essential if MI5 was to continue to do its job properly and be entrusted with the secrets of Allied services. Unless Wright was stopped, the Americans might not share their information with MI5.

Bailey's tactics were destined to fail because of the lack of an injunction in London, and, in spite of the enforcement of the order in Australia, various parts of the manuscript were leaked to the *Observer* in London and published on 22 June. The items had nothing to do with Wright's molehunts, but concerned peripheral matters that had clearly been selected for their embarrassment value: how the diplomatic missions of friendly nations had been bugged; how Lancaster House, the venue for so many international negotiations over the years, had been wired for sound; how President Nasser had been the victim of a British assassination plot. These, according to the *Observer*'s correspondent, David Leigh, were among 'the biggest potential unresolved post-war MI5 scandals' to be found in Wright's manuscript. This astonishing development took MI5 completely by surprise. How had Leigh 'obtained details of what is disclosed in the manuscript', which, after all, was the subject of a temporary injunction in Australia that, of course, was not enforceable in England?

On this occasion the foul-up had happened because MI5 had paid insufficient attention to the movements of four journalists in particular. Two of them were John Ware and Paul Greengrass, the *World in Action* producers who had compiled the television documentary on Wright, and who had also contributed to the *Observer*'s follow-up article which had appeared the next Sunday, 22 July 1984. The other two credited with the 'special report' which, obviously, had been written with Wright's help and had contained a strong flavour of both *Inside Story* and *Their Trade is Treachery*, were Nick Davies, who had compiled the *Guardian*'s controversial reports on the Bettaney trial and had now moved to the *Observer*, and David Leigh, the paper's veteran spy-watcher. Thus Wright's ghost-writer, Paul Greengrass, had an established professional connection with Leigh. Both of their names had appeared at the top of the Wright follow-up in the *Observer*, alongside Ware and Davies. In other words, instead of fighting a legal action in Australia on the narrow issue of what did and did not constitute a binding, contractual obligation of confidentiality, the Attorney-General found himself taking on much wider issues, packed with political implications that were far from trivial. Who could predict what Wright might say in court? Furthermore, the Defence had already shown it had what amounted to an open line to Fleet Street. If the *Observer*'s story was anything to go by, the Defence would concentrate on Wright's considerable embarrassment factor to force the Attorney-General to back down. Heinemann's choice of Malcolm Turnbull to lead its Defence constituted a further indication of the line to be adopted. He, too, had links with Fleet Street, having worked in London for the *Sunday Times*.

Naturally, the British government had little desire to be put in the awkward position of attempting (and perhaps publicly failing) to suppress politically damaging material. Its chosen battleground was the technical one of Wright's duties to his former employers. The fact that the employer had been the British Security Service was supposed to be incidental. The underlying, fundamental issue at stake would have been identical if Wright had been employed by British Rail. Naturally, the Defence was equally anxious to prevent MI5's involvement from becoming a side issue and allegations of law-breaking could transform the case into one about whistle-blowing. In these circumstances, there was every chance that the issue of contractual obligations would be obscured by an individual's right to call attention, in the public interest, to serious wrong-doing. If this happened, the Attorney-General anticipated a bizarre media circus in which the British national interest would be thrashed out in public and decided by an Australian judge.

The Plaintiff's fears were to be fully justified. The *Observer*'s revelations in June 1986 were credited to David Leigh, and Paul Greengrass' name was not to be mentioned publicly for some months, until he was spotted working for Heinemann's legal advisers in an undefined advisory capacity. Leigh's intervention had the effect of bringing the Australian litigation, or at least part of it, to London because Sir Michael Havers made a belated application to the High Court for an injunction to prevent extracts from *The Spycatcher* from being published in England. The temporary order, alleging breach of confidence, was granted by Mr Justice Macpherson on 27 June against the *Observer* and the *Guardian*. Its effect was to prevent any newspaper from reporting anything about MI5, whatever the source of the material, including evidence given in open court on the other side of the world. Two weeks later another judge, Mr Justice Millett, listened to three days of evidence in chambers before continuing the Attorney-General's injunction, but he limited its scope which, he said, was 'far too wide'. The papers were now free to report on matters concerning the Security Service provided it was not attributed to Peter Wright: 'Prior restraining of publication is a severe interference with the freedom of the Press but those freedoms are not absolute. They are subject to such restraints as are necessary in a democratic society in the interests of national security.' The judge rejected the argument that there was 'a compelling public interest' at stake and accepted the view expressed in yet another affidavit signed by Sir Robert Armstrong that publication of any information from Peter Wright could 'seriously damage' the work of Britain's intelligence services. In what was perhaps the first unfortunate observation of many to be heard in a long legal battle, the judge asserted that the 'security service must be seen to be leak-proof'. This view was endorsed on 25 July by the Court of Appeal, and on 29 July the Lord Chancellor, Lord Hailsham, reminded all newspapers that they too were covered by the existing injunction until the conclusion of the case in Australia.

At this stage the true nature of Wright's relationship with Chapman Pincher was known only to the two principal parties in the case, the Plaintiff and the Defence. Pincher himself must have wondered how far the litigation would go and how much would be revealed in public about his own role as Wright's one-time co-author. On 17 August, writing in the *Sunday Express*, he gave no clue to the extent of his inside knowledge:

The most devastating espionage scandal in years, involving allegations of top-level treason and criminal behaviour by MI5, is set to explode in the autumn in spite of unprecedented efforts by the Government to keep the issue under wraps . . . At the root of the developing crisis is the decision of former MI5 officer Mr Peter Wright to publish his memoirs in Australia. These memoirs are said to contain details of MI5 operations over the years. One of its key allegations is that Sir Roger Hollis, the former head of MI5, was a traitor working for the Russians.

Pincher was evidently in close touch with Heinemann's flamboyant Australian lawyer, Malcolm Turnbull, for even before the case had begun he was able to reveal how the Defence was planning to call the Cabinet Secretary as a witness and question him on the evidence he had lodged by affidavit:

Mr Malcolm Turnbull, the lawyer acting for Mr Wright's publishers, assured me that he intends a detailed cross-examination of Sir Robert. He intends to take him through Mr Wright's book 'page by page' and 'Sir Robert will be cross-examined for at least ten days and probably longer'. Among other things Mr Turnbull intends to question Sir Robert about statements made by Mrs Thatcher following the publication of my book *Their Trade is Treachery*, which made the first disclosure about the Hollis case . . . Mr Turnbull will try to get an admission from Sir Robert that his advice about Hollis was wrong and that as a result Mrs Thatcher, however unwittingly, gave the Commons a misleading statement.

Although superficially even-handed, this report can be seen to contain at least two threats aimed at the Plaintiff: Sir Robert, the head of Britain's Civil Service, was going to be grilled in the witness box for some considerable time, and would be pressed by the Defence on the kind of advice he had given the Prime Minister. Perhaps coincidentally, this article was published at about the time that the Defence surrendered a copy of *The Spycatcher* to the Plaintiff. Having read it, Sir Robert filed a third affidavit, in which he declined to comment on its content because he was unable to do so 'without causing damage which it is the purpose of these proceedings to avoid'.

A week after Pincher's comment on the forthcoming trial, he took a new approach. Whereas he had previously only mentioned the contents of Wright's manuscript in terms of what others had said it contained – 'other allegations according to a statement in the Commons by Mr Dale Campbell-Savours, include . . . '[21] – Pincher applied further pressure on the Plaintiff by disclosing material that was the subject of the Attorney-General's High Court injunction. This obviously had the effect of applying the very pressure on the Plaintiff that the restraining order had been intended to relieve, but in doing so he made a revealing admission: 'Judges here have ruled that British newspapers are forbidden to give details about the Wright book, but a dispensation in their judgement permits me to describe activities because I already knew about them before Wright began his book.'[22]

Pincher then went on to give a brief account of Operation PARTY PIECE and a few of the other controversial stories that had already been outlined, two months earlier, in the *Observer*. Whether it was his intention or not, Pincher's clear message was that he knew the stories of MI5 misdeeds and could release them at any time because he was not covered by the injunction relating to *The Spycatcher*. He had learned of them when collaborating with Wright on *Their Trade is Treachery*, so they were available for immediate use, if he so wished. The fact that he had repeated several of 'those secret sins of MI5', including the plot against Nasser, showed whose side he was on. He ended with the strange remark that, 'the row over Wright's book is less about what it reveals and more about maintaining the teeth of the Official Secrets Act which Wright, along with fellow members of MI5, signed and the Government consider binding'.[23] This conclusion made no sense because, as Pincher knew well, the proceedings in Australia were civil, not criminal, and did not involve the Official Secrets Acts. Wright had become an Australian citizen, so there could not be any question of a criminal prosecution or a request for extradition. The somewhat gratuitous comment seemed perhaps to indicate a shift in Pincher's attitude to Wright as the first day of the trial approached. There is further evidence of Pincher's changing standpoint to be found in his last news story published before the case began. In it he explained how Oleg Gordievsky, the KGB defector who had shopped Bettaney, did 'not know whether Sir Roger Hollis, the former MI5 chief, was a Soviet agent or not'.

He claims the KGB centre in Moscow never briefed him about the Hollis case or indicated they ever had a spy operating at such a high level.
  Announcing Gordievsky's ignorance of the Hollis affair once the Wright case is over, might help to substantiate Mrs Thatcher's past assurances to Parliament that Hollis was not guilty.[24]

None of these articles had any perceptible impact on the Plaintiff's determination to see the matter through, as had been discovered by Jonathan Aitken MP, who had made a last-ditch intervention to negotiate a compromise settlement between the two parties. His approach, through Sir Michael Havers, was rebuffed, and the last of the pre-trial manœuvres took place at the end of the summer when the Plaintiff conceded, for the purposes of legal argument, that the authenticity of the statements made by Wright in *The Spycatcher* would not be challenged. The arguments would focus entirely on the principles involved, or so the Plaintiff hoped. In fact, this procedural tactic was seized on by the media as an admission that Wright's central thesis, that Hollis had been a Russian spy, was indeed true. In vain the lawyers in London ineptly sought to explain why this tactic had been adopted, but it was widely interpreted as a gaffe which could only undermine the Plaintiff's case.

The first public round in the duel between Wright and MI5 took place in the Supreme Court of New South Wales when Mr Justice Powell, himself a former intelligence officer, presided over a preliminary hearing lasting three days, during which he granted the Defence an order for discovery, requiring the Plaintiff to file a number of relevant documents with the court.

The Cabinet Secretary's belated reluctance to be drawn further into the proceedings in Australia was manifested in a fracas at London Airport, where a photographer was pushed up against a wall and had his camera smashed with a briefcase. Evidently, Sir Robert Armstrong was less than enthusiastic about travelling to Sydney as a witness called by the Defence, and had reacted angrily when asked by the press outside Heathrow's VIP lounge for a picture.

By the time Armstrong and his entourage of eight, consisting of the Treasury Solicitor John Bailey; his assistant David Hogg; his private secretary; the deputy head of the Foreign Office's news department, Ivor Roberts; three solicitors, including MI5's deputy Legal Adviser; and a cipher clerk, had arrived in Australia, his intemperate behaviour had made headline news. Worse, it had ensured maximum media coverage for what was to become the public relations catastrophe the government was so anxious to avoid.

The first issue to be dealt with in Australia was the order for discovery requiring the Plaintiff to disclose documents relating to the publication of *Their Trade is Treachery* and *A Matter of Trust*. Among the items requested were MI5's files on Chapman Pincher and Sir Roger Hollis, and any relevant memos that had been exchanged between Sir Michael Havers and the Director of Public Prosecutions, Sir Thomas Hetherington. The Plaintiff had argued against their release, saying that there was a 'public interest im-

munity' on all of them. The Defence had claimed that
because Sir Roger Hollis had originally set up ASIO, there
was a strong Australian interest in establishing the truth
and getting the documents disclosed. There was more than
just the British national interest at stake, a point well
taken by the avuncular judge. After much legal wrangling,
appeals to adjourn the case and applications to overturn
the order for discovery, these papers were produced,
barely within the deadline set, but for only the judge to
see.

The case opened on 17 November 1986, in Courtroom
8D on the eighth floor of the modernistic Supreme Court
building before Mr Justice Philip Powell, and began with
four of the Cabinet Secretary's affidavits being read to the
court. The last had been sworn as recently as 6 November
and gave more compelling reasons why *The Spycatcher*
should be banned. Publication, asserted Armstrong, would
damage internal trust, adversely affect recruitment,
compromise the location of MI5's offices in London and
assist hostile intelligence services.

Cross-examination of the Cabinet Secretary on the
points made in his own affidavits proved to be the highlight
of the case, with the thirty-two-year-old Turnbull making
Armstrong respond to hours of extremely apposite and
skilful questioning. At the heart of the matter were just
two issues: 'Was the Plaintiff's attitude to the publication
of material about the Security Service consistent?', and
'Had the Prime Minister misled the House of Commons
when she had cleared Hollis back in March 1981?'

The Defence took the view that publication of *Their
Trade is Treachery* and *A Matter of Trust* had only been
possible because MI5 had collaborated with their authors.
If the Crown had allowed these books to be released, then
it was only fair that Wright should be treated in the same
way. Armstrong insisted there had been no collaboration
with the two authors, but his repeated requests for the
court to go into closed session before answering detailed
questions indicated his discomfort. In response to one
question throwing doubt on Whitehall's consistency, Arm-

strong replied that, 'the policy is consistent. Only its application varies.' When pressed on the background to the
decision to allow *Their Trade is Treachery* to be published,
Armstrong replied that the Attorney-General had decided
the matter, a claim that was to lead to a furious row in
London when his testimony was reported. In fact, MI5's
Legal Adviser had been responsible for saying that there
were no legal grounds on which to stop Pincher, and Sir
Michael Havers had never even been consulted. Once a
transcript of the proceedings had been communicated to
London, the Attorney-General insisted that Armstrong
retract his sworn evidence. To interfere or communicate
with a witness in the middle of his evidence is a hazardous
affair, but the matter was considered sufficiently important
to warrant an intervention. Rumours in Westminster
suggested that Havers had threatened to resign unless the
situation was corrected. Telephone calls were exchanged
between the Consul-General's residence in Sydney, where
Armstrong was staying, and the Cabinet Office in London,
which led, the following morning, to Armstrong giving an
apology for having misled the court. When pressed on
who exactly had advised against preventing publication of
Pincher's book, if Havers had not, Armstrong said he
could not be sure. In reality, the advice had been given by
MI5's Legal Adviser, and this news sparked off yet another
controversy in London. The Sunday newspapers competed
with each other to identify him, but only the *Mail on
Sunday* actually did so, and only in its early editions. Soon
after the printing presses had started to roll the editor was
formally requested to withhold his name. The *Sunday
Times* also agreed to change the Legal Adviser's name to
'Bernard X' so as to 'prevent him from becoming a target
for terrorists'.

The Cabinet Secretary's damaging retraction, made at
the demand of the Attorney-General, served to undermine
further his credibility which had already been damaged by
several of his remarks, including the admission that on one
occasion he had been 'economical with the truth'.

This memorable phrase had been coined by Armstrong

when he was challenged on the letter he had sent to Sidgwick & Jackson three days before the publication of *Their Trade is Treachery*, requesting two advance copies for the Prime Minister. Since Armstrong had been given an illicit copy of the page proofs some six weeks earlier, did not the letter constitute a lie, he was asked. The Cabinet Secretary, becoming increasingly ill-at-ease, responded, 'It contains a misleading impression, not a lie. It was being economical with the truth. It was misrepresenting the facts, it was misrepresentation. It was to protect a source.' In one of his original affidavits, in reply to a detailed interrogation from the Defence, the Cabinet Secretary had sworn that he had first become aware of *Their Trade is Treachery* in February 1981, a few weeks before publication, but among the Plaintiff's documents at the centre of the continuing arguments, orders and appeals over the disclosure of relevant documents was one, listed as 'B1', which had been written to Sir Howard Smith and dated 18 December 1980, containing a two-page enclosure. The Plaintiff lodged an appeal against Mr Justice Powell's order that everything on the list should be shown to the Defence, but when the Appeal Court examined the list, one of the three judges, Mr Justice Glass, experienced a slip of the tongue. Instead of referring to the 'B1' enclosure, he called it a synopsis. When it was eventually released to the Defence, it turned out to be a two-page summary of *Their Trade is Treachery*. Much to his obvious unease, Whitehall's chief mandarin was obliged to confirm that he had known about Pincher's book months, not weeks, before publication.

When the accuracy of the Prime Minister's statement on Hollis was raised, the Cabinet Secretary made another significant concession. Turnbull asked whether Mrs Thatcher's statement had been misleading because it had implied that the clues implicating Hollis could equally have pointed to Philby and Blunt. Armstrong confirmed that there had indeed been evidence of post-war penetration of the Security Service which could not be attributed to either Philby or Blunt. He said:

The Prime Minister's statement did not refer explicitly to matters considered in the course of the investigation which suggested there was continued high-level penetration of British counter-intelligence after the last years of the war.[25]

Mrs Thatcher's statement on *Their Trade is Treachery* had never been intended as a comprehensive account of the molehunts, he explained. She had correctly stated that the investigation of Sir Roger had been 'based on certain leads . . .'. Brevity was the sole reason for not giving more details: 'There are limits to the length of an oral statement that could be made. It was comprehensive in terms of what can be expected in an oral statement to Parliament.'[26]

The events in Australia were given massive media coverage in Britain and, indeed, in the rest of the world. There were also considerable political repercussions. When the case was brought up at Prime Minister's regular Question Time, Mrs Thatcher refused to discuss the matter, saying it was *sub judice*. The Speaker, who is the final arbiter in such disputes, ruled against her, stating that because the case was being held abroad there was no risk of contempt. Bowing to his judgement she simply fell back on the time-honoured convention that national security considerations prevented a reply.

An already electric political atmosphere was made even more tense by the publication in London of two new books, both written by journalists, and both directly relevant to the issues of confidentiality under scrutiny in Australia. The first, a biography of Anthony Blunt entitled *Conspiracy of Silence*, directly quoted no fewer than twenty-six retired intelligence officers in clear breach of their undertakings. Many had worked for MI5. In *The Second Oldest Profession*, author Phillip Knightley claimed that Anthony Simkins had been responsible for leaking much of the classified information contained in *A Matter of Trust*. Simkins promptly sued for libel and won 'substantial damages' and an apology from Knightley.[27]

In a separate High Court hearing, the Attorney-General embarked on a completely new case to ban *One Girl's*

War, the autobiography of Joan Miller, the wartime MI5 officer who had died in Malta in 1984. Her book, organised by her daughter from Rome, was published in Ireland and widely distributed in London. Somewhat belatedly, Sir Michael Havers obtained an injunction to stop its distribution in England, but an application made on his behalf in Dublin was rejected.

Attempts by Labour MPs to make political capital out of the government's escalating embarrassment were to badly rebound in the House of Commons. The Opposition had plenty of criticism of the government's handling of the Wright affair, and took every opportunity to play on Armstrong's ineptitude, until it was revealed that Labour's leader, Neil Kinnock, had been in direct touch with Malcolm Turnbull in Australia and some nine telephone calls had been logged in Kinnock's private office. Kinnock insisted that he had only been double-checking his facts, but the news was greeted with widespread dismay and the Prime Minister adroitly squeezed the last ounce of advantage from it. Suddenly, the case that had caused the administration so much disquiet had been transformed into an issue of Kinnock's personal reliability. It was an issue magnified to great effect and signalled a reversal in the government's ailing fortunes.

If the government seemed to wriggle nimbly off the hook, Chapman Pincher realised that his own relationship with Wright was about to be disclosed. On the very eve of the case Pincher admitted for the first time that he had known Wright. He chose an opinion column in the *Sunday Express* to say, 'It is now common knowledge that Wright was one of my major sources.'[28] In fact, this was a slight exaggeration as his involvement with Wright had been very carefully concealed and was known only to very few. Even *Too Secret Too Long*, which had been published after Wright's television appearance in July 1984, had omitted to give him credit for having co-authored *Their Trade is Treachery*. Pincher's real problems began on 20 November, after the first three days of the hearing, when the Defence tried to prove that *Their Trade is Treachery* had received some undercover support from the government. Turnbull asked Armstrong if he had 'received any reports from the Security Service concerning Victor Rothschild's role concerning *Their Trade is Treachery*'.

'I would not wish to answer that in open court,' replied Armstrong, and the public gallery was cleared so the question could be answered *in camera*. What exchanges took place behind closed doors are not known, but when he read of this incident Pincher must have realised that Turnbull was determined to show Rothschild's involvement, and presumably Pincher's too. A leak from the Plaintiff's side indicated that they were not entirely confident that *in camera* proceedings would remain confidential. Apparently, MI5 had only just realised that Turnbull's courtroom 'assistant', who had been present whenever the court sat in private, was Paul Greengrass, on leave from Granada Television.

The next day the Defence offered in evidence a copy of Pincher's letter to Wright dated 27 January 1983, in which Pincher described having discussed *A Matter of Trust* with Sir Michael Havers while out shooting. Turnbull suggested that in reality the Attorney-General was not just a friend of Pincher's, but one of his most useful sources of information. Contacted by journalists at home in Berkshire, Pincher said, 'It's utter rubbish. The conversation lasted no more than a minute,'[29] but he did admit that, 'Wright was a source, some of whose disclosures he would not publish.'

That he would be unable to extricate himself from the court case became obvious to Pincher when he had an acrimonious telephone conversation with Turnbull the following day, on Saturday, 22 November. Pincher asked Turnbull to stop circulating his confidential correspondence, but Turnbull refused:

Turnbull explained that the British government had been playing so 'dirty' that he was playing dirty too. When I asked if it mattered whether Wright's old friends like Lord Rothschild might suffer, he said that it did not because this was a do or die case which had to be won at all cost.[30]

It seems that at the conclusion of this call, in anticipation of Wright's true role as his co-author becoming public knowledge, Pincher telephoned *The Times* and issued a statement acknowledging the secret deal. In what seems to be a half-hearted attempt to protect Lord Rothschild, Pincher said he had met Wright at a secret address in this country for a few hours in August 1980. He conceded that Lord Rothschild had effected the introduction, but neglected to mention that the meeting had taken place at 11 Herschell Road, Rothschild's home in Cambridge. Pincher's admission emphasised that he had never actually paid Wright for information:

I told him that I could not possibly be involved in giving him money but that if a book was feasible and a reputable publisher could be found, it would be normal practice for half the royalties to be paid to him, provided I was not involved in the payments in any way.[31]

Pincher's bombshell had exactly the desired effect on the Defence in Sydney, and prompted Wright to issue a statement dealing with matters that were to be part of his sworn evidence. He admitted having received half the royalties of *Their Trade is Treachery*, but said Pincher was mistaken when he denied having been involved in the payments. 'I can prove, and will prove in court, that this is not true,' he insisted.

Sensitivity about whether or not money passed between Pincher and Wright was further demonstrated when Miles Copeland, a retired CIA officer, wrote a feature in *The Times* on 1 December and commented that, 'Peter Wright is sure to have enough of a best-seller to make whatever Chapman Pincher paid him look like peanuts.' Pincher immediately wrote in to protest that he had 'never paid Mr Wright anything. Mr Wright received royalties on a jointly authored book properly paid by the publishers and nothing else. '[32]

Another person ruffled by the disclosures in Sydney and Berkshire was Lord Rothschild, who overnight became the focus of intense interest from the media. Had he a statement to make on the allegation that he had introduced Pincher to Wright? Why had he brought Wright to England in 1980? What were his motives in setting up a bank account for Wright? Suddenly, the self-professed private man became the centre of attention and he did not respond well, or at least his staff didn't. In a scene reminiscent of the undignified fracas at Heathrow two weeks earlier, another Fleet Street photographer was manhandled in a scuffle with N. M. Rothschild & Sons' staff.

In spite of the pressure to make a public statement, Rothschild kept silent until 4 December when, without any warning, he sent a letter to the *Daily Telegraph* demanding that Sir Antony Duff clear his name:

Since at least 1980 up to the present time there have been innuendoes in the Press to the effect that I am 'The Fifth Man', in other words a Soviet agent. The Director-General of MI5 should state publicly that he has unequivocal, repeat unequivocal, evidence, that I am not, and never have been a Soviet agent. If the 'regulations' prevent him from making such a statement, which in the present climate I doubt, let him do so through his legal adviser or through any other recognisably authoritative source. I am constrained by the Official Secrets Act but I write this letter lest it be thought that silence would be an indication of anything other than complete innocence.

The letter took everyone by surprise, the Prime Minister included, because when she was asked by MPs to give Rothschild the clearance he had asked for, she refused. 'That letter', she said, 'is being considered in government and I cannot add anything further at this stage.' The reply stunned those present, who had expected Rothschild to be exonerated in much the same way she had dealt with the allegations against Hollis in March 1981, but she would not elaborate. Pressed by MPs on both sides of the House, she declined to say any more, but the following afternoon a short statement was released, which only served to create more dismay:

I have now considered more fully Lord Rothschild's letter to the *Daily Telegraph* yesterday, in which he referred to innuendoes that he had been a Soviet agent. I consider it important to maintain the practice of successive governments of not commenting on security matters. But I am willing to make an exception on the matter raised in Lord Rothschild's letter. I am advised that we have no evidence that he was ever a Soviet agent.

The long delay in releasing this reply, and the way in which it was delivered, late on Friday evening so that no further questions could be raised, caused considerable speculation. Why had Rothschild chosen an open letter to the *Daily Telegraph* to demand what he must have known was impossible? A public testimonial from the Director-General of the Security Service was entirely without precedent and placed the Prime Minister in a predicament. As she herself had once said, 'it is very often impossible to prove innocence'.

The 'unequivocal evidence' referred to by Rothschild had been his secret role in obtaining Philby's confession, and his tip to MI5 about Alister Watson's Communist past. But did either of these two items truly constitute the proof he believed it to be? Rothschild made no further public comment, perhaps leaving it to his friend Chapman Pincher to respond for him:

It is Rothschild's fear that treacherous reasons may be wrongly imputed against him which has finally driven him to demand full vindication from MI5. The Prime Minister's statement on Friday will not fully satisfy him.[33]

10

CONCLUSIVE PROOF

After a gruelling twenty-two days the Attorney-General's application for an injunction against Heinemann came to an end and the long-suffering judge retired to consider his verdict. The trial had been memorable for the judge's colourful but caustic criticisms of the presentation of the Plaintiff's case, and the 'labyrinthine weavings' indulged in to avoid making unnecessary admissions about MI5's molehunts. Almost everyone involved emerged with their reputations slightly tarnished. Chapman Pincher was exposed as rather less an intrepid researcher and seeker after the truth, and rather more a ghost-writer; Lord Rothschild was revealed as a man tormented by his early associations, and his inability to live with the idea that someone, somewhere, believed he was 'the fifth man'; Peter Wright emerged as an impecunious, slightly dotty old man consumed by an obsession.

In England the political repercussions damaged Neil Kinnock's credibility because of accusations of, at best, poor judgement and, at worst, disloyalty, for his contacts with the Crown's legal opponents. The government nearly lost an Attorney-General who was unwilling to be cast as scapegoat in a fiasco that he had played no part in. Even the Prime Minister must have felt a twinge of mild discomfort as Sir Robert Armstrong, pragmatic as ever, had gamefully explained to the court in Sydney why considerations of time had prevented her from giving Parliament a 'comprehensive' oral account of MI5's investigation into Hollis.

Of all, the Cabinet Secretary probably came off worst, sustaining a barrage of ridicule for his reluctance to make even the most harmless of concessions to the Defence. At one point, his Counsel intervened to prevent him from referring to the existence of SIS. Surely, the Defence pointed out, Sir Robert had already acknowledged this in his evidence the previous day, when Sir Dick White had been described as SIS's Chief. Apparently unabashed, the Plaintiff limited the damage by saying that the admission only extended to the period of White's office. This clumsy manœuvre allowed the Crown to escape from acknowledging SIS's current existence.

These semantics sometimes lent the proceedings an air of unreality and gave good entertainment value to the media, which revelled in the spectacle of Britain's most senior civil servant (and enemy of airport photographers) being forced to submit to an incisive cross-examination from someone who cared not a jot for his eminent position in England. One recurring criticism of Armstrong was his inability, as a witness of fact, to give evidence about the circumstances in which it had been decided that no obstacle would be placed in the path of *Their Trade is Treachery*'s publication. Why had no injunction been sought? Who were the faceless lawyers who had advised the government on these matters? Armstrong was unable to give satisfactory answers and incurred the court's displeasure, perhaps even to the extent of jeopardising the outcome.

That he should have been so disadvantaged is strange because he, probably more than any other, had been closely connected with the Security Service's molehunts since the day when Stephen de Mowbray had called on Downing Street alleging a cover-up in the investigation of Sir Roger Hollis. Before his appointment as Cabinet Secretary, and the Prime Minister's principal adviser on security matters, he had headed the Home Office and had been directly responsible for MI5 during the difficult years of Michael Hanley's regime, when a small group of Security

Service personnel had been found to have made rather an amateurish attempt to destabilise Harold Wilson's administration by spreading smear stories about his entourage. Armstrong knew the details of the Trend Report and had been sufficiently interested in *Their Trade is Treachery* to call on its publishers in person to receive his advance copies. But when it came to answering questions on a subject he must have been well-briefed on, he was the master of prevarication. Who was to be protected?

Although the name of Sir Roger Hollis was hardly mentioned in court, it was the continuing conundrum about his loyalty that had so motivated Peter Wright in the face of threats, illness and litigation. Others around him had their own axes to grind and latched on to whatever embarrassing incidents he could recall from his prodigious memory. But in the midst of all the claims, counter-claims and legal arguments, lay the central confirmation that there had indeed been evidence of Soviet penetration of the Security Service after the war. It was this key admission, obscured by myriad distractions, that was of absorbing interest to the molehunters, and went some way to vindicating those who believed that, though bureaucratically inconvenient, it was in the national interest to alert either politicians or the public to what was perceived as a dangerous cover-up. If politicians were so determined not to listen, other means were to be found.

The official admission to the existence of evidence indicating that MI5 had harboured a spy at a high level will now enable all the secret personal and subject files held before 1963 to be earmarked to show that they may have been compromised. This is the minimum damage control exercise required, and the one advocated for the security agencies of Australia, New Zealand, Canada and the United States at the CAZAB conference.

Having at last established and accepted the principle of penetration, there remains the issue of who was the most likely culprit. This is only of academic interest now, because Graham Mitchell, MI5's first and best candidate, died, unnoticed, on 19 November 1984.

The molehunts began as a consequence of Philby's confession in January 1963, which this book took as its starting-point. Subsequent enquiries found overwhelming evidence to show that the original suspicions were amply justified. Evidence dating back to 1945 could be found to support the proposition that an ideological traitor, in the same mould as Burgess, Maclean, Philby, Blunt, Cairncross, Long, Watson *et al.*, had been recruited before the war and had burrowed deep, leaving only the occasional traces of his duplicity. But traces there were, and quite the best spoor to be followed was that left by the ubiquitous Philby, for it allowed the field to be narrowed to just Hollis and Mitchell. One of these two individuals was a traitor. Of that truth, sixteen out of twenty-one molehunters, each an experienced counter-intelligence expert, were convinced.

That Hollis should have come under suspicion is not surprising. He was not particularly popular with his colleagues and many of his most innocent activities were sufficiently ambiguous to allow them to be interpreted to show guilt. He invariably worked late in his office. Was he photographing documents, or was he simply reluctant to go home to a wife he didn't care for? Was his long-standing liaison with his secretary a love affair or an indication of moral turpitude? He often walked home across the park: was he holding clandestine meetings with his Soviet contact, or simply fond of an evening stroll after work? He had been hesitant in telling the Prime Minister about Profumo's affair with Christine Keeler: was he trying to undermine the government, or anxious to prevent his organisation from becoming embroiled in the private lives of politicians? Was his refusal to apply for a warrant to tap Mitchell's telephone a ploy to divert attention away from himself, or a reluctance to admit to the Prime Minister that MI5 had been penetrated? Was his adverse report on Gouzenko's reliability a desperate attempt to discredit a dangerous witness or an honest opinion of the defector's value?

Some of these items look trivial, but even the most

ordinary of activities may have a dual purpose. Indeed, the best cover for espionage is routine, apparently normal behaviour. When the Krogers were unmasked as two Soviet illegals, none of their neighbours or friends could believe they were anything other than a perfectly ordinary suburban couple. Yet a search of their house betrayed a mass of sophisticated communications equipment and a wealth of espionage paraphernalia.

The underlying problem with the case against Hollis is that it was accumulated in secret by molehunters sensitive to the dangers of revealing their true purpose. Witnesses were questioned and records examined with great circumspection so as to prevent the real nature of the investigation being compromised. The picture that emerged was therefore far from complete, with undue emphasis placed on incidents and episodes that could have been represented in a different light if they had been studied openly. An obvious example is Hollis' period in the Far East. The molehunters quite reasonably took it for granted that their quarry probably had been recruited to the Soviet cause at some stage before the war and Hollis' lengthy stay in China looked promising. It was known that numerous Russian networks were operating within the European expatriate community in Shanghai, at the very time that Hollis had been a visitor, so it seemed reasonable to presume that he had somehow been drawn in at this point. The need to keep the exercise a secret prevented the molehunters from asking Hollis' ex-wife for access to her collection of his old letters, which effectively prove he had not been recruited in China. To this day, they have not been read by MI5.

Another area where the molehunters can be seen to have been side-tracked is the testimony of Gouzenko and the weight given to his mysterious ELLI. There is no disputing that there was an ELLI in England during the war but, perhaps because of the nature of the source, the molehunters became transfixed by the idea that ELLI was a GRU agent operating inside MI5, when Gouzenko's original allegation concerned 'British Counterintelligence'. Whenever he was given the opportunity,

Gouzenko embroidered a more elaborate scenario for ELLI until his knowledge of the elusive agent ended up being the principal motivation for his defection. When all his statements are analysed, as has now been done, safe from the persistent threat of litigation, Gouzenko is revealed as a classic victim of defector syndrome, craving attention and mischievously altering his stories to suit his audience. As a consequence he was able to con MI5's molehunters and Chapman Pincher. His original allegations about a mole in British counter-intelligence were entirely reasonable and can now be shown to be authentic. They can also be seen to refer to either Philby or Blunt. In other words, the molehunters were distracted into chasing a spy they already knew about.

Hollis may have been guilty of complacency, dimness, pomposity, perhaps even of incompetence, but his record stands up when accounted for like a profit and loss account. On the credit side, there are the successful wartime prosecutions of three Communist spies. The cases received scant publicity at the time, so as to avoid upsetting Britain's gallant Allies, so they are easily overlooked, but at the time of his arrest Douglas Springhall was the National Organiser of the CPGB. The two sub-agents operated by him who were also convicted of espionage were Olive Sheehan, who kept him supplied with information from the Air Ministry, where she worked in a department dealing with jet propulsion, and Captain Ormond Uren of the Highland Light Infantry, a linguist attached to the Hungarian Section of Special Operations Executive. By the time Springhall was arrested in June 1943, he had received secret information from Uren on five occasions. He was arrested on the day his sixth meeting was scheduled and was sentenced to seven years' imprisonment after a short trial *in camera* at the Old Bailey. Uren was cashiered and given seven years, and Mrs Sheehan received three months.

The Springhall prosecution was a considerable coup for the Security Service and intimately involved the CPGB which, of course, was Hollis' responsibility within F Division. The fact that MI5's operation proceeded unhindered and resulted in the arrest of three Soviet agents is not insignificant and might even be regarded as demonstrating that, whichever parts of MI5 had been penetrated by the Soviets, F2 most certainly had not. Nor is the Springhall episode to be dismissed as a trivial affair. In fact, Springhall was a key figure in the CPGB and the Party's link with its cells of undercover supporters. He visited Cambridge frequently and had been the political commissar of the British Battalion of the International Brigade in Spain which, incidentally, had been commanded by another convicted Soviet spy, Wilfred Macartney. Springhall's conviction was a severe embarrassment to the CPGB and the Soviets.

Apart from Hollis' visits to Canada to see Gouzenko, and his trip to Australia with Robert Hemner-Scales to set up ASIO, Hollis' post-war career was unremarkable except for one thing: it was not spent in the counter-espionage department where, as a Soviet mole, he would have enjoyed the greatest access to secrets and been in a position to inflict the most damage. Other agents, such as Philby and Blunt, made conscious efforts to move into sections where they could be most useful to their controllers. As the post-war Director of C Division, he was primarily responsible for advising government departments on routine security measures, known to insiders as 'locks and safes'.

Critics of Hollis point to his performance during the troubled, early 1960s to suggest his behaviour was in some ways odd. Two episodes stand out. Firstly, his reluctance to pursue the suspected spy in the Admiralty who was thought to have betrayed atomic secrets that Vassall could not have gained access to. On the face of it this is a tremendously damaging charge, but once put into its proper historical context of three separate government enquiries into security (led, respectively, by Sir Charles Romer, Sir Charles Cunningham and Lord Radcliffe) and the spate of espionage cases, one can begin to understand the Director-General's desire for a return to normality.

The first to hit the headlines was the Portland spy ring which had led to the arrest of three Soviet illegals, Gordon Lonsdale and the Krogers, and their contacts inside the Admiralty base at Portland, Harry Houghton and Ethel Gee. The investigation, following a tip from a defector, had been considered a huge success. It was quickly followed by the Vassall affair, which had considerable political implications as John Vassall had been an assistant secretary to the Civil Lord of the Admiralty, Tam Galbraith MP. The tribunal appointed to recommend improvements in the Admiralty's security procedures generated considerable public attention. Two journalists were even imprisoned for declining to name the sources of newspaper articles they had written about a supposed link between the Portland case and Vassall. In fact, there was no connection but, when yet another suspect emerged, Hollis evidently preferred to switch him away from any secrets rather than face the prospect of a fourth official enquiry. Certainly, the handful of D Branch officers who knew of his decision not to haul in the suspect for interrogation were dismayed, even contemptuous, but not, at that stage at least, apprehensive about his motives. On the profit and loss account, the Admiralty business counts as a debit, but the capture of Lonsdale and the Krogers must be a substantial credit.

Hollis' conduct throughout the Profumo affair, which was to follow closely on the heels of the Portland spy ring and the Vassall case, has also been judged harshly. Why did he keep the Prime Minister in the dark about everything that was happening? In fact, in so far as it was the Security Service's responsibility to protect the realm, the Director-General did keep the Cabinet Secretary and Harold Macmillan informed. But as Hollis was to point out to Lord Denning, once it had been established that there was no threat to security, MI5 was obliged to stand on the sidelines. Political embarrassment, or the private lives of individual ministers, were not within the Security Service's brief. Lord Denning concurred with his interpretation of MI5's charter, as laid down by the Maxwell-Fyfe directive

of March 1951. Hollis was also anxious to maintain a low
profile because one of MI5's own personnel had inadvertently sparked off the scandal by attempting to entrap
the Soviet assistant naval attaché in a 'honey-trap', using
Stephen Ward as an agent. On this occasion, Hollis' profit
and loss account should be credited with extracting MI5
from a particularly sticky situation.

Once placed in its historical perspective, Hollis' behaviour shows a hesitant style of management and a distinct
lack of self-confidence, which may not be entirely un-
reasonable given his necessary preoccupation with essentially political events. Add to this unhappy condition the
PETERS molehunt, and the scene quickly deteriorates.
No wonder Hollis was unwilling to tell Macmillan that
Mitchell, his own Deputy Director-General, who had
played a leading role in the Profumo affair, was a probable
Soviet agent and that a warrant was required to tap his
home telephone. Fortuitously, Mitchell had chosen this
moment to request an early retirement, and no doubt
Hollis welcomed the relief offered by his departure. In
hindsight, this may have been dereliction of duty or cow-
ardice, but was it anything more sinister?

While a review of Hollis' career looks unimpressive, but
not treacherous, the case to be made against Mitchell is
equally circumstantial, but rather more substantial. Having
spent the war in F3, Mitchell would not have been in a
position to compromise the successful Springhall investigation carried out in 1943. This, of course, is negative
evidence, but there are two other matters that ought not
to be dismissed lightly: the performance of the counter-
espionage division while under his command, and his inexplicable behaviour when called upon to advise the
government on the flight of Burgess and Maclean and the
possible involvement of a third conspirator.

Between 1953 and 1963, when Mitchell was either Director of D Branch or the Deputy Director-General, MI5
suffered a series of setbacks and failed to catch a single
Soviet agent by its own initiative. This incredible record is
all the more disastrous when it is realised that the single

spy who was caught in the post-war era, William Marshall, was spotted quite by chance while meeting his Soviet contact in April 1952. If an off-duty watcher, on his way home for lunch, had not stepped off his bus in Kingston at exactly the moment Pavel Kuznetsov was holding a rendezvous, it is likely that neither would ever have been discovered. Apart from this single, fortuitous episode, every other case, like the Portland spy ring and the Vassall affair, were tip-offs from the CIA. As is now known, the information which enabled Nunn May, Vassall, Lonsdale and the rest to be identified originated from defectors who had chosen to go to the Americans, although their meal-tickets were really more relevant to the British. The volume of defections, or at least offers to defect, is one good barometer of a security agency's relative freedom from contamination. Of the two defectors who did approach the British, Volkov wound up murdered and the other wisely opted for an American home at the last moment. The total lack of any defectors during the post-war years is a potent sign that MI5 itself had been penetrated by someone closely involved with counter-espionage matters. Mitchell fits this description better than Hollis.

Several operations, based on information relayed by the Americans, which ought to have had a good chance of success, failed miserably. The cases of Cairncross and Colonel Prybl were obviously betrayed, and when Cairncross was questioned about this, years later, he could not give an adequate explanation for having been deserted.

Lack of defections and the failure of particular operations do not constitute conclusive proof, nor do they directly implicate only Mitchell, but for a counter-espionage expert his scepticism about the value of defectors is distinctly odd and, as a viewpoint, has not stood the test of time. Both Vladimir and Evdokia Petrov have proved themselves to be reliable as sources of information, and tips from Mitchell's other favourite bugbear, Anatoli Golitsyn, have led to the elimination of an estimated 200

KGB agents around the world. Defectors may be fallible, and may occasionally succumb to an exaggerated sense of their own self-importance, as happened with Gouzenko, but they provide the best, most accurate, insights into the opposition's *modus operandi* apart from signals intelligence. Yet even here, with a well-established source of high-grade information, Mitchell was unenthusiastic and eventually terminated MI5's programme of analysis run jointly with GCHQ. Even though the decrypts codenamed VENONA had proved their worth by revealing clues to the identity of such spies as Fuchs and Maclean, the project was closed down and the files shelved. It was only after his premature retirement, when the study was reinstated, that the material was found to contain items of value. Perhaps more significant than Mitchell's somewhat quirky ideas about defectors and SIGINT is the indisputable fact that, during his tenure as Director D and Deputy Director-General, the Security Service experienced one operational disaster after another.

The most spectacular miscalculation was the defections of Burgess and Maclean, and both Mitchell and Hollis had the foreknowledge necessary to sabotage MI5's plan to interrogate Maclean. Burgess, of course, had been a friend of Mitchell's. The exact route of the sudden warning to Burgess, conveyed to him by telephone almost immediately after the Foreign Secretary, Herbert Morrison, had authorised Maclean's interrogation, cannot be established. It has been widely believed that Philby may have been responsible for alerting Burgess, but the time difference between Washington and London makes a direct leak, from MI5's headquarters, more probable. As the Director of C Division at the time of the escapes, there was no operational reason for Mitchell to have been informed of the Foreign Secretary's decision but, to the surprise of the molehunters, Mitchell admitted during his interrogation in 1967 that he had known of Morrison's decision. How had this knowledge come to him, bearing in mind that it was supposed to have been a closely guarded secret kept within the confines of the counter-espionage branch? Mitchell was unable to recall the exact circumstances in which he had been informed.

Some of the most damning evidence against Mitchell is on the public record, contained in the Burgess and Maclean White Paper which he drafted. Misrepresentation, blatant falsehood and subtle innuendo are all there to be seen. There can be no argument or evasion about the scale of the falsification because, as an official paper relating what are supposed to be facts, each of its constituent parts can be examined separately and subjected to a process of verification. Unlike most of the items of evidence available for review in the molehunts, these individual distortions are not open to an alternative interpretation. Unlike the 'wilderness of mirrors', where nothing is exactly what it seems and one struggles in the dark to make sense of what is not immediately obvious, there are specific matters in the White Paper that can be judged to be either right or wrong. There is no room for speculation, and each has been singled out and highlighted in Appendix 1. The most charitable view of the document is that it was a cover-up constructed to protect the reputations of more senior officers. A less generous criticism is to attribute a sinister motive to its principal author. If the first view was the sole reason for the White Paper's web of deceit, and the lies really had been inserted to avoid exposure of the organisation's shortcomings, there would not have been any compelling requirement to conceal Petrov's true role as a senior KGB officer and to denigrate his evidence. Certainly, MI5 had no need to exercise discretion about Petrov's defection, which had received enormous publicity in Australia. Naturally, the Soviets were well aware of his defection and his standing in the KGB. So why undermine his credibility by omitting to give his true status in the Embassy? His position as a mere Third Secretary was a cover for his KGB activities, as had been made perfectly clear in his testimony to the Royal Commission in Australia. His clandestine role was unmistakable and his evidence had been accepted as authentic. Indeed, the Commissioners had actually attested to his reliability. We now know that Petrov had corroborated the hearsay evidence already delivered by Goronwy Rees, yet Mitchell chose to disparage his evidence. The only logical, inescapable explanation is because Mitchell had his own, personal reasons to deflect attention away from Petrov and his testimony. The relevance of what the defector had to say on Burgess and Maclean is focused on the narrow area of remarks reportedly made by Filipp Kislitsyn and his claim that the two Foreign Office officials had not been impulsive escapees, but long-term, deep-cover moles recruited at university with the sole purpose of burrowing deep into the establishment. Why was Mitchell so keen to suppress such a claim? Was it because MI5 had never contemplated the possibility of moles until Rees had described them for the first time?

Even the most cursory reading of the White Paper reveals a strong bias against the possibility of a warning having been received by Maclean. Alternative explanations are offered, such as the idea that he had noticed that certain material was being withheld from him at work, and that 'searching enquiries' had been made to exclude the involvement of a third conspirator. In reality, Philby, Blunt and Cairncross had all been identified as probable Soviet agents. Philby had been subjected to a semi-judicial enquiry and had been sacked. Cairncross had been interrogated and required to tender his resignation. Blunt, too, had been questioned at length, but he had long since left government service so there were no immediate sanctions to be used against him. Once again, Mitchell's text is not merely disingenuous, it is downright untrue.

The fiction that Maclean was not to be interviewed 'until mid-June' is now recognised to be completely bogus. The interrogation had been scheduled for the morning of Monday, 28 May, just three days after Herbert Morrison had agreed to it. Equally false is the spurious claim that Burgess, as well as Maclean, was a suspect and that 'the security authorities were on their track'. Mitchell had obviously succumbed to an overwhelming need to deflect attention away from the possibility of a 'third man'. What had compelled him to do so?

The bland, defensive, almost prim tone of the White Paper, pontificating about what was, and was not, permissible in a free society, has the unmistakable ring of a bureaucrat justifying a monumental catastrophe, but there is much that cannot easily be categorised as a departmental cover-up. Nor can security grounds be cited because there was no possible advantage to be gained from misleading the Soviets about non-contentious issues, like the depth of Petrov's debriefings. They could have acquired that information from reading the Australian newspapers. MI5's failure to trap Cairncross also demonstrated how closely the KGB was monitoring the Security Service's progress. The only people likely to be duped by the White Paper were the British public, British politicians and any molehunters picking over the traces at a later date. Assuming that all of MI5's documents were sanitised to reflect the official line, they would have been completely useless to anyone seeking to backtrack through the files, looking for clues. That the files were doctored so they could be shown to the FBI is now generally admitted, but the result is a completely inaccurate record of the real sequence of events. Unless an individual molehunter had first-hand experience of the investigation into Maclean, he would stand little chance of discovering fresh clues from the paperwork. In this context, it is relevant to record that Peter Wright did not become a molehunter until twelve years after these events, and he only joined the Security Service's technical support section four years after the defections. If his later enquiries were to be based on alleged facts established by Mitchell after May 1951, his conclusions were bound to be way off the mark.

But could such a grand deception be put over by just one man? Why would Mitchell's two direct superiors, Hollis and White, have acquiesced in what amounted to a massive fraud? In fact, neither probably realised the scale of the misrepresentation. White's direct involvement in the Maclean investigation had been limited to the supervision, as Director of the counter-espionage division, of the individual case officers employed, and the preparation of the material with which Maclean was to be confronted at his interrogation. Once the defection had taken place, White had played a part in MI5's abortive attempt to chase after Maclean and intercept him. He had gone on to be promoted to the post of Director-General upon Sillitoe's retirement in 1953 and, therefore, had other responsibilities beyond counter-espionage. While he would have been required to endorse Mitchell's draft White Paper in 1955, he would not have had a hand in its preparation because that duty fell to his Director D Branch who had all the very latest information, including details of the Petrov defection. If Mitchell believed Petrov to be unreliable, or that MI5 would be well advised not to attach too much importance to his testimony, then Dick White would have needed to tender good arguments to overrule his Director. That the White Paper devoted no fewer than nine of its twenty-eight paragraphs to Mrs Maclean and her disappearance from Switzerland in September 1953 must have been a relief to some, even at the risk of criticism that her vanishing act had no relevance or security implications to the stated subject of the report.

As for Hollis, MI5's Director C Division at the time of the defections, he cannot have had much first-hand knowledge of what had occurred. Nor could he have contributed much, if anything, to the White Paper. As Dick White's Deputy Director-General he would have complied with his wishes, as was his practice on most matters. Responsibility for the essentially mendacious nature of the White Paper, therefore, rests almost entirely with Mitchell. He, too, was the person who advised the government to clear Kim Philby if his name should emerge in a Parliamentary Question. The Foreign Secretary's fatal reply, with the apparently gratuitous suggestion that there may never have been a third man, gave the spy what he later described from Moscow as 'the happiest day of my life'. Almost any form of words would have sufficed, but Macmillan's unqualified commitment was to handicap severely the subsequent molehunts. Governments are now more cautious in accepting the advice of the Security Service on the loyalty or otherwise of individuals and exercise greater circumspection when choosing appropriate terminology.

The events that followed the traumatic flight of Burgess and Maclean have often been obscured by side-issues and red-herrings. Gouzenko's allegations were examples of how the most dedicated of researchers can be drawn into fruitless quests in search of a mythical quarry. ELLI probably existed, but the details offered by the defector could have applied to known spies like Blunt and Philby.

Exposure of the White Paper for what it really is has not been possible in the past because of the silence of the very few who knew or suspected the truth, and the legal implications of attributing blame to a particular individual. Nevertheless, the transparent inference of *A Matter of Trust* was that Mitchell's explanation would be invaluable in settling the question once and for all. In the absence of conclusive proof, an admission would have sufficed.

POSTSCRIPT

The official view of the molehunts that paralysed the Security Service during the late 1960s, and touched off a condition close to paranoia in some MI5 officers, is that they were inconclusive. Certainly there was no evidence, in the most technical interpretation of the word, that could be presented to a court of law with the hope of obtaining a criminal conviction. And in the absence of this evidence both Roger Hollis and Graham Mitchell were declared innocent publicly, by the Prime Minister. In Hollis's case an oral statement was made; for Mitchell a written reply to a Parliamentary Question was deemed appropriate.

If, following prolonged investigation, the two chief suspects had been cleared, did it automatically follow that no hostile penetration of the Security Service had taken place? Opinions are divided. Whitehall's most convenient solution is to conclude that the 'wilderness of mirrors' probably got the better of a few misguided counter-intelligence experts who had been conditioned, by the nature of their work, to suspect treachery where there were other, more rational explanations available. They deliberately erred on the side of caution and deduced mischief as the cause of MI5's many operational failures. By pursuing the improbable, but possible, they avoided the charge of 'cover-up' but fell into the trap of actually generating suspicion. Thus by actively following up every possible lead they inevitably developed a host of new lines of enquiry. In an area notorious for its intrinsic ambiguity this is a dangerous activity. To allow it to become a dominating preoccupation is but a short step to being entrapped altogether. The molehunters eventually lose their grip on reality, trust no one, and circulate pejorative reports on entirely innocent people who have fallen under their scrutiny.

There are two fundamental objections to such a viewpoint. Firstly, it ignores the substance of the evidence available for examination. Some events are simply a matter of interpretation and analysis, and offer a variety of conclusions, but there are also those items that defy alternative definition. Only a leak from a very senior level could have allowed Philby to warn Anthony Blunt that Vladimir Petrov was on the point of defecting in Australia; Philby's carefully constructed 'confession', written under his immunity from prosecution, displayed signs of having been prepared before his final confrontation. Far from being a hastily put together document to buy a few hours of freedom, it was a sophisticated attempt to limit the damage sustained by the KGB and avoid the identification of his co-conspirators. There was a well-placed source within MI5. The admission that there was not enough evidence to mount a prosecution hardly invalidates his existence. It is a counter-espionage byword that 'smoking gun' evidence for overt legal action is extremely hard to achieve.

The second flaw in the 'unstable molehunter succumbs to irrational behaviour' proposition is the structure of the investigations conducted by the Security Service. There was no single individual, or group of renegades, that ever had the opportunity to exert such influence over the numerous cases handled over the years. Nearly two dozen separate officers were involved in the molehunts, and no fewer than three separate, independent reviews were completed at various stages. While it might be expedient for politicians and their advisers to dismiss Peter Wright as a deranged loose cannon on the deck, his contemporaries are reluctant to condemn him in those terms.

Peter Wright's eccentric appearance in Australia, shielded from the glare of the sun by a wide brimmed bush hat, gave added credence to the charge that he was unreliable. But the corollary was to cast doubt on the type of person entrusted to protect the nation's secrets. Was the slightly comical figure of Wright typical of those selected to work in MI5's K Branch? Michael Bettaney's background had not even withstood the superficial probing of the all-amateur Security Commission, and in a more recent disclosure it was conceded that the once-venerated Maurice Oldfield had himself been a practising homosexual whose behaviour had led to his security clearance being revoked in March 1980.

The truth known to those officers who originally came to believe that MI5 had harboured a spy at the top was that Mitchell was always the best candidate. The absence of a confession from him eliminated all chances of a formal trial but, in intelligence terms, they were satisfied they had nailed the right source. His own decision to take early retirement had effectively neutralised him and moved him out of harm's way. However, it was the continuing need to eliminate others from the molehunt and perhaps obtain an intelligence advantage which could be utilised against the opposition that demanded a more formal, satisfactory conclusion to the case. Mitchell's absence from MI5's headquarters had diminished his usefulness to the Soviets, but he still had a potential value for the Security Service. Interrogation and an unorthodox, informal approach both failed to achieve their objective, leaving the Security Service with a political dilemma: either to admit that penetration had once taken place, and concede the culprit was never found; or deny that MI5 had ever experienced penetration. Having been pushed on to the first course by the public allegations against Hollis, the organisation has, by confirming Mitchell's clearance, been obliged to adopt the second course. It is, of course, singularly unconvincing. The acquittal of a suspected killer does not mean a murder has not happened, even if the homicide victim's body is subsequently buried in secret.

Either way, the Security Service's molehunts led it to become engaged in a counter-productive battle with the media which was to be fought in public. Provoked by MI5's

instinctive reaction to his highly-personalised version of
the molehunts, Peter Wright responded by disclosing some
of his former employers' 'family jewels', details of some
of the more sensitive investigations conducted more than
a decade earlier. Were the enquiries which centred on
Harold Wilson and his entourage inspired by political
malice or concern for the safety of the realm? Wright saw
the matter as an instance of treason, nothing short of a
subversive plot to destabilise a Labour Prime Minister
and his administration. The Security Service management
believed it had a duty to protect the country's highest
elected official from what it perceived as the potentially
undesirable influence of those closest to him. Subversion,
as practised by highly professional renegades; or an authorised enquiry that may have involved an element of ill-
conceived mischief? It was not an issue the Security
Service, or those charged with responsibility for its supervision at the relevant time, had any desire to debate in
public.

Understandably, Mrs Thatcher, beleaguered throughout her term of office by security lapses, was unable to
answer for events that had apparently taken place during
the premiership of Sir James Callaghan. Nor did he seem
too keen to re-open an episode that, reportedly, had been
the subject of a review conducted by Lord Hunt when he
had been Sir Robert Armstrong's predecessor as Cabinet
Secretary. In whose interests was it to air such contro-
versies? Certainly not those of the Security Service, under
the stewardship of the Prime Minister's nominee Sir Antony Duff, or those of the politicians directly concerned
with the events recalled so vividly by Peter Wright. But
such considerations were never anticipated when the Security Service advised tough action through the courts to
suppress his memoirs.

If Michael Bettaney's exposure as a would-be Soviet spy
prompted Wright to take his crusade a stage further, his
case ought to be subjected to further scrutiny. As might
have been expected, the Security Commission failed to ask
the right questions. Instead of concentrating on Bettaney's

character and behaviour, greater emphasis might have
been placed on the role of the Security Service, its recruitment procedures, and the expectation of those middle-
ranking staff who have little or no prospect of
advancement. The Commission rightly highlighted the in-
built structural defects of MI5's personnel management
policy which relies on unswerving devotion with neither
reward nor promotion. In short, under the system inherited
by Sir John Jones, it offered an old-fashioned life of
tedium, with only the remotest chance of access to senior
posts. As a career model it was doomed to attract medioc-
rity unless there was an unanticipated crisis which might
enable talent to manifest itself. The principal difficulty was
persuading professionals to accept the existing arrangements, knowing that the system was already dominated
by people who had not chosen the organisation as their
first-choice career. Such a label applied to the late entry
retirees, the 'Malaya Mafia' and the diminishing contingent
of Colonial police veterans.

Bettaney was representative of a generation of Security
Service recruits, low achievers lacking the special dedi-
cation demanded. His intake suffered an attrition rate that
would not have been sustained in any other branch of the
civil service. Questions would have been raised about the
style of management and internal staff relations, but within
MI5's cloistered, stifling atmosphere, such anxieties were
rarely articulated. To do so meant jeopardising the status
quo, and one's progress up the pyramid of command and
responsibility.

The key to Bettaney's extraordinary case was not his
professed new-found political ideology, nor his apparent
contempt for the values espoused by his colleagues. In
reality it was the prospect that within a very short period
he would be obliged to submit to a routine Positive Vetting
examination, and that his latest criminal conviction would
result in disciplinary action. He may not have had any
clear picture of exactly what this might entail, and he was
probably ignorant of the very limited number of options
available to a Director-General confronted with a reject.

Outright sacking might invite retaliation, a point made by Jones to the Security Commission without much impact, and complete loss of supervision over such a disgruntled individual could risk compromising information to which previously he had enjoyed access. Knowing that he faced a limited future, Bettaney decided to be hung for a sheep as a lamb, and took advantage of the short time he had left in K Branch. His political commitment probably came later, as a self-serving justification of his appalling behaviour.

If that is indeed the explanation, rather than the semi-transparent Soviet-Marxist conversion he claimed at his trial, there should be a far-reaching review of the Positive Vetting system. The revelation that Sir Maurice Oldfield, SIS's Chief until 1978, had successfully concealed his active homosexuality from those checking his background every five years during the latter part of his distinguished career, demonstrates the urgency of the situation. Hostile penetration of any Western security or intelligence agency is an occupational hazard, but to compound the risks by inadequate employment checks seems a trifle complacent.

Positive Vetting was never intended to identify Russian spies. It was designed to spot the so-called character defects of drunkenness, indebtedness, criminal behaviour, homosexuality or membership of an extremist group, that might make a candidate susceptible to blackmail or coercion. As a broad principle it was adopted simultaneously by France, Canada and the United States. But unlike those countries, where the actual screening process was placed in the hands of the existing security authorities, Britain opted for an unusual alternative. Responsibility for carrying out Positive Vetting enquiries was rejected by the Security Service, on the advice of Graham Mitchell, and a specialist unit was created within the Ministry of Supply. In later years it was placed under the auspices of the Ministry of Aviation before returning under the Ministry of Supply's umbrella, and finally ending up with the Procurement Executive of the Ministry of Defence. In short, it was generally unwanted. Operational control was granted to a small com-

mittee drawn from SIS, the Treasury, the Intelligence
Corps and the judiciary, with a tiny field force of ex-CID
and Colonial Special Branch police officers to conduct
enquiries. The narrow terms of reference under which the
PV unit existed were so strict that it was almost impossible
for a member to recommend the rejection of a candidate
or suggest further investigation. Contact with the Security
Service was restricted to correspondence with its London
headquarters, via its 'Box 500' cover postal address, to
establish whether MI5 had a record of the candidate in its
Registry indices. Incredibly, MI5 and SIS personnel were
at first excluded from PV checks because their backgrounds
were considered too secret to be examined by outsiders. In
spite of these handicaps the unit did useful work although it
never uncovered a spy. In fact clearances were granted to a
considerable number of Soviet agents who, with hindsight,
might have merited more intensive scrutiny. As Mitchell
had pointed out upon inception, the procedure ought to
be completed in a manner which avoided accusations of
unjustified discrimination or Gestapo tactics. So far as is
known, no such charges were ever made, so to this extent
Mitchell's scheme succeeded.

PV enquiries are now rather more thorough and are
especially deep for those contemplating a career within a
secret department like MI5, SIS or GCHQ. Nevertheless,
the fact that Oldfield could have hidden his sexual proclivi-
ties until after his official retirement should give cause for
concern. This is not to suggest that he was ever disloyal.
It is simply a statement of fact relating to his five successful
efforts to deceive his colleagues when questioned about
his sexual preferences. He lied, and was believed, until he
was challenged directly and confronted with an official
report detailing his private life. The matter was eventually
considered by the Prime Minister and the Security Commission, a testament to the lack of complacency at the
highest political levels early in 1980. No doubt the recent
public statement on Anthony Blunt's treachery had been
fresh in everyone's mind and the potential for future scandal had been recognised.

Comprehensive and continuing checks conducted by MI5 itself into the background of those undertaking secret work is highly desirable so long as the procedures employed only deter those with guilty consciences. The excuse that the Security Service is too secret to undertake such mundane duties is patently absurd. Indeed, its own standards will need to be improved and facilities developed for the non-contentious dispersal elsewhere of dubious or problem staff. Stringent vetting may eliminate the more obvious potential moles with a traceable past, and it may exclude those who, even in an increasingly tolerant society, may be vulnerable to blackmail, but the future of the Security Service at least must be in a more open form of management, with an in-built mechanism to allow individual officers to express grievances. Flexibility, coupled with an opportunity for MI5 personnel to voice dissatisfaction without jeopardising their careers, would restore morale and prevent the organisation enduring the self-destructive consequences of the molehunts.

APPENDICES

1

The full text of the White Paper drafted by Graham Mitchell on the defection of Burgess and Maclean, with added emphasis on the parts now known to be untrue

Report Concerning the Disappearance of Two
Former Foreign Office Officials
The full text of White Paper, Cmd 9577, 23rd September 1955

On the evening of Friday, 25th May 1951, Mr Donald Duart Maclean, a Counsellor in the senior branch of the Foreign Service and at that time Head of the American Department in the Foreign Office, and Mr Guy Francis de Moncy Burgess, a Second Secretary in the junior branch of the Foreign Service, left the United Kingdom from Southampton on the boat for St Malo. The circumstances of their departure from England, for which they had not sought sanction, were such as to make it obvious that they had deliberately fled the country. Both officers were suspended from duty on 1st June 1951, and their appointments in the Foreign Office were terminated on 1st June 1952, with effect from 1st June 1951.

2. Maclean was the son of a former Cabinet Minister, Sir Donald Maclean. He was born in 1913 and was educated at Gresham's School, Holt, and *Trinity College*, Cambridge, where he had a distinguished academic record. He successfully competed for the Diplomatic Service in 1935 and was posted in the first instance to the Foreign Office. He served

subsequently in Paris, at Washington and in Cairo. He was an officer of exceptional ability and was promoted to the rank of Counsellor at the early age of thirty-five. He was married to an American lady and had two young sons. A third child was born shortly after his disappearance.

3. In May 1950 while serving at His Majesty's Embassy, Cairo, Maclean was guilty of serious misconduct and suffered a form of breakdown which was attributed to overwork and excessive drinking. Until the breakdown took place his work had remained eminently satisfactory and *there was no ground whatsoever for doubting his loyalty*. After recuperation and leave at home he was passed medically fit, and in October 1950 was appointed to be Head of the American Department of the Foreign Office which, since it does not deal with the major problems of Anglo–American relations, appeared to be within his capacity.

4. Since Maclean's disappearance a close examination of his background has revealed that during his student days at Cambridge from 1931 to 1934 he had expressed Communist sympathies, but *there was no evidence that he had ever been a member of the Communist Party* and indeed on leaving the University he had outwardly renounced his earlier Communist views.

5. Burgess was born in 1911 and was educated at the Royal Naval College, Dartmouth, at Eton and at Trinity College, Cambridge, where he had a brilliant academic record. After leaving Cambridge in 1935 he worked for a short time in London as a journalist and joined the BBC in 1936 where he remained until January 1939. *From 1939 until 1941 he was employed in one of the war propaganda organisations*. He rejoined the BBC in January 1941 and remained there until 1944 when he applied for and obtained a post as a temporary press officer in the News Department of the Foreign Office. He was not recruited into the Foreign Service through the open competitive examination but in 1947 took the opportunity open to temporary employees to present himself for establishment. He appeared before a Civil Service Commission Board

and was recommended for the junior branch of the Foreign
Service. His establishment took effect from 1st January
1947. He worked for a time in the office of the then
Minister of State, Mr Hector McNeil, and in the Far
Eastern Department of the Foreign Office. In August 1950
he was transferred to Washington as a Second Secretary.

6. Early in 1950 the security authorities informed the
Foreign Office that in late 1949 while on holiday abroad
Burgess had been guilty of indiscreet talk about secret
matters of which he had official knowledge. For this he
was severely reprimanded. Apart from this lapse his service
in the Foreign Office up to the time of his appointment to
Washington was satisfactory and there seemed good reason
to hope that he would make a useful career.

7. In Washington, however, his work and behaviour
gave rise to complaint. The Ambassador reported that his
work had been unsatisfactory in that he lacked thorough-
ness and balance in routine matters, that he had come to
the unfavourable notice of the Department of State because of his reckless driving and that he had had to be
reprimanded for carelessness in leaving confidential papers
unattended. The Ambassador requested that Burgess be
removed from Washington and this was approved. He was
recalled to London in early May 1951 and was asked to
resign from the Foreign Service. Consideration was being
given to the steps that would be taken in the event of his
refusing to do so. It was at this point that he disappeared.

8. Investigations into Burgess's past have since shown
that he, like Maclean, went through a period of Communist
leanings while at Cambridge and that he too on leaving
the University outwardly renounced his views. No trace
can be found in his subsequent career of direct participation in the activities of left-wing organisations; indeed
he was known after leaving Cambridge to have had some
contact with organisations such as the Anglo–German
Club.

9. The question has been asked whether the association
of these two officers with each other did not give rise to
suspicion. The fact is that although we have since learned

that Maclean and Burgess were acquainted during their undergraduate days at Cambridge, they gave no evidence during the course of their career in the Foreign Service of any association other than would be normal between two colleagues. When Burgess was appointed to the Foreign Office Maclean was in Washington and at the time Burgess himself was appointed to Washington Maclean was back in the United Kingdom awaiting assignment to the American Department of the Foreign Office. It is now clear that they were in communication with each other after the return of Burgess from Washington in 1951 and they may have been in such communication earlier. Their relations were, however, never such as to cause remark.

10. In January 1949 the security authorities received a report that certain Foreign Office information had leaked to the Soviet authorities some years earlier. The report amounted to little more than a hint and it was at the time impossible to attribute the leak to any particular individual. Highly secret but widespread and protracted enquiries were begun by the security authorities and the field of suspicion had been narrowed by mid-April 1951 to two or three persons. By the beginning of May Maclean had come to be regarded as the principal suspect. There was, however, even at that time, *no legally admissible evidence* to support a prosecution under the Official Secrets Acts. Arrangements were made to ensure that information of exceptional secrecy and importance should not come into his hands. In the meantime the security authorities arranged to investigate his activities and contacts in order to increase their background knowledge and if possible to obtain information which could be used as evidence in a prosecution. On 25th May the then Secretary of State, Mr Herbert Morrison, sanctioned a proposal that the security authorities should question Maclean. In reaching this decision it had to be borne in mind that such questioning might produce no confession or voluntary statement from Maclean sufficient to support a prosecution but might serve only to alert him and to reveal the nature and the extent of the suspicion against him. In that event he would have

been free to make arrangements to leave the country and *the authorities would have had no legal power to stop him.* Everything therefore depended on the interview and the security authorities were anxious to be as fully prepared as was humanly possible. They were also anxious that Maclean's house at Tatsfield, Kent, should be searched and *this was an additional reason for delaying the proposed interview until mid-June* when Mrs Maclean who was then pregnant was expected to be away from home.

11. It is now clear that in spite of the precautions taken by the authorities Maclean must have become aware, at some time before his disappearance, that he was under investigation. One explanation may be that he observed that he was no longer receiving certain types of secret papers. It is also possible that he detected that he was under observation. Or he may have been warned. Searching inquiries involving individual interrogations were made into this last possibility. *Insufficient evidence was obtainable to form a definite conclusion* or to warrant prosecution.

12. *Maclean's absence did not become known to the authorities until the morning of Monday, 28th May.* The Foreign Office is regularly open for normal business on Saturday mornings but officers can from time to time obtain leave to take a weekend off. In accordance with this practice Maclean applied for and obtained leave to be absent on the morning of Saturday, 26th May. *His absence therefore caused no remark until the following Monday morning* when he failed to appear at the Foreign Office. Burgess was on leave and under no obligation to report his movements.

13. *Immediately the flight was known* all possible action was taken in the United Kingdom and the French and other Continental security authorities were asked to trace the whereabouts of the fugitives and if possible to intercept them. All British Consulates in Western Europe were alerted and special efforts were made to discover whether the fugitives had crossed the French frontiers on 26th or 27th May. As a result of these and other inquiries it was established that Maclean and Burgess together left

Tatsfield by car for Southampton in the late evening of Friday, 25th May, arrived at Southampton at midnight, caught the SS *Falaise* for St Malo and disembarked at that port at 11.45 the following morning, leaving suitcases and some of their clothing on board. They were not seen on the train from St Malo to Paris and it has been reported that two men, believed to be Maclean and Burgess, took a taxi to Rennes and there got the 1.18 p.m. train to Paris. Nothing more was seen of them.

14. Since the disappearance various communications have been received from them by members of their families. On 7th June 1951, telegrams ostensibly from Maclean were received by his mother Lady Maclean, and his wife Mrs Melinda Maclean, who were both at that time in the United Kingdom. The telegram to Lady Maclean was a short personal message, signed by a nick-name known only within the immediate family circle. It merely stated that all was well. That addressed to Mrs Maclean was similar, expressing regret for the unexpected departure and was signed 'Donald'. Both telegrams were dispatched in Paris on the evening of 6th June. Their receipt was at once reported to the security authorities, but it was impossible to identify the person or persons who had handed them in. The original telegraph forms showed, however, that the messages had been written in a hand which was clearly not Maclean's. The character of the handwriting and some mis-spelling, suggested that both telegrams had been written by a foreigner.

15. On 7th June 1951, a telegram was received in London by Mrs Bassett, Burgess's mother. It contained a short and affectionate personal message, together with a statement that the sender was embarking on a long Mediterranean holiday, and was ostensibly from Burgess himself. The telegram had been handed in at a Post Office in Rome earlier on the day of its receipt. As with the telegrams from Paris to Maclean's family, there was no possibility of identifying the person who had handed it in. The handwriting had the appearance of being foreign, and was certainly not that of Burgess.

16. According to information given to the Foreign Office in confidence by Mrs Dunbar, Maclean's mother-in-law, who was then living with her daughter at Tatsfield, she received on 3rd August 1951 two registered letters posted in St Gallen, Switzerland, on 1st August. One contained a draft on the Swiss Bank Corporation, London, the sum of £1,000 payable to Mrs Dunbar; the other, a draft payable to Mrs Dunbar for the same sum, drawn by the Union Bank of Switzerland on the Midland Bank, 122 Old Broad Street, London. Both drafts were stated to have been remitted by order of a Mr Robert Becker, whose address was given as the Hotel Central, Zurich. Exhaustive inquiries in collaboration with the Swiss authorities have not led to the identification of Mr Becker and it is probable that the name given was false.

17. Shortly after the receipt of these bank drafts Mrs Maclean received a letter in her husband's handwriting. It had been posted in Reigate, Surrey, on 5th August 1951, and was of an affectionate, personal nature as from husband to wife. It gave no clue as to Maclean's whereabouts or the reason for his disappearance but it explained that the bank drafts, which for convenience had been sent to Mrs Dunbar, were intended for Mrs Maclean.

18. Lady Maclean received a further letter from her son on 15th August 1951. There is no doubt that it was in his own handwriting. It had been posted at Herne Hill on 11th August.

19. Mrs Bassett, the mother of Burgess, received a letter in Burgess's handwriting on 22nd December 1953. The letter was personal and gave no information as to Burgess's whereabouts. It was simply dated 'November' and had been posted in South-East London on 21st December. The last message received from either of the two men was a further letter from Burgess to his mother which was delivered in London on 25th December 1954. This letter was also personal and disclosed nothing of Burgess's whereabouts. It too was simply dated 'November'. It had been posted in Poplar, E 14, on 23rd December.

20. On 11th September 1953, Mrs Maclean, who was

living in Geneva, left there by car with her three children. She had told her mother, who was staying with her, that she had unexpectedly come across an acquaintance whom she and her husband had previously known in Cairo and that he had invited her and the children to spend the weekend with him at Territet, near Montreux. She stated that she would return to Geneva on 13th September in time for the two elder children to attend school the following day. By 14th September her mother, alarmed at her failure to return, reported the matter to Her Majesty's Consul-General in Geneva and also by telephone to London. Security officers were at once dispatched to Geneva where they placed themselves at the disposal of the Swiss police who were already making intensive inquiries. On the afternoon of 16th September Mrs Maclean's car was found in a garage in Lausanne. She had left it on the afternoon of the 11th saying she would return for it in a week. The garage hand who reported this added that Mrs Maclean had then proceeded with her children to the Lausanne railway station. On the same day, 16th September, Mrs Dunbar reported to the Geneva police the receipt of a telegram purporting to come from her daughter. The telegram explained that Mrs Maclean had been delayed 'owing to unforeseen circumstances' and asked Mrs Dunbar to inform the school authorities that the two elder children would be returning in a week. Mrs Maclean's youngest child was referred to in this telegram by a name known only to Mrs Maclean, her mother and other intimates. The telegram had been handed in at the Post Office in Territet at 10.58 that morning by a woman whose description did not agree with that of Mrs Maclean. The handwriting on the telegram form was not Mrs Maclean's and it showed foreign characteristics similar to those in the telegrams received in 1951 by Lady Maclean, Mrs Maclean and Mrs Bassett.

21. From information subsequently received from witnesses in Switzerland and Austria, it seems clear that the arrangements for Mrs Maclean's departure from Geneva had been carefully planned, and that she proceeded by

train from Lausanne on the evening of 11th September, passing the Swiss – Austrian frontier that night, and arriving at Schwarzach St Veit in the American Zone of Austria at approximately 9.15 on the morning of 12th September. The independent evidence of a porter at Schwarzach St Veit and of witnesses travelling on the train has established that she left the train at this point. Further evidence, believed to be reliable, shows that she was met at the station by an unknown man driving a car bearing Austrian number plates. The further movements of this car have not been traced. It is probable that it took Mrs Maclean and the children from Schwarzach St Veit to a neighbouring territory in Russian occupation whence she proceeded on her journey to join her husband.

22. There was no question of preventing Mrs Maclean from leaving the United Kingdom to go to live in Switzerland. Although she was under no obligation to report her movements, she had been regularly in touch with the security authorities, and had informed them that she wished to make her home in Switzerland. She gave two good reasons, firstly that she wished to avoid the personal embarrassment to which she had been subjected by the Press in the United Kingdom, and secondly, that she wished to educate her children in the International School in Geneva. It will be remembered that Mrs Maclean was an American citizen and in view of the publicity caused by her husband's flight it was only natural that she should wish to bring up her children in new surroundings. Before she left for Geneva the security authorities made arrangements with her whereby she was to keep in touch with the British authorities in Berne and Geneva in case she should receive any further news from her husband or require advice or assistance. Mrs Maclean was a free agent. The authorities had no legal means of detaining her in the United Kingdom. Any form of surveillance abroad would have been unwarranted.

23. In view of the suspicions held against Maclean and of the conspiratorial manner of his flight, it was assumed, though it could not be proved, that his destination and

that of his companion must have been the Soviet Union or some other territory behind the Iron Curtain. Now Vladimir Petrov, the former *Third Secretary of the Soviet Embassy in Canberra* who sought political asylum on 3rd April 1954, has provided confirmation of this. Petrov himself was not directly concerned in the case and his information was obtained from conversation with one of his colleagues in Soviet service in Australia. Petrov states that both Maclean and Burgess were recruited as spies for the Soviet Government while students at the University, with the intention that they should carry out their espionage tasks in the Foreign Office, and that in 1951, by means unknown to him, one or other of the two men became aware that their activities were under investigation. This was reported by them to the Soviet Intelligence Service who then organised their escape and removal to the Soviet Union. Petrov has the impression that the escape route included Czechoslovakia and that it involved an aeroplane flight into that country. Upon their arrival in Russia, Maclean and Burgess lived near Moscow. They were used as advisers to the Ministry of Foreign Affairs and other Soviet agencies. Petrov adds that one of the men (Maclean) has since been joined by his wife.

24. Two points call for comment: first, how Maclean and Burgess remained in the Foreign Service for so long and second, why they were able to get away.

25. When these two men were given their appointments nothing was on record about either to show that he was unsuitable for the public service. It is true that their subsequent personal behaviour was unsatisfactory, and this led to action in each case. As already stated Maclean was recalled from Cairo in 1950 and was not re-employed until he was declared medically fit. Burgess was recalled from Washington in 1951 and was asked to resign. It was only shortly before Maclean disappeared that serious suspicion of his reliability was aroused and active inquiries were set on foot.

26. The second question is how Maclean and Burgess made good their escape from this country *when the security*

authorities were on their track. The watch on Maclean was made difficult by the need to ensure that he did not become aware that he was under observation. This watch was primarily aimed at collecting, if possible, further information and not at preventing an escape. In imposing it a calculated risk had to be taken that he might become aware of it and might take flight. It was inadvisable to increase this risk by extending the surveillance to his home *in an isolated part of the country* and he was therefore watched in London only. Both men were free to go abroad at any time. In some countries no doubt Maclean would have been arrested first and questioned afterwards. In this country no arrest can be made without adequate evidence. At the time there was *insufficient evidence*. It was for these reasons necessary for the security authorities to embark upon the difficult and delicate investigation of Maclean, taking into full account *the risk that he would be alerted*. In the event he was alerted and fled the country together with Burgess.

27. As a result of this case, in July 1951 the then Secretary of State, Mr Herbert Morrison, set up a Committee of inquiry to consider the security checks applied to members of the Foreign Service; the existing regulations and practices of the Foreign Service in regard to any matters having a bearing on security; and to report whether any alterations were called for. The Committee reported in November 1951. It recommended, among other things, a more extensive security check on Foreign Service officers than had until then been the practice. This was immediately put into effect and since 1952 searching inquiries have been made into the antecedents and associates of all those occupying or applying for positions in the Foreign Office involving highly secret information. The purpose of these inquiries is to ensure that no one is appointed to or continues to occupy any such post unless he or she is fit to be entrusted with the secrets to which the post gives access. The Foreign Secretary of the day approved the action required.

28. A great deal of criticism has been directed towards the reticence of Ministerial replies on these matters; an

attitude which it was alleged would not have been changed had it not been for the Petrov revelations. Espionage is carried out in secret. Counter-espionage equally depends for its success upon the maximum secrecy of its methods. Nor is it desirable at any moment to let the other side know how much has been discovered or guess at what means have been used to discover it. Nor should they be allowed to know all the steps that have been taken to improve security. These considerations still apply and must be the basic criterion for judging what should or should not be published.

ERRORS IN THE WHITE PAPER

1 Maclean was an undergraduate at Trinity Hall, not 'Trinity College', Cambridge.

2 Apparently, 'there was no ground whatsoever for doubting his [Maclean's] loyalty', but in fact Maclean had openly expressed his sympathy for the Soviet cause while at university and had made no secret of his CPGB membership. He had even written to *Granta*, Cambridge's undergraduate magazine, openly expressing his pro-Communist views.

3 'There was no evidence that he had ever been a member of the Communist Party', but in reality several people had told MI5 of Maclean's CPGB membership.

4 'From 1939 until 1941' Burgess was not 'employed in one of the war propaganda organisations'. He was, successively, a member of the Secret Intelligence Service, Special Operations Executive and a part-time MI5 agent. His employment at the BBC had merely been a semi-transparent cover story.

5 'No legally admissible evidence' had been contained in the VENONA intercepts implicating Klaus Fuchs, yet he had been interrogated on the strength of them, and a confession had been extracted which proved sufficient to obtain a conviction.

6 The authorities had plenty of 'legal power' to stop Maclean from leaving the country.

7 The Security Service had no intention of delaying Maclean's interrogation 'until mid- June'. It had been scheduled for 28 May.

8 The defections had led MI5 to form a 'definite conclusion' about Philby, Blunt, Rees and Cairncross.

9 'Maclean's absence' was known to the authorities on Friday, 25 May, not 'Monday, 28th May' as claimed.

10 To say his absence 'caused no remark until the following Monday morning' ignores MI5's abortive efforts over the weekend to trace Maclean in France.

11 MI5 did not ask for help from the French police 'immediately the flight was known', but delayed for some days. It is not explained how Burgess, who supposedly 'was on leave and under no obligation to report his movements', had apparently been identified as one of 'the fugitives' whom the continental security authorities had been asked to 'intercept'.

12 Vladimir Petrov's cover in the Soviet Embassy was as a diplomat with the rank of Third Secretary. His true position was the NKVD's *rezident* for all Australia. No mention is made of his wife's NKVD role, nor her corroboration of her husband's testimony.

13 The claim that MI5 had doubts about both Burgess and Maclean before their defection, and had been 'on their track', is untrue. Only Maclean had become a suspect, Burgess had never come under suspicion.

14 In many cases, where observation is intended only to monitor times of arrival and departure (and not total surveillance on all contacts), it is easier to undertake such operations 'in an isolated part of the country'. In any event, this description hardly suits Tatsfield in Kent.

15 There may have been 'insufficient evidence' to warrant a formal arrest, but there was no obstacle to questioning Maclean or inviting him to help the police with their enquiries. MI5's professed inability to have Maclean arrested in England is contradicted by the previously stated claim that a request had been made to 'intercept' him in France.

16 The implication is that MI5 feared that Maclean 'would be alerted' by the nature of the surveillance mounted upon him although, by this time, it was known that he had been warned by someone, an insider, who knew of the investigation.

17 Considering Burgess, Maclean, Philby and Blunt had all reported to Moscow on the circumstances of the defection, MI5's reluctance to tell the government the full story seems, at best, inappropriate.

2

Arthur Martin's letter to *The Times* published on 19 July 1984 following Peter Wright's television interview

Sir. In Monday's *World In Action* programme about the security service my former colleague, Peter Wright, said that he was '99 per cent certain that Sir Roger Hollis was a spy'.

I think that was an exaggeration. My recollection is that, while Hollis fitted the circumstantial evidence more closely than any other candidate, the case against him was not conclusive.

It was the evidence of continued penetration of the service after Blunt retired in 1945 until at least the early 1960s which carried complete conviction among those working on the case.

When in 1969 the interrogation of Hollis failed to produce a conclusive answer, it would have been normal practice to continue the search but to widen its scope: if it was not Hollis, who was it?

Instead, the investigating team was disbanded and the case allowed to lapse. It was that decision, I believe, which led to a decade of unease which, as the programme showed, still festers today. For it is inconceivable that the security service would have allowed an investigation to lapse if similar evidence of penetration had been discovered in any other department of government.

It has been suggested from time to time that yet another

official enquiry into the case should be made. In my view this would be pointless. No amount of re-examination can resolve the case; only new evidence will do that. New evidence, if it comes, will be by chance or renewed security service effort.

In the article in your issue of July 17 you quote the comment of a very senior former counter-intelligence officer to the effect that Mr Wright's action 'is a very serious crime'. That may be. I remember Peter Wright as a dedicated officer, deeply concerned by the threats to his country.

Yours, A. S. MARTIN

NOTES

1: Immunity Accepted
1 Foreign Secretary's statement, 7 November 1955
2 Peter Wright interview, *World in Action*, 16 July 1984
3 Peter Wright manuscript notes

2: Operation PETERS
1 Michael Straight, *After Long Silence* (Collins, 1983), p. 72
2 *Ibid.*, p. 104
3 *Ibid.*, p. 167
4 *Ibid.*, p. 167
5 Goronwy Rees, *A Chapter of Accidents* (Chatto & Windus, 1972), p. 219
6 *Ibid.*, p. 226
7 Peter Wright, *World in Action*

3: Operation FLUENCY

1 Kim Philby, *My Silent War* (MacGibbon & Kee, 1968), p. 133
2 Peter Wright, *World in Action*

4: Smoking Gun Evidence: DRAT
1 Philby, *My Silent War*, p. 115
2 Gouzenko transcripts
3 Igor Gouzenko, *This Was My Choice* (Eyre & Spottiswode, 1948), p. 140
4 *Ibid.*, p. 138
5 Chapman Pincher, *Too Secret Too Long* (Sidgwick & Jackson, 1984), p. 104
6 Lord Rothschild, *Random Variables (Collins, 1984), p. 203*
7 *Ibid.*, p. 204

5: Cover-Up

1 Chapman Pincher, *Inside Story* (Sidgwick & Jackson, 1978), p. 17
2 *Ibid.*, p. 18
3 *Ibid.*, p. 190
4 Rees, *A Chapter of Accidents*, p. 207
5 *Ibid.*, p. 209
6 Patrick Seale and Maureen McConville, *Philby: The Long Road to Moscow* (Hamish Hamilton, 1973), p. 130
7 Richard Deacon, *The British Connection* (Hamish Hamilton, 1979)
8 *Ibid.*, p. 75
9 *Ibid.*
10 Rees, *op. cit.*, p. 208
11 Andrew Boyle, *The Climate of Treason* (Hutchinson, 1979), p. 430
12 Mrs Thatcher, 15 November 1979

6: Other Connections

1 Rees, *A Chapter of Accidents*, p. 154
2 Pincher, *Sunday Express*, 30 November 1986
3 *Ibid.*
4 David Mure, *The Times*, 31 December 1979
5 *Sunday Times*, 20 January 1980
6 Andrew Boyle, *The Times*, 23 February 1980
7 *Sunday Times*, 20 January 1980
8 Rothschild, *Random Variables*, p. 204
9 Flora Solomon, *From Baku to Baker Street* (Collins, 1984), p. 226
10 Pincher, *Sunday Express*, 30 November 1986
11 *Ibid.*
12 *Ibid.*
13 *Ibid.*, 7 December 1986
14 Peter Wright, *The Times*, 9 December 1986
15 Pincher, *Inside Story*, p. 17
16 Pincher, *Sunday Express*, 30 November 1986
17 *Ibid.*
18 Pincher, *Inside Story*, p. 153
19 Pincher, *Sunday Express*, 30 November 1986
20 J. C. Masterman, *On the Chariot Wheel* (OUP, 1975), p. 359
21 *Ibid.*, p. 361
22 John Whitwell, *British Agent* (Kimber, 1966)
23 Pincher, *Sunday Express*, 30 November 1986
24 *Ibid.*, 14 December 1986
25 *Ibid.*
26 Peter Wright statement, *The Times*, 9 December 1986

27 Pincher, *Sunday Express*, 30 November 1986
28 *Ibid*.
29 *Ibid*.
30 Pincher, *Inside Story*, p. 92
31 *Ibid*.
32 *Ibid*., p. 89
33 *Observer,* 30 November 1986
34 *Ibid*.
35 Peter Wright statement, *The Times*, 9 December 1986
36 Chapman Pincher, *Their Trade is Treachery* (Sidgwick & Jackson, 1981), p. x

7: Their Trade is Treachery
1 Pincher, *Their Trade is Treachery*, p. 1
2 *Ibid*., p. 14
3 *Ibid*., p. 89
4 *Ibid*., p. 138
5 *Ibid*., p. 132
6 *Ibid*., p. 138
7 *Ibid*., p. 136
8 *Ibid*., p. 42
9 *Ibid*., p. 43
10 *Ibid*., p. 81
11 *Ibid*., p. 101
12 *Ibid*., p. 121
13 *Ibid*., p. 88
14 *Ibid*., p. 80
15 *Ibid*., p. 145
16 *Ibid*., p. 232
17 Mrs Thatcher's statement on Hollis, 26 March 1981
18 *Ibid*.
19 *Daily Mail*, 27 March 1981
20 Peter Wright, *World in Action*, 16 July 1984
21 *Daily Mail*, 27 March 1981
22 Pincher, *Their Trade is Treachery*, p. 19
23 *Ibid*., p. 131
24 John Allen letter, *People*, 23 November 1986
25 *Daily Telegraph*, 27 October 1981
26 Pincher, *Their Trade is Treachery*, p. 99
27 *Ibid*., p. 100
28 *Ibid*.
29 *Ibid*.
30 *Sunday Times*, 8 November 1981
31 *The Times*, 26 October 1981
32 Gouzenko transcripts
33 Gouzenko, *This Was My Choice*, p. 268
34 *Ibid*., p. 300
35 *Ibid*.
36 June Callwood, *Emma* (Beaufort Books, 1984), p. 124
37 Peter Wright, *World in Action*
38 Gouzenko, *op. cit*., p. 280
39 *Ibid*.

40 *Daily Mail*, 10 October 1981
41 *The Times*, 21 October 1981
42 *Ibid*., 23 October 1981
43 Pincher, *Their Trade is Treachery*, p. 83
44 Pincher, *The Times*, 12 December 1981
45 Sir Charles Cunningham, *The Times*, 16 December 1981
46 Anthony Glees, *Listener*, 29 October 1981
47 *Ibid*.
48 Anthony Glees, *The Times*, 3 April 1982
49 *Ibid*.
50 *Ibid*.
51 *Ibid*.
52 Pincher, *The Times*, 5 April 1982
53 Pincher, *Their Trade is Treachery*, p. 3
54 Pincher, *The Times*, 5 April 1982
55 Glees, *The Times*, 3 April 1982
56 *Ibid*.

8: A Matter of Trust
1 *The Times*, 3 January 1985
2 Burgess and Maclean White Paper (Cmd 9577), 23 September 1955
3 Parliamentary reply from Harold Macmillan, 25 October 1955
4 White Paper
5 *Ibid*.
6 Michael Thwaites, *Truth Will Out* (Collins, 1980), p. 131
7 Vladimir and Evdokia Petrov, *Empire of Fear* (André Deutsch, 1956), p. 272
8 *Ibid*.
9 White Paper
10 Pincher, *Their Trade is Treachery*, p. 286
11 *Ibid*., p. 290
12 *Ibid*., p. 6
13 *Ibid*., p. 5
14 Petrov, *op. cit.*, p. 210
15 Pincher, *Their Trade is Treachery*, p. 19
16 Nigel West, *A Matter of Trust* (Weidenfeld & Nicolson, 1982), p. 107
17 *Observer*, 7 December 1986
18 *The Times*, 1 December 1986
19 Pincher, *Sunday Express*, 30 November 1986
20 *Ibid*.
21 See also the *Sunday Mirror*, 30 January 1986

9: The Wright Affair
1 Security Commission Report (Cmd 9514), p. 17
2 *Ibid*., p. 4
3 *Ibid*., p. 17

4 Pincher, *Their Trade is Treachery*, p. 235

5 *Ibid.*, p. 221

6 Security Commission Report, p. 31

7 *New Society*, 31 May 1984

8 *Ibid.*, 14 June 1984

9 *Observer*, 22 July 1984

10 *The Times*, 23 July 1984

11 *Observer*, 22 July 1984

12 *The Times*, 30 July 1984

13 *Sunday Times*, 22 July 1984

14 *Ibid.*

15 *Ibid.*

16 *Observer*, 29 July 1984

17 *The Times*, 3 August 1984

18 *Sunday Times*, 27 July 1984

19 *Daily Telegraph*, 3 August 1984

20 *Ibid.*, 25 February 1985

21 Pincher, *Sunday Express*, 17 August 1986

22 *Ibid.*, 24 August 1986

23 *Ibid.*

24 *Ibid.*, 9 November 1986

25 *Guardian*, 21 November 1986

26 *Ibid.*

27 *The Times*, 20 December 1986

28 Pincher, *Sunday Express*, 16 November 1986

29 *Daily Express*, 22 November 1986

30 *Sunday Express*, 7 December 1986

31 *The Times*, 24 November 1986

32 *Ibid.*, 12 December 1986

33 Pincher, *Sunday Express*, 7 December 1986

INDEX